OBSERVATIONAL STRATEGIES FOR CHILD STUDY

DISCARD

K
6

OKANAGAN COLLEGE LIBRARY
BRITISH COLUMBIA

OBSERVATIONAL STRATEGIES FOR CHILD STUDY

D. MICHELLE IRWIN
M. MARGARET BUSHNELL

60667

Holt, Rinehart and Winston

New York   Chicago   San Francisco   Dallas

Montreal   Toronto   London   Sydney

The authors gratefully acknowledge the following authors, publishers, and photographers for permission to reprint their work:

p. v- Charles Bradshaw Bushnell, born April 14, 1899 and Hilma Frimodig Clark, born March 8, 1891.

p. 1- Photo by D. Michelle Irwin.

p. 21- Photo of G. Stanley Hall, courtesy of Clark University; Photo of Charles Robert Darwin, courtesy of Down House and Royal College of Surgeons of England; Photo of Lawrence Kelso Frank, courtesy of Merrill-Palmer Institute.

p. 61- Photo by D. Michelle Irwin.

p. 77- Darwin and his son, Doddy. Photo courtesy of Down House and the Royal College of Surgeons of England.

p. 95- A photographic anecdote 50 years ago: unwrapping the new truck. Watch the child on the tricycle take part and take over. Photos from Child Development Institute, Teachers College, Columbia University.

p. 106- Quotes from *Recording and Analyzing Child Behavior* by Herbert F. Wright, used with permission of the author.

p. 101- Quotes reprinted by permission of Bank Street College from *Life Ways of the Two-Year-Old*, by Louise Woodcock and from the "Foreword," by Barbara Biber from the book of the same title.

p. 105- Quotes reprinted by permission from *Kinesics and Context*, by R. Birdwhistell, University of Pennsylvania Press, 1972.

p. 125- Flo and her son Flint (facing camera), with his younger sister Flame. Photo by Pat McGinnis © National Geographic Society.

p. 137- Quotes from *Social Interaction*, by Muzafer Sherif. Used by permission of the author.

p. 147- Mildred Parten observed scenes like these when she did her research on children's social interactions 50 years ago. Photos from Child Development Institute, Teachers College, Columbia University.

p. 175- One of the early event sampling studies was Helen Dawe's study of children's quarrels. Photo reprinted by special permission of American Guidance Service from the *Peabody Early Experiences Kit* by Lloyd M. Dunn, L. Chun, D. Crowell, Leota Dunn, L. Halvei, and E. Yackel.

p. 187- Lab assignment 22 adapted from D. E. Barrett and Y. M. Yarrow, © The Society for Research in Child Development.

p. 199- Photo of boy and teacher. Photo by Sally Gale, courtesy of *Young Children*, 1968.

p. 210- Chart reprinted from Fels Parent Behavior Rating Scale No. 7.2.

p. 229- By the time these observers were recording behaviors at the Teachers College Child Development Institute (Columbia University), a number of observational strategies were available to them. Photo courtesy of Myron Papiz.

pp. 233-235- Quotes and grids from N. Flanders, *Analyzing Teacher Behavior*, © 1970 Addison-Wesley, Reading, Mass., pp. 5 and 34. Reprinted with permission; Physical Environment Inventory from The SRI Preschool Observation Instrument, reprinted with permission.

p. 236- Quotes from *Learning to Look: A Handbook on Classroom Observation and Teaching Models*, by Jane Stallings, © 1977 by Wadsworth Publishing Company, Inc. Reprinted by permission of the publisher.

Table 10.1- Summary of the Major APPROACH Behavior and Setting Categories, used with permission of the author, Bettye M. Caldwell.

p. 249- Photos by D. Michelle Irwin and M. Margaret Bushnell.

pp. 62, 148, 153, 178, 180, and 250- Quotations reprinted from P. H. Mussen, ed. *Handbook of Research Methods in Child Development*, 1960, by permission of John Wiley and Sons.

Front cover photo by D. Michelle Irwin and back cover from Child Development Institute, Teachers College, Columbia University.

Library of Congress Cataloging in Publication Data

Irwin, D. Michelle
  Observational strategies for child study

  Bibliography: p. 265
  Includes index
  1. Child psychology—Research. 2. Observation (Psychology) I. Bushnell, M, joint author.
II. Title. III. Title: Child study.
BF722.I78   155.4   80-11703
ISBN: 0-03-045726-2

Copyright © 1980 by Holt, Rinehart and Winston
All rights reserved
Printed in the United States of America
0 1 2 3 4   1 4 0   9 8 7 6 5 4 3 2

This book is lovingly dedicated to
HILMA FRIMODIG CLARK
and
CHARLES BRADSHAW BUSHNELL
who observed and shaped our own growth and development.
These two people were born in the 1890s when child study was
just beginning. Since then, fewer children have died as
infants and many children have been better fed, housed, and
educated as a result of advances made during their lifetime.
Their lives have spanned the first manned flight at Kitty
Hawk and the landing of the first man on the moon.
They have witnessed the impact of radio and radar;
of the telegraph, telephone, and television;
of antibiotics and antiballistic missiles.
Just as they were babies during the era of baby biographies,
so they became senior citizens as developmentalists turned their
attention to the process of aging. We hope that we can approach
each new stage of our lives with the same resilience
and the same grace, humor, and gentleness
that characterize these two very special people.

Preface

Katherine Read Baker wrote in her Preface to Anne Shaaker Schulman's *Absorbed in Living, Children Learn:*

> The first and continuing task of every student of child development is to learn to observe and record observations of child behavior. It is not easy to learn to see objectively and in depth, to record one's observations and finally to organize and interpret them. (1967, p. vii)

Most of us need to learn to be good observers. Few of us are "born" observers. And along with learning to be good observers, we need to learn to consider, wonder, question, check, remember, compare, hypothesize, test, correct, synthesize, and interpret.

Whether you are teaching or research oriented, you will do well to sharpen your observation skills. Although your purposes in studying a child may differ from someone else's you will find that the techniques and processes of observation are similar whatever the observational environment—be it the natural environment of the home or classroom or the engineered environment of the laboratory.

Your ability to be a good observer—to see what's happening—can make a critical difference to what you do. And what you do about what you see can make a critical difference to the child. That's what this book is all about.

When we think of learning to observe, we generally think of learning to *see* what's happening. This is as it should be. The majority of our information comes to us through our eyes. Of course, the other senses work for us as well—to warn and inform us:

"I smell smoke."

"I hear someone coming."

And taste, touch, and motion are other sensing "devices" that help us know more about people and places around us.

But our focus in this book is on helping you to become more visually and perceptually alert to children. The art and science of studying children is relatively recent, dating back only about 100 years. And the development of observational strategies is even more recent, with most of the techniques we use now dating back no more than about 50 years.

It is our aim not only to familiarize you with these key strategies (narrative descriptions, sampling technqiues, rating scales, and observational systems) but also to point out when and how each strategy developed and evolved. In the process, you will learn something about the history of child study and become acquainted with some of its leaders.

And it is appropriate that these leaders have come from a number of disciplines: education, psychology, home economics, medicine, law, anthropology, economics, biology, and physiology, among others. All these fields touch on the growth and development of the human being and, thus, have made contributions to our knowledge about children. Your own observation course may be a part of the child development sequence in the department of education, home economics, psychology, or medicine. It could be either an undergraduate or a graduate school offering. You might be using the entire book as a text for an observation course or you might be using selected chapters as part of a child development course.

The book is organized as a text-lab manual. Because we believe that the only way to become a better observer is to work at it, laboratory assignments are included in each chapter and are designed to help you discover your own strengths and develop sound observational skills.

The first three chapters are concerned with some of the reasons for learning to observe; the historical background of child study, including some key theories and approaches to studying children; and an outline of observational strategies.

Chapter Four discusses the first strategy—the diary description or baby biography. Other narrative techniques—anecdotal records, running records, and specimen descriptions—are covered in Chapter Five. Chapter Six outlines the use of narrative descriptions in case and field studies. Chapters Seven and Eight introduce time sampling and event sampling, respectively. Here, as elsewhere, both classic and modern studies using these techniques are described. With very few exceptions, we have gone back to the original material in reviewing the historical works that have contributed to observational child study, rather than relying on secondary sources.

Chapter Nine is devoted to checklists and rating scales. Observation systems are presented in Chapter Ten, with special focus on: (1) Flanders' Interaction Analysis System; (2) Caldwell and Honig's APPROACH; and (3) Stallings' SRI system. The final chapter discusses some of the questions to be considered in selecting an observational strategy for your own use.

At the close of the presentation of each observational strategy, there is a discussion of the advantages and disadvantages of that strategy. Each chapter ends with a brief list of annotated references for students who want to explore a topic in greater depth.

Every author can list individuals—teachers, students, friends, and relatives—who have offered advice, encouraged efforts, and in many ways supported the hours of "book" work. We would like to make special mention of two such groups. We are particularly indebted to the students at the University of North Carolina, Greensboro, who have used the early draft of this text and who helped to identify the weak spots in our presentation and in our assignments, and to the reviewers whose thoughtful suggestions helped make this a stronger book.

D. Michelle Irwin
M. Margaret Bushnell

Contents

Chapter One

Why Observe?

Observation serves at least two important functions in our lives: By helping us to learn, it helps us survive in the present and prepare for the future. We learn by looking at what happens around us. We accumulate visual information that makes life easier and safer—information that helps us survive. Perhaps the survival function of seeing was more obvious in the past than it is now. Or perhaps we have simply developed different kinds of survival techniques for a different world.

We are all familiar with stories by and about frontiersmen, pioneers, natives, people in any natural environment whose knowledge of their surroundings is subtle and deep. The ability to see a broken twig on a path, a movement among the trees, and the ability to identify friend or foe at a distance is part of what we call survival technique in that natural environment.

Our contemporary environment and our personal interests indicate what we will observe. If we sail, we are attuned to signs of waves and weather that can affect our well-being. If we are serious about gardening or farming, we become expert at reading the subtle signs plants give off to indicate the state of their health as well as reading weather signals that can mean changes we need to prepare for. If we are city residents, we probably pay very little attention to first-hand weather signals. We depend on the weatherman on TV to tell us what to expect—whether or not we should carry an umbrella. Unlike our country cousins, our own livelihood is not threatened by an unseasonal snow; our winter food supply is not jeopardized by a prolonged dry spell. We rarely need to read weather signals to survive in the urban environment.

Observation for survival is of a different order for the city dweller. We learn to identify and steer clear of potentially hostile or dangerous "people" situations. We are wary on crowded—or deserted—subway platforms. At night we are alert in poorly lit areas and places where muggings are apt to occur. These are survival techniques for our man-made environment.

Modern life, especially urban life, with its sensory overload of lights, noise, smells, and movement often calls for us to screen out, rather than take in, stimuli. Survival becomes a process of ignoring the majority of stimuli to focus on the appropriate or relevant few. Centuries of fine tuning, developed in human beings, have been essentially washed out in a few brief generations of amplified input. We have been programmed over the centuries to hear twigs snap and are, instead, bombarded by deafening decibels of noise—whether from city subways or country chain saws and snowmobiles. Our sensitive faculties for observations have been changed and diminished by our "noisy" visual environment as well: billboards, flashing neon lights, highway signs, and signals. Modern technology sets up an additional barrier which enables us to distort reality. We can hear and see things larger than life on TV where seeing is not always believing. TV is the most unnatural of all environments; people pretend to be people. We are too often observers not of life, but of imitations of life. Rather than simply learning to observe and then observing to learn, the television generation must learn to sort out visual fact from fancy.

Children may watch an older sibling make a paper airplane and fly it. They may then go to a movie and see Peter Pan fly. They get up the next morning and watch Captain Kangaroo demonstrate how to make and fly a kite. Children need to sort out the facts from fanciful entertainment. They can fly the paper airplane or the kite, but, despite Peter Pan's example, they cannot jump out the window and fly.

Some of our observational learning is intentional, as in learning to make a paper airplane. Some of our observational learning is incidental, or accidental. For example, we often copy the body language or physical mannerisms of those around us, but are quite unaware that we are doing so. Some of our observational skills are instinctive; we are born with a predisposition to attend to sudden movement or visual changes around us. Other skills need to be learned and perfected through practice.

Once we have trained ourselves to become keen observers, we can turn our attention to becoming shrewd interpreters of what we observe. What we see and what we think about what we see will naturally raise questions in our minds about what action we might take. Identifying, recording, hypothesizing, questioning, theorizing, changing—these are all part of the cycle of discovery for every observer.

Observation in Research and Teaching

Each day teachers and researchers take part in this cycle of discovery. Students tend to think of teaching and research as separate processes. Researchers work in laboratories or field settings, use strange sounding words like *vicarious reinforcement* and *tertiary reactions* to describe concepts, apply statistical tests like correlations and analysis of variance to the data they gather to see if the findings are significant or have happened by chance, and then write all of this in what often seems like a stuffy and boring report meant to plague unsuspecting students.

The concerns and techniques of the researcher and the teacher are more similar than many students realize. Whether in the laboratory or the classroom, children's actions and reactions can be observed, identified, and in some way recorded either formally or informally. We may deliberately watch and record events or simply observe and make mental notes. Likewise, the theorizing and testing out of ideas which are part and parcel of the formal research process, are also part of the teaching process. If Peter is having trouble learning fractions, we try to think of math games that will help him understand the concept and the process. If one idea doesn't work, we try another until we hit on the right solution. Whether formal or informal, the cycle of discovery is a part of good teaching, good research, and learning for both children and adults.

Direct observation (watching what people do naturally in various natural environments) is an important part of the discovery process for at least five reasons. First, *observation is a means of generating hypotheses or ideas.* The perceptive teacher will observe how children spend their free time—what activities they pursue, what games they play, which heroes they imitate or emulate. The teacher uses the activities that are already of high interest (intrinsically motivating) to the children to stimulate their curiosity about other areas of learning. If, for example, the teacher observes the fifth-graders digging channels in the sand area, he or she may decide to use that activity to help illustrate how irrigation canals were constructed in desert areas to make the desert bloom. The teacher generates ideas about how to extend learning and make it more interesting and meaningful by observing the children to find out "where their heads are at," and what they already understand and enjoy.

Ethologist N. Blurton-Jones feels that observation is also an important part of the research process. It not only leads to productive hypotheses or ideas, but can also save research time. He feels that "a long . . . observational phase may . . . save time on experimental tests of very unrealistic hypotheses" (1972, p.10). For example, a researcher who is interested in children's fear of potentially dangerous situations may find that below a certain age, children have no fear of the selected situations. The researcher then knows that it would be fruitless to include children below a certain age in the study.

It is not mere chance that so many theories have developed out of an individual's own experiences observing life around him or her. Jean Piaget's observations of his own children in the 1920s caused him to conduct experiments by asking the children what they thought and why. He then challenged their responses to see if they really understood the concept they were dealing with. These simple observations and spontaneous experiments formed the beginnings of his theory of cognitive development.

Sigmund Freud's observations of his clinical patients led to his theories about personality development. Konrad Lorenz's hours of watching waterfowl as a child led to his ethological studies on imprinting, the newborn bird's instinctive acceptance of any moving object as the "mother" during a brief critical period right after birth. Ignaz Semmelweis's observations of women dying of puerperal or childbed fever led to his eventual discovery in 1847 that infectious material was spread from the doctors' contaminated hands to women during childbirth, causing infection and death.

A second reason for observation's being central to the research and teaching processes is that *it is a means of answering specific questions.* If Ms. Matthews notices that Dwight seldom gets his work in on time, she may observe his behavior to find out why and, in so doing, learn that he spends most of his time wandering around talking to others. Muzafer Sherif et al. (1961) had some ideas about peer group formation. They tested these ideas out by setting up a summer camp and observing how the groups structured themselves and how children responded to such situations as competitive games. Another researcher, Mary Ainsworth (1966), wondered what effects maternal deprivation in infancy had on a child's later adjustment. She located children who had been deprived of maternal attention and affection as infants and carefully observed such factors as age of infant or child at separation, length of separation, and kinds of alternative care available.

A third reason for using observation in research and teaching is that *it provides a more realistic picture of behavior or events* than do other methods of information gathering. A teacher may learn a great deal about a child's abilities from the tests of basic concepts given at the preschool level or from the various achievement tests given in the public schools. But he or she may have a more complete understanding of the child's ability to use a concept by observing the child's actual behavior in the classroom. The teacher may learn, for example, that Karen can count to ten but does not understand what *three* means if she is asked to put three blocks in the box.

Research is often divided into two major categories: experimental and naturalistic. Experimental research is done in a laboratory setting where factors that might influence the behavior under investigation can be controlled as much as possible. Naturalistic research is done in the child's natural environment. The researcher observes whatever behavior or events occur and does not try to control or manipulate any of the factors that might influence the behavior being studied.

Observation plays a key role in both types of research. Researchers who are proponents of naturalistic methods of child study use the term *direct observation* to distinguish between experimental and naturalistic uses of observation. Direct observation looks at freely-occurring behavior in the natural setting where there is nothing artificial or contrived. Therefore, the findings have greater generalizability than many experimental laboratory studies do. The researcher can use information gathered in direct observational study to predict what would happen in similar circumstances or situations. The laboratory researchers, on the other hand, know that they can safely predict what will happen in other laboratory situations *similar to the one created,* but are less confident (or should be) about generalizing the information to the "real" world where many additional factors intervene to influence behavior.

A fourth function of observation is *to help us better understand children's behavior.* This is important for good research and for good educational practice. Not only does the observant teacher gain insight into children's feelings and actions, but also into a child's learning style. By observing how children interact with one another and with the materials presented, the astute teacher gains valuable clues about how individual children process information for their own use. For example, there are children who need to be shown how to mix blue and yellow to get green. There are other children who need only to be told how to do it. There are still others who learn almost incidentally, simply by observing others or by experimenting on their own. Some children prefer to learn by words; others prefer to learn through visual images—pictures or photographs—for example. Both words and pictures are symbols of reality. Each child exhibits his or her own preferred learning style if the teacher will just watch for clues.

The skills of teacher and researcher are sometimes combined in a single person. Susan Isaacs was such a person. Her observations of children's social and intellectual behavior in the classroom have greatly increased our understanding of these areas of development. Isaacs indicates that her material was gathered in a school under natural conditions, not in a laboratory where behavior was manipulated. She also mentions the value of making observations without a predetermined focus: "By looking for particular answers to particular questions, we run the risk of missing other perhaps more significant facts which might transform our problem and make our previous questions idle" (1930, p. 3).

As a result of carefully recorded observations of children, Susan Isaacs was able to group her observations into categories and draw conclusions about some of the characteristics of children's social and intellectual behavior at different ages or stages, and about the factors that influence those behaviors.

A fifth function of observation is *evaluation,* either informal teacher evaluation of educational efforts in the classroom or a formal observational system. Evaluation can involve the informal observations of a teacher's performance, notes on children's responses to a new activity or a different method of presentation, or observation of a single child. When a child in a class exhibits a great deal of aggressive behavior, for example, the perceptive teacher will watch for situations in which the aggression occurs and try to determine what sets off the behavior and what reinforces it. The teacher may determine that the child behaves aggressively to get attention and will not pay attention when the child behaves thus, instead selecting more positive, prosocial behaviors to reward with attention. Or the child may behave aggressively because he wants to join an activity that the other children are engaged in but does not know how to. The teacher's task in this case would be to help the child learn positive methods of approaching others. In either case, once the teacher has instituted a plan of action, he or she needs to continue to observe carefully to see how the plan is working.

One of the most extensive formal observational systems developed for classroom evaluation is the Stanford Research Institute's observational system used by Jane Stallings and her associates (1973) to study Follow Through programs. (See Chapter 10 for a discussion of the SRI system.) Most evaluation studies in the past used measures of IQ gain, test performance in academic areas, and language proficiency to evaluate the gains brought about by intervention programs. Stallings felt that a better test of the effects of a program would be to ask the program sponsor or developer to state the goals of the program and list a series of statements describing the program in action. She then took the list of descriptors and observed classrooms to see how the actual program matched the intent of the sponsor. The observations measured different features of the program such as physical environment, classroom interaction, activities provided, and teacher behaviors. This kind of evaluation not only allows the evaluator to judge how well a program is implemented but also to look at how programs are different and alike.

Summary

Observation serves two important purposes: It is both an aid to survival and an instrument to facilitate learning. Some of our observational learning is planned, and some is accidental. Some of our observational skills are instinctive, particularly those related to survival needs; other skills need to be learned and perfected through practice.

Observation is an important skill to master for at least five reasons:

1. It is a means of generating hypotheses or ideas.
2. It is a means of providing a realistic picture of behavior or events.
3. It is a means of answering specific questions.
4. It is a means of helping us to better understand children's behavior.
5. It is a means of evaluation.

Observing Passive vs. Active Subjects

One of the goals of direct observation is to record events and behavior to accurately reflect what occurred. Some of the observational strategies that we will be studying require that the observer write a narrative description of what is being observed. Other strategies let the observer use a shorthand form of recording, such as checklists and rating scales.

Narrative descriptions require a careful eye and a quick pen. The following exercises will help you prepare for the kind of narrative descriptions that will be described in Chapters 4 and 5. The first assignment will help you appreciate the kinds of skills demanded by different categories of subjects. You will do four brief (three-minute) observations, each of a different kind of subject.

Part I: Passive Subjects

Procedure: Observe any building of your choice for three minutes. Write down your observations in order.

Date_____ Time_____ Setting/Location _____

Descriptive Statements:

1.

2.

3.

4.

5.

6.

7.

8.

9.

10.

One of the goals of narrative observational descriptions is to describe the event, scene, or behavior observed in such a manner that someone who was not present at the time could either identify what you had observed (in this case which building you had observed) or could visualize what had occurred. The descriptive statements that you have written should clearly distinguish the building you observed from other buildings. Indicate (by number) which descriptive statements clearly differentiate your building from other buildings.

It is not enough simply to distinguish one object or event from another. We must also be able to describe how it is like other objects or events. This kind of comparative description—a statement of similarities and differences—is what allows us to discuss how one object or event fits in with or relates to others of the same general category.

Procedure: Observe a tree of your choice for three minutes. While you are observing, write down a series of descriptive statements that define the tree as part of a recognizable group or category and that also identify the tree as a unique "individual" within the group.

Date_____Time_____Setting/Location _____

Descriptive Statements:

1.

2.

3.

4.

5.

6.

7.

8.

9.

10.

Which descriptive statements identify your tree as part of a recognizable group or category of trees? _____

Which statements identify it as a unique individual within the category? _____

Part II: Active Subjects

Buildings and trees are easy subjects for observation because they stand still. This means we can observe them for as long as we like at any time we like. There will be changes over time in these objects. Buildings weather and eventually decay if they are not properly maintained. Deciduous trees change color with the coming of colder weather and then lose their leaves entirely only to bud again with the return of warm weather. These changes happen slowly, however, allowing us to observe with relative leisure. People are not as accommodating. They are active subjects, often on the move. This means that people demand more of the observer.

Procedure: Observe an infant under six months of age for three minutes. While you are observing, write down a series of statements that describe the infant and his or her behavior.

Date_____Time_____Setting/Location _____

Descriptive Statements:

1.

2.

3.

4.

5.

6.

7.

8.

9.

10.

Identify the statements that describe the infant as a person (physical characteristics, etc.) _____

Identify the statements that describe the infant's behavior. _____

As infants grow into toddlers and then preschoolers, they complicate our observational task even further. First they become mobile moving around with seemingly endless energy and then they become verbal. Trying to describe a conversational three-year-old who is darting in and out of a play area can be an exhausting and challenging task.

Procedure: Observe a preschool child (two to five years of age) for three minutes. Write down a series of statements that describe the child and his or her behavior.

Date_____Time_____Setting/Location _____

Descriptive Statements:

1.

2.

3.

4.

5.

6.

7.

8.

9.

10.

Part III: Analysis and Comparison

Now that you've had a chance to observe a range of subjects from very passive to very active, let's compare them and see what kind of observational skills are required by each:

1. Which observation was easiest to do? Why?

2. Which observation provided the most raw material for description? Why?

Observations are not random or capricious but are guided by the nature of the questions, the setting, and the natural selectivity of our own knowledge or perceptions. As observers, we employ a kind of *systematic strategy* in making our observations.

3. Consider the things you noticed, the number of descriptive statements you used, and the order or sequence of your observations. What does this tell you about what is most important or most apparent to you?

4. Compare your observations with those of several classmates. What similarities and differences do you notice? How do you explain this?

5. The directions for observing the building instructed you to write down your observations in the order that they occurred to you. The directions for observing the tree asked you to make statements that both identified the tree as part of a group and as a unique individual within that group. The instructions for observing active subjects also asked you to describe behavior. How did the instructions influence your observations in each instance?

6. Consider how the setting itself influenced your observation. For example, what was around the building? Where was the tree? Who was near the child? We tend to view things in context. Behavior in church is viewed differently than the same behavior seen on a playground. Which of your statements would have been the same regardless of setting and which were influenced by the setting? Specify by statement topic and number (e.g. Building: Statement # 3) those that were influenced by setting.

The first assignment should have helped you to become aware of the different observational skills required by passive and active subjects. It should also have helped you to learn about the systematic and selective nature of observation and how your own feelings and knowledge influence what you notice. Finally, you should be more aware of how the setting itself affects the observation.

Observer Point of View

The first assignment demonstrates how subtle changes in the directions given to the observer can influence both how the observer records statements and what he or she notices. Sometimes the directions are not so subtle. This observation is designed to help you better understand how the directions shape the kind of observation you do.

Part I: Thumb-Nail Description

Procedure: Observe a child between five and ten years of age for five minutes. While you are observing, write a series of descriptive statements that adequately and accurately describe the child.

Date_____Time_____Setting/Location _____

Descriptive Statements:

1.

2.

3.

4.

5.

6.

7.

8.

9.

10.

Write a short summary paragraph based on your observation which would provide a thumb-nail sketch of the child for someone who has never seen him or her.

Part II: Focused Observation

Procedure: Observe the same child for another five minutes as if you were an observer on a research team studying aggressiveness in children. As in Part I, your task is to write a series of descriptive statements that you feel adequately and accurately describe the child. Assume that the person reading this description *will not* have read the description you gave in Part I.

Date_____Time_____Setting/Location _____

Descriptive Statements:

1.

2.

3.

4.

5.

6.

7.

8.

9.

10.

Write a short summary of your observation, again describing the child for someone who has never seen him or her.

Part III: Analysis and Comparison

1. Compare the two observations. How did the specific focus influence your second observation?

2. What elements are common to the general and the specifically focused observations?

3. Which are different?

4. What factors other than the nature of the directions could account for the differences?

In 1968 Robert Rosenthal and Lenore Jacobsen conducted an experiment to see what effect prior information would have on teacher behaviors and attitudes. They selected a random group of children and told the teachers that tests given these children had indicated that the children had high academic potential and would probably show a burst of achievement during the year. Their study, *Pygmalion in the Classroom*, indicates that the children did, in fact, do better than their classmates of the same ability, who had not been labeled as children likely to spurt ahead. The authors refer to this as an example of how self-fulfilling prophesy works in the classroom.

We need to be careful not to let directions bias our observations. When we are told to observe aggressiveness, we need to be careful not to let that direction make us see aggressive behavior where there is none. It is easy to let suggestion shape our descriptions and labels. We must make our observations as factual as possible and try to avoid being caught up in a mood or influenced by suggestions, whether these suggestions come in the form of helpful information or directions that can bias what we see.

Three teacher requests for observational information are given below. Analyze each of these requests for possible biasing effect. If you feel that a request does bias the observer, underline the portion of the request at fault, describe its potential influence on the observer, and rewrite that portion of the request so that it will still yield the needed information without biasing the observer.

1. Alex seems to have trouble sticking to a task. He spends more time out of his seat than in it and can't seem to settle down. Would you please observe his behavior and tell me whether I am overreacting or if he really does wander around all the time?

2. Mrs. Jones has a great deal of trouble letting Rebecca go when she brings her to nursery school. She seems to be ambivalent about whether she wants Rebecca to be with the other children or wants Rebecca to need her presence. It often takes her as long as twenty-five minutes to say goodbye. I can't stay to watch the process as I have to attend to the other children. Can you observe when she brings Rebecca next week and tell me what the total process includes?

3. Paul is a new child in the after-school day care program. He was in a car accident when he was two years old and is paralyzed in his left leg. He wears a leg brace and uses crutches. He doesn't seem to interact much with the other children. I can't tell if this is because he is shy and not ready to interact or if the other children are ignoring him and not inviting him to participate. Could you observe him on Thursday and Friday to see what kind of interaction is occurring?

Describing the Setting

You have already learned that the setting itself can have an influence on how you perceive the object or event you are observing. The next step is to gain skill in being able to describe the features of the setting likely to either influence the observed behavior itself or our own perceptions of the observed behavior.

Part I: Environmental Description

Procedure: Roger Barker's (1968) text, *Ecological Psychology*, extensively describes concepts and methods for studying the environment of human behavior. Barker talks about the interaction between the individual and the environment and also the fact that the structure of the environment influences behavior. Your task in this assignment is to observe two different environments and then analyze what components within the environments give the individuals operating in these environments cues as to what behavior is expected or permitted. Your description of each environment should include the physical boundaries of the setting and the arrangement of objects within the setting—i.e. a map of the setting, the activities or behaviors occurring within the setting, and any other information about the setting you feel is important. You might include weather or temperature conditions and nearby settings that could influence behavior (an ambulance across the street could influence behavior on a playground, for example). Ratio of materials to children, boys to girls, adults to children could also be important factors to mention. Your first observation should be of a preschool or public school classroom; the second should be of a children's sports event (e.g., Little League, soccer, a playground game, a neighborhood game of hopscotch).

Date_____Time_____Setting/Location _____

1. Description of the classroom:

Observer _____

Date_____Time_____Setting/Location _____

2. Description of the sports activity:

Part II: A Comparison and Analysis

1. What features of each environment give the strongest clues as to what kind of behavior is expected or allowed?

   Classroom   Sports Activity

2. Some environmental cues have certain meanings because of social expectations; other cues are purely physical. Put an asterisk (*) in front of each statement listed above that is a physical environment cue with no specific social expectation attached to it. What does this tell you about how behavior in settings is defined?

3. Consider the behavior that you observed in each setting. What elements of behavior are the same in the two settings? What do you think accounts for the similarities?

Chapter Two

Observation and Child Study

A Historical Perspective

"I don't know what to expect; I'm completely in the dark."

"Out of sight, out of mind."

"I can't make him understand. He seems to have a blind spot."

"Can you explain it again? I don't see what you mean."

"Now I see what you're driving at."

The metaphor of vision is commonly used to convey understanding—or lack of it. We learn by looking. We are all, to a greater or lesser degree, observers of life.

The Art and Science of Observation

The great artists through the ages have been careful observers of life around them. The unknown artists who created the Altamira cave paintings over 10,000 years ago and the present-day Picassos all have looked at people and places with acute perception.

The great scientists through the ages have also been thoughtful observers of life around them. Because scientists have wanted to see more, and see more clearly, they have developed ways of seeing *beyond* and *within* and *over*. They have extended the eye by creating the microscope, the telescope, the periscope, and the X-ray. Because they have wanted to look longer and see it again, they invented the camera and the video recorder.

As a result of new or different "vision," the basic and accepted facts of the universe can change dramatically. So, in 1610, when Galileo discovered the telescope, he began to accumulate evidence about the earth and its spatial environment. It was a revolutionary idea when he stated that the sun, not the earth, was at the center of our system. What had been a geocentric universe before the time of Galileo, with the earth at the center of an onion-like (layered) system, became a heliocentric universe with the sun at the center. And in the philosophical revolution that followed, the psychocentric universe emerged with man at the center. Attention began to focus on the inner self rather than on outside influences like planets, destiny, fate, or the gods. The role of the individual as possessor of inner forces affecting the direction of his or her own life began to surface. A new interest in the human being, and the forces that influence, move, and shape that human being, developed. Alexander Pope wrote at the beginning of the eighteenth century, "The proper study of mankind is man." We would add only *woman* and *child* to that statement.

The study of the human being is both an art and a science. It calls for the ability to look objectively and creatively at a subject along with the need to treat the results of our looking with precision and imagination. Much of the knowledge we have gathered about human behavior and development has come through observation.

The observer needs to approach the study of human behavior with an open eye and learn to process what is seen with an open mind. With this combination of vision and perception, the observer-artist-scientist can begin to understand human behavior as well as the factors that shape it.

The Beginnings of Child Study

The first record we have of a study of a child is Swiss. In 1774 Johann Heinrich Pestalozzi published observations he had written on the development of his three-and-a-half-year-old son. In 1787, a German named Dietrich Tiedemann cataloged his son's first three years. But nearly a century passed before any appreciable volume of work on the subject of the child developed. Perhaps the very fragility of the infant's life was a factor. It was difficult to focus much serious attention on the development of an infant whose life span was often measured in weeks or months. The history of the Richardson family, recorded on a gravestone in an old cemetery in New Orleans, Louisiana, serves as a good example. Ella Oliver (1857-1932) and John Patton Richardson (1851-1891) had six children born to them between the years of 1879 and 1888:

November 1879: Marguerite Callaway born
August 1881: Susie born
March 1883: Ella born
September 1883: Ella died at six months of age
May 1884: Marguerite Callaway died at four years, six months of age
December 1884: Little Sister born
August 1885: Little Sister died at eight months of age
March 1886: Edmund born
November 1888: Mary Oliver born
June 1890: Mary Oliver died at one year, seven months of age
June 1894: Susie died at twelve years, ten months of age

Only Edmund lived to adulthood (1886-1965). With such a poor survival rate, it is no wonder that the first careful observers of infant development were fathers, and later mothers, whose hopes for their child's survival were great enough to allow them to watch and record and interpret.

For centuries, concern had been expressed for the education and proper upbringing of children, starting with earliest infancy. A great deal of literature had been generated, almost as far back as we want to go, out of this need to direct parents and teachers in their responsibilities to the church and the state in training their children. Especially influential in the eighteenth and nineteenth centuries were such works as John Locke's *Some Thoughts Concerning Education* (1693), Jean Jacques Rousseau's *Emile* (1762), Johann Pestalozzi's *How Gertrude Teaches Her Children* (1801), and Friedrich Froebel's *Education of Man* (1826).

Concern for what was to be taught to children, what they needed to know, and how they needed to behave, continued (and continues) as a legitimate, important topic. But interest in children themselves, the *knowers* and *behavers*, did not occur until the nineteenth century. Three men were largely responsible for the growth of interest in child study: Charles Darwin, G. Stanley Hall, and Lawrence K. Frank.

Charles Robert Darwin (1809—1882)

Charles Darwin is usually credited with creating the tangential strain we have come to recognize as the scientific study of the child. William Kessen, in his book *The Child* (1965), states that starting with Rousseau (the mid-1700s) the child had been recognized as a part of society; beginning with Darwin (a hundred years later) the child became a part of the scientific endeavor.

From the publication of *The Origin of Species* to the end of the nineteenth century, there was a riot of parallel-drawing between animal and child, between primitive man and child, between early human history and child. The developing human being was seen as a natural museum of human phylogeny and history; by careful observation of the infant and child, one could see the descent of man (Kessen, 1965, p. 115).

Darwin suggested that by observing the development of the infant, one could catch a glimpse of the development of the species itself.

Not only did Darwin's evolutionary theory spark scientific interest in the child, but his own notes on his infant son also drew attention to a newly emerging method of child study. In 1840, Charles Darwin, a good scientist-father, began a journal on the development of his son, William Erasmus (Doddy), born when Darwin was thirty-one years old. These notes were not published until 1877, almost a hundred years after Pestalozzi's 1774 publication. These early journals or developmental diaries became known as "baby biographies" because they detailed the early life of children. Darwin's fame gave the "baby biography" public attention and made it an important means of child study.

Granville Stanley Hall (1846—1924)

The second individual who made a significant contribution to the development of child study was G. Stanley Hall. Hall played a major role in defining and encouraging the newly emerging field of child study. In 1883, Dr. Hall wrote a book entitled *The Content of Children's Minds*, an early scientific study of the child. Hall also extended the existing methods of studying children by perfecting the questionnaire, a method based on asking a child a series of questions. This method launched hundreds of studies of child development. Another of Hall's direct contributions to child study was to found several journals including *The American Journal of Psychology* so that early researchers would have a public means of sharing their work with others.

Hall became president of Clark University in 1889 and made it a famous center for child study. He was the teacher of many men who would become leaders in education and psychology, and greatly influenced their interest in child development. One of his students was John Dewey, who advocated educational reform within a movement known as Progressive Education. Arnold Gesell was another student who became a pediatrician and cataloged the ages when different behaviors like walking, talking, and catching a ball emerged in the natural development of children. A third student, Lewis Terman, became a leader in the area of mental testing or psychometrics. Terman and Maud Merrill, a colleague at Stanford University, revised Alfred Binet's test of intellectual ability and called the revision the Stanford-Binet. Terman also developed the intelligence quotient or IQ as a standard index of intellectual ability.

G. Stanley Hall also introduced American educators and psychologists to European leaders whom he felt were making important contributions to the area of child study. He hosted Sigmund Freud's only visit to the United States in 1909. Freud was the founder of psychoanalysis, a theory of personality development and a therapeutic method that focuses on the thoughts and feelings of the individual and views the first five years of life as the most important for shaping the personality. Hall also introduced Wilhelm Preyer, the European master of the baby biography method, to the American public and encouraged scores of mothers to keep records of their infants' development to add to Preyer's growing collection of data.

In 1896, W. T. Harris, the first U.S. Commissioner of Education, praised Dr. Hall's efforts:

The present widespread study in this country of the child in school and in the family is due, more than to any one else, to the enthusiastic efforts of Dr. G. Stanley Hall. The study has become so general and is so wisely managed at various centres that new harvests of observations are reaped annually or semiannually (Compayré, 1896, p. vi).

Thanks to Darwin's influence and Hall's enthusiasm and promotion, by the turn of the century child study was firmly launched as a legitimate area of study in human development.

Once launched, child study grew by leaps and bounds. From 1900 to 1950 we learned more about children than in all previous centuries combined. Two important reasons for this increase in knowledge about child development were the creation of child development institutes and the increase in funding for child study. Lawrence K. Frank was the moving spirit behind both.

Lawrence Kelso Frank (1890-1968)

Lawrence K. Frank was a young economist who gave a vigorous push to the scientific study of the child. Frank recognized that "a sound program of child rearing and child care (was) dependent upon research in these fields" (Senn, 1975, p. 14). Larry Frank had an opportunity to help promote research on child rearing and child care when he was given the task of developing the Laura Spelman Rockefeller Memorial child development grants in the 1920s. In a letter describing his work, Larry Frank wrote:

When I proposed the child study program and indicated how it would be implemented through research centers and fellowships for the training of personnel and by a concurrent program of parent education all over the country, [Beardsley] Ruml [Director of the Rockefeller Memorial] asked me to undertake the development of this program and persuaded the trustees to approve and make the grants that I proposed (Senn, 1975, p. 15).

The first grant was accepted by Dean James E. Russell of Columbia University's Teachers College in 1924 to establish a child study institute there. In 1925 a similar grant was given to the University of Minnesota, $50,000 per year, supplied in decreasing amounts for fourteen years ending in 1939. In 1927 the University of California at Berkeley received its grant for an institute. Money also went to Gesell's Clinic of Child Development at Yale, to the Iowa Child Welfare Station, and to others. Larry Frank wrote:

I was able to promote these child study centers by taking advantage of the growing awareness of the importance of childhood and the increasing concern for improvement in the nurture and education of children as aroused by Dewey and Parker, by Hall, and also by Freud who became known in this country before the First World War and whose theories emphasizing the crucial significance of early childhood were being discussed in the 1920s (Senn, 1975, p. 18).

With the Rockefeller grants, the focus of child study moved from the home, with one child as subject, to the university centers where, for the first time, impressive numbers of preschool children were available for observation and study. The shift in the location of child study from the home to the child development institutes brought with it a shift in the age of children who were studied. Infants had been the focus of the baby biographers; preschoolers enrolled in the laboratory nursery schools became the focus at the child development institutes.

Because Frank was committed to the idea that parent education was a vital component in child welfare, and because he could fund institutes willing to pursue this idea, child development and family relations became linked and are linked to this day, particularly in a number of university home economics departments. Frank's insistence on an interdisciplinary focus in child study institutes also guaranteed that researchers would be attracted from many disciplines. His idea was to "wring the best from all the human sciences—biology, sociology, anthropology, psychiatry, medicine, physiology—and effect a joint effort to understand the normal development of an individual" (Senn, 1975, p. 24). This not only brought people together from diverse backgrounds, but also promoted child study as an important area of concern in a wide array of disciplines as members of the interdisciplinary teams published the results of their studies in the journals of their separate areas of study.

Perspectives on Child Study

The growing interest in child study soon led to a variety of explanations or theories about how children develop. Theories are a handy summary of ideas designed to describe, explain, and predict what will happen in a given situation. There are many theories about how children develop. Most theories select a major aspect or component of development on which to focus. The three theories that have been most influential in child study are *psychoanalytic theory*, *learning theory*, and *cognitive-developmental theory*. Psychoanalytic theory focuses on feelings and attitudes; learning theory deals with observable behavior; cognitive-developmental theory is concerned with the child's conceptual or intellectual development.

Psychoanalytic Theory

Psychoanalytic theory began with the work of Sigmund Freud at the end of the nineteenth century. Freud was a medical doctor who became interested in helping people to better understand and then solve their emotional problems, many of which seemed to accompany their physical ailments. This interest eventually took him away from treating diseases of the body to treating diseases of the mind. He called his method of treatment and the theory that he developed psychoanalysis, or analysis of the mind.

Freud's thesis was that an individual possesses two minds, one conscious and the other unconscious. The conscious mind uses a variety of techniques that Freud called *defense mechanisms* to keep painful or unpleasant memories and thoughts from becoming conscious. The aim of analysis is to bring unconscious thoughts out into the open where they can be dealt with. The process by which this occurs is called the "free association" of thoughts. "The patient undertakes to report to the analyst without exception whatever thoughts come into his mind and to refrain from exercising over them either conscious direction or censorship" (Brenner, 1957, p. 8).

Freud's theory is known as a *psychosexual* theory of personality development because Freud felt that biological and psychological energy were localized in a bodily zone of development. According to Freud, the body zone shifts as the child grows older; this idea led him to postulate a stage theory of development. The individual matured by going through a series of stages that are fixed in order. Each stage builds on the stage that came before it and each prepares the individual for the next stage in sequence. The first stage occurs in infancy and is known as the *oral stage*. The primary source of pleasure comes from stimulation of the oral regions of the body, primarily the mouth. The major focus of activity is on feeding during the oral stage. The second stage occurs during toddlerhood and is called the *anal stage*. The dominant region of pleasure shifts to the anus and activities focus on toilet training. At about age three the child's interest shifts to the genital region of the body and the child enters the *phallic stage* of development. During the elementary school years, the child is in a *latency period* that is essentially quiet; drives are relatively stable. Adolescence brings the *genital stage* with a focus on sexual development and reproduction.

Each stage contributes to the individual's personality. There are traits that are characteristic of certain stages; for example, passivity is associated with the oral stage; compulsiveness and possessiveness are associated with the anal stage. Freud felt that the individual's basic personality was shaped very early in life, somewhere around five years of age. The events of childhood, therefore, are of major significance in shaping the person's feelings about the self and in developing thoughts and attitudes that will govern his or her adult behavior. Much of the time spent in psychoanalysis is devoted to helping the individual remember and understand the events of childhood.

Children perceive the world very differently from adults, in part because they lack the cognitive or mental ability to understand all that they see and hear (as we shall learn from the cognitive developmentalists) and in part because their experience is limited and they have fewer events to compare or use as a standard for judgment. The task of psychoanalysis is to unravel the misunderstandings and misperceptions of childhood and put them into proper perspective for appropriate adult functioning. Psychoanalysis thus became a theory and a therapy, a way of thinking about an individual's development and a way of treating problems and anxieties.

James A. C. Brown summarized the impact of Freud's theory on Western thought as follows:

> Like Copernicus and Darwin, the men with whom he compared himself, Freud revolutionized our way of looking at ourselves, and like them he may well come to be regarded rather as a moulder of thought than as a mere discoverer of facts . . . The fact is that each of these men happened to live at a time when the current of opinion was changing as traditional beliefs disintegrated, and that their work heralded or helped to hasten this change because it was in accord with new trends of thought (1961, pp. 2-3).

A student of Freud's named Erik Erikson took on the task of extending Freud's psychosexual stages to include what Erikson called the psychosocial learning that occurs at different stages in the individual's development. Erikson drew on both psychoanalysis and cultural anthropology and extended the stages into adulthood and old age. His "Eight Stages of Man" draws on Freud's ideas of psychosexual development but places emphasis on the cultural and social factors that influence development at each stage. This view has become more popular than Freud's theory and is used as a major theory in child development texts today. Erikson views each stage as having a psychosocial crisis to be resolved rather than as having a body zone that is the focus of pleasure. He outlined these stages in a book called *Childhood and Society*, first published in 1950 and revised in 1963.

Erikson views infancy as a time when infants either learn to *trust or mistrust* those around them and by extension the world in general, depending on how well their basic needs are met. Toddlerhood presents the conflict of *autonomy versus shame and doubt* and is affected by how others respond to the infants' own attempts to gain some self-control over their behavior. The preschool years are concerned with *initiative versus guilt* as children learn to undertake, plan, and do things for themselves. If children are rewarded for independent behaviors, they feel a sense of initiative; if children are punished, they feel a sense of guilt. The psychosocial crisis of the elementary school years relates to *industry versus inferiority*, depending on whether children feel a sense of mastery over things and a level of social competency or develop feelings of inadequacy instead. Adolescence is a period of *identity versus identity diffusion* as individuals strive to become their own persons. Erikson has devoted a great deal of attention to the identity crisis of adolescence. It is the subject of his book, *Identity, Youth and Crisis* (1968), and is the part of his theory that he is best known for.

Interpersonal commitment is emphasized in the early adulthood psychosocial crisis of *intimacy versus isolation*; the individual either develops a meaningful relationship with another person or does not. The middle years of adulthood focus on a commitment to improving the life conditions of future generations (specifically one's own children) as opposed to becoming self-serving. Erikson calls this stage *productivity versus self-absorption*. The final stage of adulthood, *integrity versus despair*, is centered on whether or not the individual can accept the facts of his or her life and face death without great fear.

Both Freud and Erikson present dynamic views of personality development, views that deal with causes and effects of behavior. Both theorists view development as proceeding in stages, each stage with its own conflict to resolve. Both feel that the individual's personality is shaped or determined by how the individual deals with these conflicts or tensions. The two differ in their basic orientation toward the role of biological and cultural factors. Freud tends to ignore culture; Erikson feels that culture is a key factor in influencing personality development.

Learning Theory

Behaviorism, S-R (stimulus-response) theory, and social learning theory are all variations of basic learning theory. This group of closely related theories comprises the bulk of what is known as experimental psychology, psychological theory and research based on the experimental method.

The roots of learning theory go back at least as far as Aristotle (Fourth Century B.C.) and can be traced through major work done by John Locke in 1693 to the turn of the twentieth century when Ivan Pavlov and Edward Thorndike were writing the first laws of learning theory. It was John Broadus Watson, however, who made learning theory popular with researchers and the general public.

Watson, known as the father of behaviorism, rejected the psychoanalytic emphasis on studying thoughts and feelings. He believed that psychology should study only behavior that can be observed and measured. Behaviorism, as one would expect, focuses on behaving rather than on feeling or thinking or knowing. The particular interest of behaviorists is to discover how different behaviors are learned. Behaviorists believe that learning takes place through a process of training called conditioning.

The principles of conditioning depend upon a basic relationship between different events or behaviors. One set of events or behaviors is called stimuli because they trigger other behaviors. The behaviors that are triggered are called responses. Some stimuli automatically trigger certain responses; a loud noise, for example, triggers a startle or fear response. Other stimuli have to be trained or conditioned to trigger the same response.

In 1920, Watson and his research assistant Rosalie Raynor, in their famous experiment involving Albert and a white rat, demonstrated how conditioning occurs. They took an eleven-month-old infant named Albert who had been reared in a hospital and presented him with a white rat. Albert showed no fear of the rat. Watson then set about to use conditioning to teach Albert to be afraid of the white rat. The rat was the unconditioned stimulus because it did not automatically trigger a fear response. Albert, like most infants, was afraid of loud noises, however, so every time Watson showed Albert the white rat, he struck a bar of steel very sharply and created a loud noise. The noise was the conditioned stimulus because it elicited the fear response. Soon Albert showed fear whenever he saw the white rat because he had learned to associate the white rat with the feared loud noise.

Watson took his experiment one step further and presented other white furry objects to Albert: a white rabbit and a bearded Santa Claus mask. Albert showed the same fear responses to these objects even though they had never been paired with the loud noise. This is an example of *stimulus generalization*, a key concept in behaviorism's attempt to demonstrate how learning takes place. According to the behaviorists, responses like Albert's fear of white rats are learned in relation to a specific stimulus and then generalized to a whole range of stimuli similar to the original one.

OKANAGAN COLLEGE LIBRARY
BRITISH COLUMBIA

John Watson believed so strongly in the power of conditioning that he said:

Give me a dozen healthy infants, well-formed, and my own specified world to bring them up in and I'll guarantee to take any one at random and train him to become any type of specialist I might select—doctor, lawyer, artist, merchant-chief and, yes, even beggar-man and thief, regardless of his talents, penchants, tendencies, abilities, vocations, and race of his ancestors (1930, p. 82).

Another important principle of learning theory is the value of reinforcement. In 1911 Edward Thorndike demonstrated that whenever a response is reinforced or rewarded, the likelihood of the response occurring again under similar circumstances is increased. The more the response is practiced and subsequently reinforced, the more likely it is that it will become a part of the person's behavior.

Burrhus Frederick Skinner used Thorndike's discovery about the value of reinforcement to show how behavior could be shaped or molded by reinforcing responses that are closer and closer to the desired end behavior. For example, if Joe has trouble attending to a task for more than two minutes and the teacher wants to extend his attention span to ten minutes, she will start by praising (reinforcing) him when he can attend for three minutes, then four, then five and so on, gradually extending the time he must attend in order to get reinforced until he has reached the desired goal of ten minutes.

The most recent addition to the concepts used by learning theorists to explain how behaviors are learned are imitation and modeling. A large number of learning theorists have contributed to this addition to learning theory, known as social learning theory, because most of the learning studied by these researchers occurs in the social environment. The man most generally recognized as the major spokesman for this group is Albert Bandura (1924-).

Imitation refers to watching what another person does and then copying or imitating that behavior. Modeling does not need to rely on direct imitation of another person's behavior but involves a person identifying with a model and behaving more or less the way he or she perceives that the other person would behave. The individual learns to *inhibit* or avoid certain behaviors that he or she might otherwise produce if the model is seen being punished for those behaviors. For example, if grandchildren go to visit their grandparents and one of them throws his coat on the floor and gets scolded for doing so, the other children are less likely to throw their coats on the floor. Conversely, if a model is reinforced for doing things that the person is not likely to have done otherwise, *disinhibition* occurs and the person is more likely to produce the behavior, good or bad. If one of the grandchildren carries his dishes to the sink after dinner (and they don't do this at home) and is praised (reinforced) by the grandmother, the other grandchildren are more likely to do the same. Or, if a child steals money from the family piggy bank and is praised by peers for cleverness, another child might be inclined to do likewise.

Both Skinner and Bandura have contributed heavily to *behavior modification* as a direct application of learning theory to educational and clinical settings. Behavior modification is used to modify or change deviant or undesirable behaviors. It can be applied to groups, but is most frequently applied to a single individual.

The procedure for behavior modification involves identifying the target behavior, observing the child to see what behavior patterns exist and what seems to be reinforcing the target behavior, and then working out a modification program that essentially involves ignoring the undesirable behavior and reinforcing the more desirable, alternative behavior. K. Eileen Allen, Florence Harris, Don Baer, and their associates at the University of Washington and the University of Kansas have pioneered research on the use of behavior modification in the preschool. Through the use of behavior modification, they have successfully demonstrated that aggressive behaviors, thumb sucking, nail biting, isolate behaviors, crying, and passivity, to name but a few, can be decreased and more appropriate prosocial behaviors reinforced to take their place.

Cognitive-Developmental Theory

The father of cognitive psychology is Jean Piaget, a Swiss philosopher and epistemologist born in 1896. Piaget was a precocious child who showed an interest in science at a very early age. His first interest was in biology and zoology, and before he was twenty-one he had published twenty papers on mollusks. He had earned his bachelor's degree by the time he was eighteen and his doctorate in natural sciences at twenty-one. He read widely in philosophy, biology, sociology, religion, and psychology and quickly became interested in epistemology, the study of knowledge. This interest led him to a career in psychology. Piaget spent several years gaining experience in the field. He worked in a psychiatric clinic, studied at the Sorbonne, and worked as an assistant in the mental-testing laboratory of Alfred Binet. It was there, working under the direction of Binet's collaborator, Theodore Simon, that Piaget became interested in children's incorrect answers to questions. He began to investigate this and in so doing launched himself on a course of study that was to consume the rest of his career. By 1921, he had published four papers on mental testing. The quality of one of these was impressive enough to land him the job of director of studies at the Institute Jean-Jacques Rousseau at the University of Geneva (now the Institute des Sciences de l'Education), a position he held until his retirement. He continues to be actively involved in research and writing.

Piaget employed the clinical method that he had learned in his brief psychiatric experience, adapting it to an informal interview procedure. Claparede described this procedure as the art of questioning.

(It) does not confine itself to superficial observations, but aims at capturing what is hidden behind the immediate appearance of things. It analyses down to its ultimate constituents the least little remark made by the young subjects. It does not give up the struggle when the child gives incomprehensible or contradictory answers, but only follows closer in chase of the ever-receding thought, drives it from cover, pursues and tracks it down till it can seize it, dissect it and lay bare the secret of its composition (J. Piaget, 1955, p. xv).

Piaget used this procedure first to study children's causal reasoning, conceptions about the world and everyday phenomena, and understanding of moral judgments. He also used it to study the intellectual development of his own children. These observations and questions provided him with the data that launched his theory of cognitive development. An example of his questioning procedure is:

Questioner: You have already seen the clouds moving along? What makes them move?
Sala (8): When we move along, they move along too.
Q: Can you make them move?
S: Everybody can, when they walk.
Q: When I walk and you are still, do they move?
S:Yes.
Q: And at night, when everyone is asleep, do they move?
S: Yes.
Q: But you tell me that they move when somebody walks.
S: They always move. The cats, when they walk, and then the dogs, they make the clouds move along. (Flavell, 1963, p. 286).

Piaget's theory resembles Freud's theory of psychoanalysis in some respects. Like Freud, Piaget emphasizes the importance of biological forces in the child's development. The biological forces are not Freud's sexual energy but relate instead to biological adaptation. Piaget defined adaptation in terms of *assimilation*, taking in information from the environment and *accommodation*, adapting existing ideas or thought structures to adjust to the new information.

Another common thread between Freud and Piaget is that both felt that the "givens" inherited at birth (heredity) plus physical maturation (growth) interact with experience to shape the child's thought. Freud chose to use this base to study drives and instincts. Piaget used it to study how the individual organizes information. Both generated a stage theory of development and according to both, the stages are irreversible: The child must go through stage one before going on to stage two. It is also impossible to skip a stage; the child cannot go directly from stage two to stage four; he or she must go through stage three on the way.

A third area of similarity between Freud and Piaget is that both used clinical rather than experimental methods and both dealt with matters of the mind rather than with overt behavior. Freud studied the structure of the personality, the child's feelings and emotions. Piaget studied the structure of the intellect, the child's knowledge about things.

Steve Yussen and John Santrock (1978) identify three major features of Piaget's ideas. First, Piaget's investigations of intellectual development are more concerned with how a child thinks than with either what he thinks about or how much he knows. The first differentation separates him from Freud, the second from the intelligence theorists who attempt to measure intelligence with IQ tests and other psychometric methods. Second, Piaget is not interested in how all children the same age are alike or different in their level of cognitive development, but rather in the general nature of children's thought. Third, Piaget tends to concentrate on what Yussen and Santrock call ideal thought, the kind of thinking a child could do if there were no distractions or interruptions and if the child's concentration and motivation were both good.

Piaget has identified four main periods of developmental thought. The first is called the *sensory-motor* period. This period lasts from birth to about two years of age and is subdivided into six stages and several substages. During this period children progress from the reflex-action stage that characterizes newborn infants to the initiating-action stage in which infants elicit a response from the environment (kicking a mobile in their crib to make it move) to the active exploration of the environment stage and the beginning of a symbol system or means of communication (usually single words like *more, daddy*). As the name implies, many infants' actions during this period are sensory and motor in nature and through experience with the environment they gradually learn to coordinate the two systems.

The second period is called the *pre-operational* period. It starts at about age two and lasts until six or seven years of age. During this period, the children's symbol system expands as they master language, allowing them to deal with the world in symbolic ways rather than just through motor activity. They can talk about what they see, hear, feel, and think and soon can even communicate through written symbols. A key feature of children's thought at this stage is its *egocentric* quality. Children tend to view everything from their own perspective as if the world revolved about them. They also tend to think that others see things and think about them in the same manner that they do. They are also confused by changes in things. If a beaker of water is poured into a container of a different shape, children are unable to realize that the amount of liquid itself has not changed although the shape has. When children reach the third period of cognitive development, *concrete operations*, they are better able to organize their thoughts. In addition, the thoughts themselves are more stable and less likely to change. Concrete operations lasts from about seven to eleven years of age. During this stage, children begin to move away from egocentric thought and are able to *role-take*—to put themselves in the place of someone else and consider how the other person would feel or think or what the other person would do in a situation. Children are limited, however, by their need to have concrete events or objects to think about, hence the name concrete operations. They will not be able to move away from the world of concrete experiences until they reach the period of formal operations, the fourth period of cognitive development.

Formal operations develop in most people sometime between eleven and fourteen years of age. During this period adolescents can deal with reality as well as with hypothetical, what-if situations. They can use probability, complex reasoning, and logic.

As mentioned earlier, the mechanism for moving children from one stage to another is adaptation. Borrowing from biology, Piaget views adaptation as an interaction between the organism and the environment. It involves the concepts of *assimilation* (taking in new information) and *accommodation* (changing existing ideas to fit in new evidence or information). At each stage, children organize the information they have into some system and operate on the basis of that system. Because assimilation and accommodation are constantly occurring, children are constantly seeking *equilibration* or balance. If a new piece of information or a new concept throws previous ideas into conflict, children must somehow try to resolve the conflict by reorganizing their thoughts until there is equilibrium again.

One of the chief factors that distinguishes Piaget's theory of development from either the learning theorists or the Freudian psychoanalysts is that Piaget views children as responsible for their own forward movement. As Nathan Isaacs says, "We owe to him a striking fresh picture of the child himself as the architect of this (intellectual) growth" (1972, p. 15). Children are not so much shaped by what others do and say as by how they view the world conceptually. This is why Piaget is interested in the processes of thought. Children's experiences with life and their own operations on those experiences are responsible for knowledge and understanding. In this respect, Erik Erikson's notion of psychosocial stages of development comes closer to Piaget's view of development than does Freud's, since Erikson feels that both biological and cultural factors must be considered in the development of personality.

Approaches to Studying Children

The theories that we have just discussed all have a well defined set of laws or principles that were developed to describe, explain, and predict behavior and development. Not all researchers work out of a theoretical base. Some prefer to focus on how the data are collected. They feel that how the data are gathered is the most important factor in being sure that the results of their investigations will allow them to describe, explain, and predict behavior.

Ecological and Ethological Psychology

Two approaches to studying children that are becoming increasingly popular are the ethological and ecological approaches to child study. Ethological and ecological psychologists both share a common belief that individuals must be studied as they react and interact in the natural environment, not in a laboratory or on an analyst's couch, or during an interview.

Ecological psychology is rooted in Gestalt psychology, which asserts that the child is more than just a summation of language, perception, social behavior, reasoning, and so on. It is the way all the pieces work together that defines the complexity of the individual.

Growing out of this assumption that the whole is greater than the sum of its parts, ecological psychologists rejected the narrow focus of the experimentalists as too fragmented and artificial. Their interest was in the interaction of the organism with its natural environment, in the totality of behavior and the myriad factors which interact to shape it.

The methods of the ecological psychologists were first developed by Roger Barker and his associates in the early 1950s at the Midwest Psychological Field Station at Lawrence, Kansas. Barker wanted to study behavior in the real-life settings in which people lived and moved and acted and reacted. He believed that this was the only way that psychologists could discover the laws of behavior. Therefore, he had to develop a method for collecting data. The extensive field records developed by anthropologists like Franz Boas, Ruth Benedict, and Margaret Mead offered descriptions of behavioral patterns in the natural environment but their focus was on discovering the cultural laws governing behavior, in cultural patterns as reflected by behavior. Barker was more interested in discovering the psychological laws governing behavior. To do this, he adapted the continuous, narrative description technique used by earlier researchers and renamed it specimen description. Specimen descriptions involve recording everything that the individual does or says with as much information about the context (people involved, circumstances that might be influencing the behavior, and so on) as possible. This information is later divided into logical segments (eating dinner would be an example of a segment) and then analyzed.

Ethological psychology borrows heavily from the concepts and methods of biology and in many universities is referred to as human biology or sociobiology. Much of the modern impetus for ethology has come from Konrad Lorenz and Nikolaas Tinbergen and their associates at the Max Planck Institute for Behavioral Physiology in Seewiesen, West Germany. Lorenz was first known for his 1935 work in imprinting with graylag geese—the discovery that young geese when first hatched will follow or imprint on whomever or whatever they first see.

The method of both the ecologists and the ethologists is direct observation, observing freely occurring behavior in the natural environment. J. D. Carthy (1966) describes the method of direct observation used in ethological studies as follows:

The first aim of the study of the behavior of a particular animal is to record it in all its detail, correlating it with the stimuli which evoke the different sections of it . . . Such a complete catalogue of behaviour is called an ethogram (p. 1).

Many of the ethograms, detailed descriptions of behavior, describe motor movements, facial gestures, body posture, and so on.

There are many similarities between ecological and ethological approaches to child study. Both prefer to observe and measure behavior rather than to manipulate it. Both are concerned with describing behavior in the natural setting. Both are particularly appropriate for studying "uncooperative" subjects like infants, young children, and emotionally or mentally disturbed children. Hutt and Hutt (1970) identify four important characteristics that differentiate the two approaches:

1. Ecologists tend to focus on large units of behavior—molar actions—like playing the piano, eating dinner, or playing in the sand box. Ethologists focus on smaller units of behavior—molecular actions—like facial expressions, gestures, body posture, and eye gaze.
2. Ecologists tend to think of behavior episodes that have a specific goal to achieve. Ethologists do not focus on goals but rather on the motor patterns used by the person being observed.
3. Ecologists include inferential statements relating to the person's attitudes, intentions, and motives—the "psychological habitat" of the person. They feel that this is important in trying to describe the environment from the perspective of the person being observed. Ethologists regard this as unscientific.
4. Ecologists are advised to include words that describe the quality of actions. "Give the *how* of everything," Wright says (1967, p. 50). Ethologists would not allow such phrases in their descriptions, in part because they view them as ambiguous and in part because they are not behavioral descriptions (pp. 22-24).

The Perspectives Applied

The theories and approaches to child development covered in this chapter represent different ways of viewing development. The particular perspective that a person holds greatly influences how he or she approaches a problem, how it is conceptualized, and how it is studied. The same question asked of representatives of each perspective would not yield the same answer. In fact, the answers might give one reason to ask if, indeed, they all heard the same question.

Let us consider the question, "What is the nature of moral development in children?" Learning theory would look at moral behavior as a reflection of moral development and would study areas such as resistance to temptation, not cheating when you're behind in a game and no one is looking, for example. Psychoanalysis would focus on moral feelings and would study the internalization of values. Cognitive-developmental theory would concentrate on moral judgment, studying the child's understanding of concepts like fairness, justice, right, and wrong, and what kind of punishment would be appropriate for the crime. Ecologists would observe situations involving moral areas and record the individual's behavior and the environmental context in which it occurs, or would glean the information from specimen records already collected. Ethologists would select specific behaviors to observe, like altruism or empathy, and would ask how these behaviors developed and what function they play in the life of the individual or the preservation of the species.

Whatever the perspective, it can shed light on the problem at hand. The more we know about the area of child development, the better equipped we are to understand the nature of the child. Perhaps it is a bit like the story of the blind men and the elephant. One man touched the elephant's trunk and said, "I know what the elephant is; it is like the snake that can curve and curl around itself." The second blind man reached up and touched the elephant's tusk and said, "No, the elephant is not like a snake; it is more like the smooth limb of a tree. An elephant is more like a beautifully curved tree." The third blind man went up to the elephant and put his hands on the elephant's side. "Oh no, the elephant is neither like a snake nor like the limb of a tree. It is rough and wide and tall—like a wall. An elephant is like a wall." The fourth blind man went up to the elephant and touched the elephant's large, fan-shaped ear. "Gentlemen, you are all mistaken. The elephant is like a large leaf from the shade trees we rest beneath in the heat of the day." And so, each man had a piece of the truth, a perception that was helpful but also incomplete. Only by sharing the insights, and accepting the additional "realities" of the others, could the picture become complete.

Research Strategies in Child Study

As the field of child study matured, a variety of research methods were developed to meet research requirements. Most of these methods can be sorted into one of six general categories:

1. *Naturalistic Research*—in which no controls or manipulations are exercised. The subject is observed doing what comes naturally, in the natural environment.
2. *Experimental Laboratory Research*—in which various factors are carefully controlled or manipulated in order to determine the effect on specific responses in the laboratory.
3. *Experimental Field Research*—in the natural environment, in which one or more factors are controlled or manipulated to the extent that the situation will permit in order to determine the effect on specific responses.
4. *Case Studies*—or case histories, in which detailed information is systematically collected about a single individual, family, or group from observations, testing, and various records that have been kept over time.
5. *Tests and Surveys*—which collect data on various aspects of human growth and development in an attempt to provide normative information about these dimensions.
6. *Interviews or Clinical Methods*—used to gather information about what people say, do, feel, or think. Jean Piaget developed the interview method into an approach that combines observation and manipulation, called the *methode clinique*, in which children are observed, often in a natural setting like the home, playground, or classroom, and are asked nonstandardized questions. In other words, instead of asking a specific series of questions that must be put to everyone in the same order, as is the case with IQ testing, the interviewer asks the child a question and the child's answer gives the interviewer clues as to what questions to ask next. The probing is open-ended and tailored to the subject.

Let's look at a problem and see how it could be studied by each of the methods and what kind of information would be derived from using each method. Suppose that the State Department of Education wants to develop a new educational television series for the K-3 level. They want to be sure that the material will be interesting enough to hold the children's attention. Some of the staff members feel that they should use a cartoon format because children are "hooked" on cartoons. Other staff members feel that people should be used to make a stronger connection between learning from classroom teachers and learning from television characters. The director of the project decides to do a short research study to see if she can gain some information that will help the group decide which format to use.

A design that is based on the *naturalistic approach* to research might focus on at-home observations of children's television viewing behavior. Children enrolled in kindergarten through third grade would be observed for a specified period of time. The observer would note down each of the programs that the children themselves selected, how long they watched each program, whether or not they attended (actively watched), and whether the program used cartoon characters, people, or a combination of the two.

A second researcher might elect to do an *experimental laboratory* study. His plan is to select a task for the children to do (sorting blocks according to shape or color) and then reward a child for doing the task by letting each child select one of six television videotapes to watch. Two would have cartoon characters, two would use people and two would have both cartoon and real people. The researcher feels that if the child can select only one show, he or she will pick the one that is most appealing and that if enough children are observed, he will have a reasonably good index of the type of characters children prefer.

A third researcher might decide to do an *experimental field* study. She decides that she can observe the program preference of the children more efficiently by observing several children at once. She knows that the local airport has individual TV sets in the waiting area. She also knows that a television can be an attractive object for children. She plans a class field trip to the airport (natural environment). The children are told that they will be able to go inside one of the planes and talk to the pilot. When they get to the airport, they find that there is a slight delay and they will have to wait for twenty minutes before they can board the plane. The stewardess tells them that they can each watch TV on their own TV set in the lounge while they wait. In this way, the researcher and her team can gather information on the children's viewing preferences.

A fourth researcher decides to do a *case study* of several children, perhaps two from each grade. She plans to use information from a variety of sources: home observations, interviews with parents about their children's viewing preferences, and interviews with the children themselves. She also plans to study these children across a longer period of time, in this case for the entire school year, to see if the children's viewing preferences are stable or if they change during the year.

The fifth researcher decides to do a *survey* of viewing preferences. She lists all of the children's TV programs on a sheet of paper and asks parents to identify the ones their children watch. Then she selects the dozen programs most watched and asks children a series of prearranged questions about the characters on those programs.

The last researcher selects a design somewhat similar to the one above, but chooses to *interview* the children to find what they think about the different programs and characters. She might ask whether a child would prefer to watch "The Flintstones" or "The Brady Bunch." She is less interested in the actual choice than in why the child selected one over the other. Her questions would, therefore, probe into the child's reasons behind his or her choice.

Most questions interesting to researchers can be studied using any one of the six methods. The results from each of the six methods are apt to be somewhat different because each looks at different pieces of the behavior for different purposes. This leads researchers to draw different conclusions about the information they have gathered. Therefore, it would be desirable to use a variety of methods within the same study, but few researchers have the time or money to do this. As a result, it is important for a researcher to be careful in describing the method he or she uses so that others reading the report of the study can better assess the results.

Most of the exercises in this book will draw from naturalistic methods of research, in part because we feel that it offers the richest information base, in part because it provides the easiest access for students, and in part because learning the various observational techniques developed for direct observation of children is the best way to master them so that they can be successfully and appropriately applied in other research situations.

Direct observation (the observation of freely occurring behavior in the naturalistic environment) is always a part of naturalistic research but need not be limited to naturalistic research. It is also a method employed in experimental field research and it is a method that contributes to case studies. Many people use observational research as a synonym for naturalistic research. This is inappropriate because, with the exception of tests, surveys, and some physiological types of research, all methods involve some form of observation. The chapters that follow will explore the development of various observational strategies—how they have contributed and continue to contribute to our knowledge and understanding of child development.

Summary

The great artists and scientists through the ages have been careful observers of life around them. While human beings have been the subject of discussion and speculation throughout recorded history, it is only since the late 1700s that we have actually studied children as subjects worthy of our attention. It was not until the late 1800s that child study became a science of its own under the guiding influence of Charles Darwin and G. Stanley Hall. Lawrence K. Frank furthered the growth of child study by helping to establish the child development institutes in the 1920s and by providing funding for research through the Laura Spelman Rockefeller Memorial.

The nature of an observational study is often influenced by the researcher's or teacher's attitudes about how children develop, how they learn, what factors influence their behavior, and so forth. Most of our "scientific" attitudes can be described as belonging to a particular theory, philosophy, or approach to child study. Three theories and two approaches to studying children were outlined in this chapter.

Psychoanalytic theory originated with Sigmund Freud. Freud focused on the attitudes and feelings that we call personality. He believed that there is a psychosexual basis for development governed chiefly by unconscious sexual drives. He saw development as progressing through a series of stages; oral, anal, phallic, latency, and genital, each of which is governed by a different body zone. Freud felt that the individual's basic personality is shaped by about five years of age and that this personality governs much of his or her adult behavior.

Erik Erikson postulated a psychosocial theory of personality development that is the product of both biological and cultural determinants. Erikson's "Eight Stages of Man" extend from infancy to old age. Each stage involves a psychosocial dilemma or crisis that must be resolved by the child. Unlike Freud, Erikson does not view the personality as essentially fixed at five, but rather as a constantly evolving personality responding to the resolution of each psychosocial stage.

Learning theorists study overt behavior in an attempt to discover the laws that govern learning and behavior. They view learning as a product of factors such as various stimulus-response associations, reinforcement, shaping, imitation, and modeling. Behavior modification is an application of learning theory frequently used in educational and clinical settings as a means of modifying or changing undesirable or deviant behaviors.

Cognitive-developmental theory is a stage theory of cognitive or intellectual development derived from the observations and studies of Jean Piaget. Piaget views cognitive growth as a function of the individual's adaptation to the environment. Through assimilation and accommodation, the individual constantly restructures his or her concepts and thought structure to achieve equilibration. Like the psychoanalysts, Piaget views cognitive development as a series of qualitatively different stages: sensory-motor, preoperational, concrete operations, and formal operations.

Ecological psychology is method-based rather than theory-based. It views development as an interaction between the organism and the environment and studies it in natural rather than laboratory settings. The major method of observation is the specimen description.

Ethologists are interested in the biology of behavior. They study both animals and man in an attempt to learn how different species adapt to their environments. Behavior is viewed as a product of adaptation to the environment, but unlike the cognitive-developmentalists who seek to describe the various stages of concept development, the ethologists seek to understand the origin and function of behavior. Changes in species behavior are viewed as an evolutionary process. The ethologist's main unit of study is the ethogram or catalog of behavior patterns.

As interest in the field of child development grew, so did the variety of ways researchers study children. Six research methods were summarized in this chapter:

1. Naturalistic Research
2. Experimental Laboratory Research
3. Experimental Field Research
4. Case Studies
5. Tests and Surveys
6. Interviews or Clinical Methods

Observation plays a key role in most of these research methods. The chapters to follow will explore the creation and use of these observational strategies as they relate to child study today.

SUGGESTIONS FOR FURTHER READING

Students interested in reading original source material about the beginnings of child study will find the following books of interest:

Hall, G. Stanley, and his pupils. *Aspects of Child Life and Education.* New York: Appleton, 1907. A collection of child studies from the turn of the century conducted by the "father of child study" and his students.

Kessen, William. *The Child*. New York: Wiley, 1965. A collection of original articles (some abridged) about the development of ideas about children from John Locke to Jean Piaget. Useful introductions and commentaries by Kessen.

Summaries of the development of child study can be found in the following:

Biehler, Robert F. *Child Development: An Introduction*. Boston: Houghton Mifflin, 1976, Chapters 1-4. An excellent but long (179 page) review of the people, methods, and theories that have shaped the field of child development.

Frank, Lawrence K. The beginnings of child development and family life education in the twentieth century. *Merrill-Palmer Quarterly*, 1962, 8 (4), 207–228. This review traces the history of early nursery schools and child development institutes, the research that grew out of the early centers, and efforts at parent education. The best brief summary available.

Sears, Robert R. Your ancients revisited: a history of child development. In E.M. Hetherington, ed., *Review of child development*, vol. 5. Chicago: University of Chicago Press, 1975, pp. 1-73. An admirable overview of the development and flowering of the field, with some speculation about the future as well. A must for the serious student.

Senn, Milton. Insights on the child development movement in the United States. *Monographs of the Society for Research in Child Development*, 1975, 40 (3-4, Serial No. 161). A valuable supplement to Robert Sears's history of child development, this monograph presents information and insights gained from taped interviews of more than eighty leaders in child development research since 1920, with particular emphasis on the people and forces that shaped the field.

Students interested in reading more about the theories and approaches to child study will find the following books of interest:

Psychoanalytic Theory

Brenner, C. *An Elementary Textbook of Psychoanalysis*. New York: International Universities Press, 1955. A readable and reliable introduction to psychoanalytic theory that should be read prior to reading Freud.

Brown, J. A. C. *Freud and the Post-Freudians*. Baltimore: Penguin Books, 1961. A well-written little book which shows Freud's relationship to the broader psychoanalytic theory offered by the leading neo-Freudians.

Erikson, E. H. *Childhood and Society*, 2d ed. New York: Norton, 1963. A far-ranging classic that includes Erikson's studies of childhood among the Sioux and Yurok Indians, his preliminary work on adolescence and psychohistory, and his psychosocial theory of development, "the eight stages of man" (outlined in Chapter 7).

Freud, S. *New introductory lectures on psychoanalysis*. Translated by W. J. H. Sprott. New York: Norton, 1933. Freud's writings are voluminous. A good introduction to his work written toward the end of his writings; also includes his later revisions of his psychoanalytic theory of personality development.

Learning Theory

Bandura, A. *Social Learning Theory*. Englewood Cliffs, N.J.: Prentice-Hall, 1977. The most recent exposition of social learning theory by the man who, along with the late Richard Walters, was one of its principal architects.

Hilgard, E. R., and G. H. Bower, *Theories of Learning*, 4th ed. New York: Appleton, 1975.

Hill, W. F. *Learning: A Survey of Psychological Interpretations*, 3d ed. New York: Crowell, 1977. Both of these books present the major learning theories from Thorndike to cybernetics. Hilgard and Bower also include a comparison of learning principles embedded in Freud's psychodynamic theory of personality with traditional theories of learning. Hill includes a chapter on developmental aspects of learning with a passing nod to Piaget. Students reading learning theories for the first time would do well to start with Hill; those with a basic background will find Hilgard and Bower enlightening.

Skinner, B. F. *Walden Two*. New York: Macmillan, 1948. A novel demonstrating operant learning theory applied to the social control of behavior. It is of interest both for its coverage of Skinnerian theory and for the issues it raises about the uses and abuses of behavioral control.

Cognitive-Developmental

Flavell, J. H. *The Developmental Psychology of Jean Piaget*. New York: Van Nostrand, 1963. A scholarly review of the theory and works of Jean Piaget through 1962. Most appropriate for graduate students who have already had an elementary introduction to Piaget.

Ginsberg, H., and S. Opper. *Piaget's Theory of Intellectual Development: An Introduction*. Englewood Cliffs, N.J.: Prentice-Hall, 1969. A well-written, readable introduction to Piaget. A good introduction or review.

Piaget, J., and B. Inhelder. *The Psychology of the Child*. Translated from the French by Helen Weaver. New York: Basic Books, 1969. Piaget has written hundreds of articles, monographs, and books. This one, written with his chief collaborator, is one of the most readable and covers the broad range of topics subsumed under cognitive theory.

Ecological

Barker, R. G. *Ecological Psychology*. Stanford: Stanford University Press, 1968. An overview of the methods and concepts of ecological psychology. Students will benefit most if they have a basic understanding of research design and statistics before reading Barker.

Ethological

Eibl-Eibesfeldt, I. *Ethology: The Biology of Behavior*, 2d ed. New York: Holt, Rinehart and Winston, 1975. Translated by Erick Klinghammer. A comprehensive and well-written survey of ethology covering both human and animal research.

Surveys of Child Development Theories

Baldwin, A. L. *Theories of Child Development*. New York: Wiley, 1967. This text has been out for only slightly more than a decade but is already a classic in child development. Appropriate for students who have already had introductory child development, the only shortcoming of this book is that it needs updating to describe the developments of the last ten years.

Maier, H. W. *Three Theories of Child Development*, 3d ed. New York: Harper & Row, 1978. Maier gives in-depth coverage to three theories of child development: the cognitive theory of Jean Piaget, the affective theory of Erik Erikson, and the behavioral theory of Robert Sears. The newly revised third edition also contains a section dealing with the application of these theories to education and the helping professions.

Thomas, R.M. *Comparing Theories of Child Development*. Belmont, Calif.: Wadsworth, 1979. This text is the best available overview of child development theories. Thomas traces two major historical views of the child, and then presents, discusses, and evaluates fifteen theories or descriptions of child development and four educational applications of child development theory.

Research Strategies in Child Study

The researcher has a variety of research methods available. Each method has its own set of advantages and disadvantages. The researcher must select the one method that best fits his or her needs, time, and budget. This assignment is designed to help you learn how questions interesting to parents, teachers, and researchers can be studied utilizing a variety of methods.

Part I: Strategies

Procedure: There has been a great deal of interest in recent years in the diets of young children and how diet affects behavior, attitudes, cognitive development, and physical growth. The most recent questions have to do with what effect the artificial flavorings, preservatives, and colorings in processed foods have on behavior and development. Consider each of the six strategies for child study outlined in the chapter and briefly identify how one might use each strategy to study diets of children and/or effects of diet on behavior and development. Write a brief paragraph for each method, identifying what you would study and how you would measure the important variables or factors.

1. Naturalistic Research

2. Experimental Laboratory Research

3. Experimental Field Research

4. Case Study

5. Tests and Surveys

6. Interviews or Clinical Methods

Part II: Follow-Up Studies

Often researchers get ideas for studies by reading about the investigations of other people. Sometimes they plan a study to follow up on the original researchers' findings. They may choose to use the same method and extend the study to include other factors or variables or they may select an entirely different method arguing that the original study overlooked a critical point.

Procedure: In 1939 Dr. Clara M. Davis reported a study in the *Canadian Medical Association Journal* that was to become a classic study on diet in young children. Read "Results of Self-Selection of Diets in Young Children" reprinted following this lab sheet and answer these questions about the study:

1. Write a short abstract (250 words) of the study. Your abstract should include the problem studied, method used, and major findings.

2. Unfortunately, this study has often been misquoted and unwarranted implications drawn from it. Identify the erroneous conclusion(s) which could be drawn from the study.

3. What is the critical fact that people who make the mistake you have identified are ignoring?

4. A number of interesting follow-up studies could be developed to carry this research one step further. Follow-up studies are designed either to confirm or disprove other possible explanations for the results, or to ask another question so that the results of the two studies can be compared in the hope of gaining a broader understanding of the question or topic being studied. Briefly outline a follow-up study that you feel would shed new light on the results of self-selection of diets by young children.

5. What are the major differences between the original study and your follow-up study?

Results of Self-Selection of Diets by Young Children

Clara M. Davis

Originally published in *Canadian Medical Association Journal,* 41 (September 1939), 257–261.

The self-selection of diet experiment had for its subjects infants of weaning age, who had never had supplements of the ordinary foods of adult life. This age was chosen because only at this age could we have individuals who had neither had experience of such foods nor could have been influenced by the ideas of older persons and so would be without preconceived prejudices and biases with regard to them. The children concerned were studied for six years.

The list of foods used in the experiment was made up with the following considerations in mind. It should comprise a wide range of foods of both animal and vegetable origin that would adequately provide all the food elements, amino-acids, fats, carbohydrates, vitamins and minerals known to be necessary for human nutrition. The foods should be such as could generally be procured fresh in the market the year around. The list should contain only natural food materials and no incomplete foods or canned foods. Thus, cereals were whole grains, sugars were not used nor were milk products, such as cream, butter, or cheese.

The preparation of the foods was as simple as possible. All meats, vegetables and fruits were finely cut, mashed or ground. Most of the foods were served only after being cooked, but lettuce was served only raw, while oat meal, wheat, beef, bone marrow, eggs, carrots, peas, cabbage and apples were served both raw and cooked. Lamb, chicken, and glandular organs, all of local origin and not Federally inspected, were cooked as a measure of safety. Cooking was done without the loss of soluble substances and without the addition of salt or seasonings. Water was not added except in the case of cereals. Combinations of food materials such as custards, soups, or bread were not used, thus insuring that each food when eaten was chosen for itself alone.

The list of foods was as follows:

1. Water
2. Sweet milk
3. Sour (lactic) milk
4. Sea salt (Seisal)
5. Apples
6. Bananas
7. Orange juice
8. Fresh pineapple
9. Peaches
10. Tomatoes
11. Beets
12. Carrots
13. Peas
14. Turnips
15. Cauliflower
16. Cabbage
17. Spinach
18. Potatoes
19. Lettuce
20. Oatmeal
21. Wheat
22. Corn meal
23. Barley
24. Ry-Krisp
25. Beef
26. Lamb
27. Bone marrow
28. Bone jelly
29. Chicken
30. Sweetbreads
31. Brains
32. Liver
33. Kidneys
34. Fish (haddock)

The entire list could not, of course, be gotten ready and served at one time and was therefore divided and served at three (in the early weeks, four) meals a day, this arrangement providing a wide variety at each meal. Both sweet and sour (lactic) milk, two kinds of cereals, animal protein foods, and either fruits or vegetables were served at each meal according to a fixed schedule. Each article, even salt, was served in a separate dish, salt not being added to any, nor was milk poured over the cereal. All portions were weighed or measured before serving and the remains weighed or measured on the return of the tray to the diet kitchen.

Food was not offered to the infant either directly or by suggestion. The nurses' orders were to sit quietly by, spoon in hand, and make no motion. When, and only when, the infant reached for or pointed to a dish might she take up a spoonful and, if he opened his mouth for it, put it in. She might not comment on what he took or did not take, point to or in any way attract his attention to any food, or refuse him any for which he reached. He might eat with his fingers or in any way he could without comment on or correction of his manners. The tray was to be taken away when he had definitely stopped eating, which was usually after from twenty to twenty-five minutes.

The results of this six-year study of self-selection of diet by young children from the time of weaning on may, for the purpose of this discussion, be conveniently grouped under three heads: (1) The results in terms of health and nutrition of the fifteen children; (2) the adequacy of the self-chosen diets as judged by nutritional laws and standards; (3) the contributions made by the study to our understanding of appetite and how it functions.

Like the lives of the happy, the annals of the healthy and vigorous make little exciting news. There were no failures of infants to manage their own diets; all had hearty appetites; all throve. Constipation was unknown among them and laxatives were never used or needed. Except in presence of parenteral infection, there was no vomiting or diarrhea. Colds were usually of the mild three-day type without complications of any kind. There were a few cases of tonsilitis but no serious illness among the children in the six years. Curiously enough, the only epidemic to visit the nursery was acute glandular fever of Pfeiffer with which all the children in the nursery came down like ninepins on the same day. During this epidemic when temperatures of 103 to 105° F. prevailed, as with colds, etc., trays were served as usual, the children continuing to select their own food from the regular list. This led to the interesting observation that just as loss of appetite often precedes by twenty-four to forty-eight hours every other discoverable sign and symptom of acute infection, so return of appetite precedes by twelve to twenty-four hours all other signs of convalescence, occurring when fever is still high and enabling the observer to correctly predict its fall. This eating of a hearty meal when fever is still high is often not in evidence when children are put on restricted diets during such illness, but the correctness of the observation has been amply confirmed in the Children's Memorial Hospital where a modification of the self-selective method of feeding prevails. During convalescence unusually large amounts of raw beef, carrots, and beets were eaten. The demand for increased amounts of raw beef and carrots can be easily accounted for but we are still curious about that for beets, and inclined to wonder whether they may furnish an anti-anaemic substance (iron?) from the fact that beets were eaten by all in much larger quantities in the first six months or year after weaning than ever again save after colds and acute glandular fever.

Some of the infants were in rather poor condition when taken for the experiment. Four were poorly nourished and underweight; five had rickets. Two of these five had only roentgenological signs of rickets, and one mild clinical rickets as well, while the other two were typical textbook cases. The first infant received for the study was one of the two with severe rickets, and, bound by a promise to do nothing or leave nothing undone to his detriment, we put a small glass of cod liver oil on his tray for him to take if he chose. This he did irregularly and in varying amounts until his blood calcium and phosphorus became normal and x-ray films showed his rickets to be healed, after which he did not take it again. He had taken just over two ounces in all. No other of the 15 children had any cod liver oil, viosterol, treatment by the ultra-violet rays, or other dietary adjuvants at any time during the study, and all four of the other cases of rickets were healed in approximately the same length of time as was the first. Regardless, however, of their condition when received, within a reasonable time the nutrition of all, checked as it was at regular and frequent intervals by physical examinations, urine analyses, blood counts, haemoglobin estimations and roentgenograms of bones, came up to the standard of optimal so far as could be discovered by examinations.

However, as I may be thought to have been unduly biased in my estimate of this rollicking, rosy-cheeked group, Dr. Joseph Brennemann's appraisal of them may be of interest. In his article, "Psychologic aspects of nutrition," published in an early number of the *Journal of Pediatrics,* he says, "I saw them on a number of occasions and they were the finest group of specimens from the physical and behavior standpoint that I have ever seen in children of that age."

But all is not gold that glitters. Carefully controlled laboratory experiments with animals have shown that growth and nutrition throughout the entire growth period may be satisfactory on diets that are slightly deficient in some of the essentials, and that such slight deficiencies only became evident as lessened vigor, fertility, and longevity in adult life. Long as was the time these children remained on the study—none less than six months, and all but two from one to four and one-half years—but a fraction of the growth period was covered. One might, therefore, raise a skeptical eyebrow and say, "The examinations of these children do not by any means prove that all, some, or any of them were indeed optimally nourished; or that any of their diets were in fact adequate in the scientific sense. Whether appetite was or was not a competent guide to their eating can only be shown by checking their diets with nutritional laws and standards."

Such checking of each of the fifteen diets in its entirety (the grand total of all meals eaten by the children was nearly 36,000) gave, in summary, the following results:

QUANTITIES OF FOOD EATEN

The average daily calories furnished by the diets during each six months' period were in every instance found to be within the limits set by scientific nutritional standards for the individual's age. So, too, were the average daily calories per kilogram of body weight, except in the few instances in which infants, undernourished before weaning, exceeded the standard in their first six months' period on the experiment. Finally, the law of the decline of calories, per kilogram of body weight, with growth was followed without exception and in orderly fashion as shown by curves made on a monthly basis. Quite possibly it is the close conformity of the diets to these quantitative laws and standards that accounts for the fact that there were after the first six months' period of each child no noticeably fat or thin children, but a greater uniformity of build that often obtains among those of the same family.

POTENTIAL ACIDITY AND ALKALINITY OF THE DIETS

Maintenance of the acid-base balance of the blood requires that potentially acid constituents of the diet must be at least balanced by constituents of potential alkalinity, and most authorities agree that a moderate excess of potentially alkaline ones is desirable. Regarding the relation of this law to dietary practice, H. C. Sherman says that while an upset of the acid-base balance resulting in ketosis may occur when the proportions of carbohydrates, proteins, and fats in the diet are out of the proper relation to each other, "it is presumably rare in normal individuals on self-chosen diets." This proved to be the case with the diets of the children. In the diet of one child there was an exact balance of potentially acid and potentially alkaline constituents during his first and only six month's period. In the diets of the other fourteen there was a moderate preponderance of the potentially alkaline in every month's period.

THE DISTRIBUTION OF CALORIES

Nutritional science has been much concerned with the problem of the proper distribution of calories among the three dietary constituents—fat, carbohydrate, and protein—and especially about the percentage of calories to be allotted to protein with which carbohydrates and fats are not interchangeable as body-builders. Authorities vary somewhat in the percentages they allot to protein for children below the age of five years, *i.e.,* in general, from 10 per cent to 17 per cent. For the self-chosen diets, the *average* distribution of calories per kilogram of body weight (regardless of variations in children's age) was protein 17 per cent, fat 35 per cent and carbohydrate 48 per cent. The individual range for the protein in the group was from 9 per cent to 20 per cent. All diets showed a decline in protein per kilogram of body weight in accordance with the change in the relation of body-building requirements to energy requirements that comes with growth and increased activity. Quality of protein is, however, no less important than quantity. The protein of the diets was in every case protein of the highest biological value, having been predominantly derived from such animal sources as milk, eggs, liver, kidney, and muscle meats.

Because of the extent to which the essentially energy furnishing fats and carbohydrates are interchangeable in nutrition, few authorities make any allocation of the remaining 83 per cent of calories between them. The average distribution for these in the diets as a group (fat 35 per cent, carbohydrate 48 per cent) differs but slightly from that advocated by Rose.

As yet no statistical analysis of the diets has been made for their vitamin and mineral contents, but with all vegetables fresh, all cereals whole grains, ground by the old stone process, eggs, liver and kidney eaten freely, fresh fruits eaten in amazingly large quantities, and the salt used, an unpurified sea salt containing all the minerals found in the body, the probability of any deficiency in vitamins or minerals is slight indeed. In fact, the quantities of fresh fruit, carrots, and potatoes and of eggs, liver, and kidneys in practically all the diets preclude, on the basis of their known vitamin content, any shortage of Vitamins A, B, C, and G. For the adequacy in vitamin D and calcium of the diets of children who took none or little milk for considerable periods of time we cannot speak so surely from an off-hand consideration of the quantities of foods eaten. We can, however, call in evidence the roentgenograms of these children's bones which showed as excellent calcification as those of the others.

Regarding the calcification of bones in the group, Dr. W. E. Anspach, Roentgenologist of the Children's Memorial Hospital, has written in a personal communication to your essayist, "The beautifully calcified bones in roentgenograms of your group of children stand out so well that I have no trouble in picking them out when seen at a distance." That such "beautiful calcification" of bones was achieved by all, regardless of whether or not they had rickets when admitted, would seem difficult to account for, had adequate calcium or vitamin D been lacking.

The diets, then, were orthodox, conforming to nutritional laws and standards in what they furnished. The children actually were as well nourished as they looked to be.

Such successful juggling and balancing of the more than thirty nutritional essentials that exist in mixed and different proportions in the foods from which they must be derived suggests at once the existence of some innate, automatic mechanism for its accomplishment, of which appetite is a part. It is certainly difficult to account for the success of the fifteen unrelated infants on any other grounds.

Also, such success with the nutritional essentials suggests the possibility that appetite indicated one orthodox diet in terms of foods and the quantities of them, comparable to the diet lists of paediatricians and nutritionists. But to this possibility the self-chosen diets give not a scintilla of support. In terms of foods and relative quantities of them they failed to show any orthodoxy of their own and were wholly unorthodox with respect to paediatric practice. For every diet differed from every other diet, fifteen different patterns of taste being presented, and not one diet was the predominantly cereal and milk diet with smaller supplements of fruit, eggs, and meat, that is commonly thought proper for this age. To add to the apparent confusion, tastes changed unpredictably from time to time, refusing as we say "to stay put," while meals were often combinations of foods that were strange indeed to us, and would have been a dietician's nightmare—for example, a breakfast of a pint of orange juice and liver; a supper of several eggs, bananas and milk. They achieved the goal, but by widely various means, as Heaven may presumably be reached by different roads.

This seemingly irresponsible and erratic behavior of appetite with respect to selection of foods from which the essentials were obtained stamps it as the same Puckish fellow we have always known it to be. Why, then, were his pranks beneficent in the experiment when so often harmful elsewhere? Or to put it baldly, as I hope many of you are doing, what was the trick in the experiment? This brings us to the discussion of what we learned about appetite and its workings, which throws light on the question of its competencies and fallibilities.

Selective appetite is, primarily, the desire for foods that please by smelling or tasting good, and it would seem that in the absence of such sensory information, i.e., if one had never smelled or tasted a food, he could not know whether he liked or disliked it. Such proved to be the case with these infants. When the large tray of foods, each in its separate dish, was placed before them at their first meals, there was not the faintest sign of "instinct" directed choice. On the contrary, their choices were apparently wholly random; they tried not only foods but chewed hopefully the clean spoon, dishes, the edge of the tray, or a piece of paper on it. Their faces showed expressions of surprise, followed by pleasure, indifference, or dislike. All the articles on the list, except lettuce by two and spinach by one, were tried by all, and most tried several times, but within the first few days they began to reach eagerly for some and to neglect others, so that definite tastes grew under our eyes. Never again did any child eat so many of the foods as in the first weeks of his experimental period. Patterns of selective appetite, then, were shown to develop on the basis of sensory experience, i.e., taste, smell, and doubtless the feeling of comfort and well-being that followed eating, which was evidenced much as in the breast-fed infant. In short, they were developed by sampling, which is essentially a trial and error method. And it is this trial and error method, this willingness to sample, that accounts for the most glaring fallibility of appetite. From time immemorial adults as well as children have eaten castor oil beans, poisonous fish, toad stools and nightshade berries with fatal results. Against such error, only the transmission of racial experience as knowledge can protect. Such error affords additional proof that in omnivorous eaters there is no "instinct" pointing blindly to the "good" or "bad" in food. And since every trial and error method involves the possibility of error, the problem of successful eating by appetite is that of reducing possible errors to those that are most trivial by a prior selection of the foods that are made available for eating.

Appetite also appears to have fallibilities with processed foods which have lost some of the natural constituents and which have become such important features of modern diet, e.g., sugar and white flour. Certainly their introduction into previously sound primitive diets has invariably brought with it a train of nutritional evils, and their widespread excess in civilized diets is decried by nutritional authorities. Whether the evils are due to innate fallibilities of appetite with respect to these products, or whether appetite in such cases is merely overruled by extraneous considerations of novelty, cheapness, ease of procurement and preparation, etc., has not been determined.

We had hoped to investigate this problem in a small way by an experiment with newly weaned infants in which both natural foods and their processed products were simultaneously served, but the depression dashed this hope.

By this time you have all doubtless perceived that the "trick" in the experiment (if "trick" you wish to call it) was in the food list. Confined to natural, unprocessed and unpurified foods as it was, and without made dishes of any sort, it reproduced to a large extent the conditions under which primitive people in many parts of the world have been shown to have had scientifically sound diets and excellent nutrition. Errors the children's appetites must have made—they are inherent in any trial and error method—but the errors with such a food list were too trivial and too easily compensated for to be of importance or even to be detected.

The results of the experiment, then, leave the selection of the foods to be made available to young children in the hands of their elders where everyone has always known it belongs. Even the food list is not a magic one. Any of you with a copy of McCollum's or H. C. Sherman's books on nutrition and properties of foods, could make a list quite different and equally as good. Self-selection can have no, or but doubtful, value if the diet must be selected from inferior foods. Finally, by providing conditions under which appetite could function freely and beneficently as in animals and primitive peoples, the experiment resolved the modern conflict between appetite and nutritional requirements. It eliminated anorexia and the eating problems that are the plague of feeding by the dosage method.

Asking the Question

The questions we seek to answer are motivated by many different concerns. A researcher might be interested in the environmental factors that encourage aggressive behavior. A teacher might be interested in how to help an aggressive child learn to develop more positive interactions with his classmates. A parent might be interested in what control techniques to use in disciplining aggressive behavior toward a younger sibling. We already know that it is important to ask questions in a manner that does not unduly influence or bias the answer. It is also important to be clear about how we are using or defining terms. Aggressiveness might mean physical abuse, verbal hostility, assertiveness, or a drive for achievement.

Kerlinger (1973) says that "it is necessary, then, to define fairly precisely and unambiguously what is to be observed. If we are measuring *curiosity* we must tell the observer what curious behavior is. If *cooperativeness* is being measured, we must somehow tell the observer how cooperative behavior is distinguished from any other kind of behavior. This means that we must provide the observer with some form of operational definition of the variable being measured; we must define the variable behaviorally" (p. 541). An operational definition is a definition that lets everyone operate from the same base of understanding. It defines a term so that everyone understands how it is being used by the person defining it. This does not always mean that everyone agrees with the definition; but it does mean that in a particular situation the term has a specific meaning.

Researchers must give careful attention to operational definitions. They often relate the definition to a particular theory or perspective and to terms or concepts frequently used within that theory or concept. Ethologists, for example, feel that aggression is an innate human behavior and that rituals and sports serve as a means of releasing and channeling aggression. Their choice of words to describe aggression will reflect this biological perspective.

Teachers do not need to be as precise in defining terms, nor do they have to relate the definitions to theory or to previous work of other people. They do, however, need to be clear about what they mean by a term. Particular caution is needed when the term can easily mean several different things.

Your task in this assignment is first to review some definitions of aggression and then develop your own operational definition of aggression.

Part I: Analyzing Definitions

Procedure: Each of the behaviors identified below has been classified as "aggressive" by some researcher studying aggression. Consider each behavior and identify the ambiguities or confusions that could occur by taking the behavior at face value. How could the definition be rewritten to eliminate these ambiguities?

1. A child hitting another child.

    Possible Ambiguity:

    How To Eliminate the Ambiguity:

2. Angry outbursts.

    Possible Ambiguity:

    How To Eliminate the Ambiguity:

3. Rejecting and/or putting down another person.

    Possible Ambiguity:

    How To Eliminate the Ambiguity:

4. Destruction of another person's property.

    Possible Ambiguity:

    How To Eliminate the Ambiguity.

Part II: Developing an Operational Definition

1. Now that you have analyzed some brief descriptions of what others have meant by aggression, try to develop your own operational definition of aggression.

2. Having defined aggression, think of a question about aggression in children that you could study observationally. Write the question in a manner that clearly states both the question being asked and what you mean by aggression.

Observing and Hypothesizing

A common criticism of researchers and evaluators is that they have training in research theory, design, method, and statistics but have never seen a real live child. This is an exaggeration, but it is true that many studies go directly from the drawing board to a pilot study. The pilot study is designed to try out the methods: instructions given the child, scoring procedures, length of the session or observation, and so on. Seldom does the pilot study address itself to whether or not the study itself is worthwhile, or whether the method selected actually measures or is relevant to the behavior in question. Blurton-Jones feels that a preliminary observation phase (before the pilot study is designed) saves time by eliminating unproductive or unrealistic hypotheses or ideas. In Chapter 1 we identified one of the values of observation as a means of generating hypotheses or ideas. Your task in this assignment is to observe to gain some ideas.

Procedure: A half hour is a very short preliminary observation period, but it is enough to give you a flavor of what can be learned from observing behavior and events around you. Select something that you are interested in to observe. It might be the way different children approach learning a new activity, how a coach motivates players in a workout with the football team, how efficiently time is used by clerks in a fast-food store, parental control techniques used in supermarkets, how children explore the zoo—or anything else you can think of. Spend at least half an hour observing the behavior or setting you have identified. Make notes on whatever interests you or seems important to you. Then reflect on what you have observed and think about questions that would be productive for investigation.

Date_____Time_____Setting/Location _____

Focus of Observation _____

Transcribe the notes or comments that you made in the course of your observation in the space below.

1. Based on what you observed, identify a question you feel warrants further study. For example, if you observed how young children explore the zoo, you may have found that most of the children simply darted from cage to cage and didn't really stop to look at anything. The goal seemed to be to get to the next cage first, wait for your friend to catch up, and then take off for the next cage. You might also have noticed that all of the information about the animals was designed for older children and adults. Your question for investigation might then be: "How would young children respond to the zoo if there were materials designed especially for them, picture signs at their level, hands-on experiences with barnyard animals, touch tables with sea life?"

2. What hypothesis or prediction would you make about what the results of the study would show? For example, your hypothesis might be: "The amount of random behavior (defined in terms of running around rather than looking at the animals) would decrease if there were signs and experiences specially designed for younger children."

3. What basis do you have for your hypothesis?

4. What method (from the six child study methods outlined in this chapter) would you select to study your hypothesis? Why?

Chapter Three

Observational
Strategies

Over the years, a number of observational strategies have been developed to meet the needs of researchers and teachers in a variety of situations. From the beginning, researchers have recognized the fact that observation is both a scientific tool and an everyday skill of value to teachers and parents as well as to researchers. Herbert F. Wright (1960), one of the leading proponents of direct observation and naturalistic research, identified six methods of direct observation that have been used in child study.

Wright reviewed all of the child-development research published in major journals from their beginnings in 1890 to 1958. He found 1409 empirical (scientific) studies with children or adolescents as subjects. Only 8 percent of these studies used direct observation methods. This does not mean that only 8 percent of the studies used observational techniques, but that only 8 percent were observations of *freely occurring behavior in the natural environment*. Wright does not identify the methods used for the remaining 92 percent, but one can safely assume that most research occurred in experimental laboratories. Many of these studies may have used some of the same observational techniques identified by Wright as methods of direct observation, but used them in a laboratory rather than in a natural setting.

The six commonly used observational methods identified by Wright are listed below:

1. *Diary Descriptions* had their beginnings with Pestalozzi in 1774 and emerged as a major child-study method with the baby biographies in the period from 1890-1920. Diary descriptions record developmental changes as they occur. The biographer or journalist may record general development or may focus on specific areas of development like language or sensory-motor skills. Most diaries were kept by relatives of the child because the method demands prolonged and frequent contact with the child.

2. *Specimen Descriptions* are similar to diary descriptions in that they are narrative records. They differ in that they provide more complete details of *single episodes* of behavior covering "intensively and continuously the behavior and situation of the child during more or less extended behavior sequences" (Wright, 1960, p. 73). Fletcher B. Dresslar first used this technique in 1901 in his "A Morning's Observation of a Baby." This method is not limited to people who have constant access to an individual child, but can be used by any observer. A briefer version of specimen description is the anecdotal record in which a single relatively brief event is recorded, often after the fact rather than on the spot. It does not contain the same richness of detail, but preserves the essence of what occurred.

3. *Time Sampling* was developed by Willard Olson in the mid-1920s to study nervous habits exhibited by school children in the classroom. This method allowed the observer to narrow his attention from recording everything, as in specimen descriptions, to recording selected aspects of behavior as they occurred within specified intervals of time. Behavioral categories are identified in advance and then the observer records the frequency of occurrence within each time interval. Time sampling was quickly adopted by experimentalists who found the ease of recording, coding, and analyzing data more suitable to laboratory studies than the laborious and costly specimen descriptions.

4. *Event Sampling* was used by Ernest Horn as early as 1914 in his study of student participation in classroom recitation, but did not blossom until Florence L. Goodenough described it as a research method in 1928. It differs from time sampling in that it is free of any time constraints. This method involves recording each instance of a particular behavior or event as it occurs. Helen C. Dawe used it in 1934 in her classic analysis of 200 quarrels of preschool children. Researchers since then have used it both in laboratory and natural settings to study just about every aspect of child behavior. Along with time sampling, it has become the major observational technique of child development research.

5. *Rating Scales* (or *Trait Rating* as Wright calls them) were described by Haggerty, Olson, and Wickman (1930) in their behavior rating scales. This method, used heavily in clinical and experimental research, selects specific dimensions of behavior to observe and then uses a battery or scale to judge the child's behavior. The observer thus both observes and judges behavior against some predetermined criteria. For example, the teacher may rate a child on how frequently he asks for help in completing assignments using a scale with intervals ranging from *never needs help* to *always needs help*.

6. *Field-Unit Analysis* grew out of the work of Roger Barker and Herbert Wright (1951) who had long advocated specimen records as the best means of preserving the behavior stream—descriptions of on-going behavior and identification of the environment in which the behavior occurs. One of the major criticisms of specimen descriptions in research was the time needed to transcribe the notes, code the data, and assemble it into a form manageable for analysis. Field-unit analysis divides the behavior stream into consecutive units as they occur and provides on-the-spot coding. This method is used mainly in child development research growing out of ecological psychology, an approach that investigates the interactions between the organism and the environment. Field-unit analysis has grown into a variety of observational systems which share in common the need for a comprehensive yet efficient means of data collection. Our discussion of observational strategies will focus on observational systems rather than on field-unit analysis.

Wright's taxonomy or means of classifying observational methods focuses on *how the data are obtained* and what the distinguishing features are for each method of obtaining data. Richard Brandt (1972) has developed a taxonomy that focuses on *how the data are recorded*. His taxonomy includes three general methods of recording data:

1. *Narrative types* of data include "all data that merely reproduce behavioral events in much the same fashion and sequence as in their original occurrence" (Brandt, 1972, p. 80). Wright's diary and specimen descriptions would fit this category.

2. *Checklist notations* require the observer to impose some sort of structure on the observation by selecting and defining behaviors ahead of time so that the observer can simply check their occurrence rather than describe the behavior as required by the narrative types of data gathering. Wright's time and event sampling and field-unit analysis can be treated in checklist fashion, although

event sampling and field-unit analysis may also involve some narration.

3. *Rating scales* require the observer to make some sort of interpretation of what has been observed and information is recorded that reflects observer judgment. This overlaps with Wright's trait rating method of observation.

All of the observation methods mentioned in both the Wright and Brandt taxonomies were developed for direct observation of people and events in the natural environment. They are not, however, limited to naturalistic research.

Observation Guidelines

Given the visual and perceptual difficulties of becoming a good observer, trying to attend to everything that may be important, plus the challenge of selecting the method that best meets your need, it is appropriate to try to formulate some guidlines for both.

The earliest writers on the topic were busy reminding their readers of the difficulties of becoming a good observer and reporter of human behavior, but they had very little to say about how to do it. In emphasizing the difficulty of studying the child, Compayré wrote: "But in the case of the child one phenomenon has no sooner shown itself than it gives place to another" (1896, p. 10). There is no way to stop motion, do an instant replay, or ask a child to repeat an utterance. Action continues whether or not the observer is ready for it to do so. This recognition of the difficulty of studying a child led most early researchers to say that professional training was needed to guarantee useful notes or documentation.

William Stern, an early twentieth-century writer of psychology textbooks, admitted that mothers were probably best at the task of observing and recording their observations, but he was quick to add that scientific training was needed to make a good observer. Stern and others felt that mothers might be too close to their children to observe and report dispassionately; however, this disability was evidently not shared by fathers! Stern indicated that observations might also be made by other relatives, including fathers, and by teachers, doctors, and psychologists.

Stern (1930) carefully and thoughtfully developed some guidelines for the inexperienced observer:

1. *Make a clear distinction between what is actually seen or heard and conclusions drawn from it.* In everyday life, people have a tendency to explain, excuse, embroider, and expound on what they see and hear. An observer must clearly separate observed fact from interpretation.

2. *Try to interpret what you observe from the child's viewpoint rather than imposing adult perceptions on the material.* The ability to get into a child's head is a rare one. Some adults seem to have a talent for putting themselves in a child's place. But most adults need to be wary when interpreting a child's actions; too often the interpretation is a better reflection of how adults reason and react than it is of a child's response.

3. *Draw no conclusions which cannot be positively justified by the actual observation.* This touches on a common weakness in us all. We are all apt to go a bit beyond the actual evidence if we have a hunch that something might be true (p. 35).

To these few suggestions made by Stern, we might add others to consider when doing any kind of observational work.

1. *Describe, in writing, the purpose and procedure involved in your observation.* By having to think of the right words to describe your intentions and plans, you will help clarify the task for yourself and for others who may read your observations.

2. If your observation involves being in a school classroom (other than your own), *be sure you have the approval of the school principal and classroom teacher for your work.* This is just common courtesy. If your subject is at home, or in any other supervised environment, get the approval of the supervising adult before proceeding with your observation. For most research in public, naturalistic settings (supermarkets, playgrounds, etc.) where there is no need to acquaint anyone with your plans, simply be certain that your observation is unobtrusive. Be as discrete as you can in such instances. If your observation is part of a research project you will need to clear your project with parents or special committees, such as Human Subjects Committees within the university.

3. Most universities have committees set up to review and approve all experimental research that directly involves children in order to safeguard them from potentially harmful or unpleasant experiences. Gerald Levin (1973) suggests that students *design studies in which participation benefits the child.* He says, "If you feel you must study unhappiness, study it naturalistically or seek to reduce it" (p. 71). If you are doing your observation within a naturalistic framework, you will not be asking children to participate in any direct way, and this guideline will not apply.

4. If your observation is done in a classroom, get the teacher's advice on where to position yourself. *It is usually desirable to adopt a low profile by selecting an unobtrusive vantage point for observing and by sitting rather than standing.* The same would be true if you were to observe on the playground. From time to time, children will come up to an observer who is a stranger to them and attempt to engage the observer in activity or conversation. When that occurs, it is usually best to explain that you are busy doing your work and suggest that they go to their teacher instead. If there is a situation involving danger to a child and the observer is the only adult in the immediate area, then the observer should step in (if, for example, a swing is about to hit a child in the head). In situations involving arguments between children, the observer should not intervene. If adult attention is required, the observer should simply inform a nearby teacher.

5. *Information gathered on individual children or situations should be treated confidentially and with respect.* It is unprofessional to use material from your research in social conversation, and names of individuals involved should always be

protected. Notice how careful Barker and Wright (1967) are to state that real names and place names have been disguised in their book *Midwest and Its Children*. They say, "All names of persons and communities in the book are code names used to protect the privacy of the individuals concerned" (Barker and Wright, 1955, Preface).

6. *Take down exact words whenever possible and note exact behavior, including body language.* After the observation period, read your notes and correct or modify them while your memory of the observation is still relatively fresh. If you are unsure of your data at any point, indicate this in the margin to help you evaluate its use later on.

7. *Be as objective as possible in your work as observer.* As Robert Watson and Henry Lindgren (1973) point out, ". . .all observation remains subjective because it depends upon the organism of the observer. We attempt to make it as objective as possible by arranging conditions of observation so that the human element can be minimized (although never eliminated)" (p. 44). One of the problems with objectivity is that as observers we have our own biases. These biases often lead us to see what we expect to see or what we want to see. Another problem is that we become accustomed to seeing certain things and take them for granted. In so doing we fail to notice their importance or significance. A third problem with objectivity is that we tend to assume that other people are like ourselves; we interpret behavior on the basis of our own feelings. To check yourself on your own objectivity, review your observations for assignments seven and eight at the end of this chapter.

8. *Avoid letting your own feelings about the subject of your observation color or slant your observation.* This guideline addresses another aspect of objectivity. Specifically it means that we should avoid giving higher ratings or emphasizing the more positive behaviors of subjects we like and likewise need to guard against giving lower ratings or focusing on the more negative aspects of subjects we don't like. Researchers call this the *halo effect*; if we like a person or an object we tend to see only good things, and vice-versa.

9. *In recording your observational notes, there are several points of information that need to be on every sheet you use.* These are:
   a. identity of observer
   b. name or description of subject for later identification (such as subject's age or birthdate, sex, plus any special characteristics important to the research—age of siblings, socioeconomic level of family, handicapping conditions, and so on)
   c. date and time of the observation
   d. the setting or location (classroom, playground, research room, supermarket, etc.)

Most of the assignments in this book do not require the observer to actually engage the children observed in conversation or in any kind of experimental activity. Students are well advised, however, to learn the ethical standards published by the American Psychological Association (APA) governing research with children. These guidelines are as follows:

Table 1   Ethical Standards for Developmental Psychologists*

Children as research subjects present problems for the investigator different from those of adult subjects. Our culture is marked by a tenderness of concern for the young. The young are viewed as more vulnerable to distress (even though evidence may suggest that they are actually more resilient in recovery from stress). Because the young have less knowledge and less experience, they also may be less able to evaluate what participation in research means. And, consent of the parent for the study of his child is the prerequisite to obtaining consent from the child. These characteristics outline the major differences between research with children and research with adults.

1. No matter how young the subject, he has rights that supersede the rights of the investigator of his behavior. In the conduct of his research the investigator measures each operation he proposes against this principle and is prepared to justify his decision.
2. The investigator uses no research operations that may harm the child either physically or psychologically. Psychological harm, to be sure, is difficult to define; nevertheless, its definition remains a responsibility of the investigator.
3. The informed consent of parents or of those legally designated to act *in loco parentis* is obtained, preferably in writing. Informed consent requires that the parent be given accurate information on the profession and institutional affiliation of the investigator, and on the purpose and operations of the research, albeit in layman's terms. The consent of parents is not solicited by any claims of benefit to the child. Not only is the right of parents to refuse consent respected, but parents must be given the opportunity to refuse.
4. The investigator does not coerce a child into participating in a study. The child has the right to refuse and he, too, should be given the opportunity to refuse.
5. When the investigator is in doubt about possible harmful effects of his efforts or when he decides that the nature of his research requires deception, he submits his plan to an *ad hoc* group of his colleagues for review. It is the group's responsibility to suggest other feasible means of obtaining the information. Every psychologist has a responsibility to maintain not only his own ethical standards but also those of his colleagues.
6. The child's identity is concealed in written and verbal reports of the results, as well as in informal discussions with students and colleagues.
7. The investigator does not assume the role of diagnostician or counselor in reporting his observations to parents or those *in loco parentis*. He does not report test scores or information given by a child in confidence, although he recognizes a duty to report general findings to parents and others.
8. The investigator respects the ethical standards of those who act *in loco parentis* (e.g., teachers, superintendents of institutions).
9. The same ethical standards apply to children who are control subjects, and to their parents, as to those who are experimental subjects. When the ex-

perimental treatment is believed to benefit the child, the investigator considers an alternative treatment for the control group instead of no treatment.

10. Payment in money, gifts, or services for the child's participation does not annul any of the above principles.

11. Teachers of developmental psychology present the ethical standards of conducting research on human beings to both their undergraduate and graduate students. Like the university committees on the use of human subjects, professors share responsibility for the study of children on their campuses.

---

*Statement of Division of Developmental Psychology of the American Psychological Association, *Newsletter*, 1968, pp 1–3. Copyright 1968 by the American Psychological Association, and reproduced by permission of the Division on Developmental Psychology.

Summary

A variety of observational strategies exist. Herbert Wright has classified these strategies or techniques according to method. The six methods identified by Wright are diary descriptions, specimen descriptions, time sampling, event sampling, trait rating (rating scales), and field-unit analysis (which we have expanded to observational systems). Richard Brandt has classified the techniques according to how the data are recorded: narrative data, checklist notations, and rating scales. This book will deal with both taxonomies.

The final section of the chapter outlines guidelines for observers and ethical considerations for research with children.

Suggestions for Further Reading

Brandt, R.M. *Studying Behavior in Natural Settings*. New York: Holt, Rinehart and Winston, 1972. This text, devoted to naturalistic observational research, provides a good overview of the methods and uses of direct observation. Chapters 2, 4, and 5 review the ethical considerations involved in naturalistic study, Brandt's taxonomy of observational measures, and a discussion of tests, questionnaires, and interviews.

Wright, H.F. Observational child study. In P.H. Mussen, ed. *Handbook of Research Methods in Child Development*. New York: Wiley, 1960, pp. 71–139. This important chapter focuses on observational child study—"research methods that leave nature and society to their own devices" (p. 71). Wright briefly traces the development of observational studies and methods, starting with the diary description (baby biography), and gives the procedures, advantages, and disadvantages of each method. A section on problems common to all methods of observational child study covers observer influence, reliability, instrumental aids, and descriptive categories. Even today, twenty years after it was written, Wright's chapter is still the best available summary of the various direct observation methods.

Fact vs. Inference

We have discussed the need to be objective in reporting observational information. Now it is time to check your own objectivity. This is one of the most important skills to develop in becoming a good observer.

Part I: Field Notes

Procedure: Visit the waiting room of a local pediatrician and unobtrusively observe for twenty minutes. Take careful notes on what goes on in the waiting room during the time you are there. Your notes should describe the interactions, conversations, and any other information that you feel would help a reader picture the situation. (Be sure to get permission from the doctor or nurse before doing the observation.)

Date_____Time_____Setting/Location _____

1. Identify by age (approximate), sex, and relationship (i.e., mother of two-year-old boy, nurse, and so on) each of the people in the setting.

2. Observer's notes:

Part II: Analysis of Subjective and Objective Statements

It is easy to make inferences about behaviors or situations we have observed. In part we do so as a shorthand means of communication. It is easier to say that "She sat dejectedly at the end of the table" than to say that "She sat by herself at the end of the table; her shoulders were hunched over; her eyes looked down at the table; and the corners of her mouth drooped." In part we infer feelings or motives because it is the message we get as we observe. Sometimes, however, these messages are more a reflection of our own feelings than they are of the feelings of the person being observed. Sometimes we are lacking important information which would change our perception, and sometimes we are just plain wrong.

It is important to separate observable fact from observational inference. Observable facts describe what is happening—events that everyone can agree upon, like who is in the setting, the sequence of events, what an individual says, how long a person spends doing something, and so on. Inferences are subjective words or phrases which suggest the quality of an action or what the behavior means or how a person feels. They are often words that evaluate rather than describe what is happening. Words like *aggressive, isolated, fearful, shy,* or *reluctant* are words that carry emotional overtones and as such are inferences about how a person feels or behaves.

Procedure: Analyze the notes you have just made and list all of the words or phrases that are descriptive in the OBJECTIVE statement column and all words or phrases that are inferential in the SUBJECTIVE column.

Objective Statements	*Subjective Statements*

1. Look at the inferential statements you have made. Does there seem to be any pattern to the things you infer or are they just general inference? Discuss.

2. Rewrite each of the inferential statements to make each one a descriptive statement.

Drawing Inferences

Not all inferences are bad. Inferences can be useful if they help us generate ideas for research, plan better for the individual needs of children in a class, or do a better job of analyzing a situation. The important consideration to keep in mind is whether or not the inferences or conclusions can be substantiated from the data. Would another person arrive at the same conclusion if he or she were to read the observational notes?

If we write, "She sat dejectedly at the end of the table," we have not given the naive reader (someone who did not observe what actually happened) enough information for that reader to decide whether or not her behavior indicated that she felt dejected. We have simply told the reader that this was the case.

We need to give the reader descriptive information that is recorded as objectively as possible. This information needs to be complete enough so that we can draw conclusions or inferences from the data. The important point to remember is to infer at the end of an observation not during it.

Procedure: The kind of observation done of an active, speaking individual is quite different from one that focuses on an infant or young animal. When observing a nonverbal or preverbal subject, the observer must find clues in the behavior and nonverbalized expression. This exercise will give the observer experience in recording nonverbal clues and in interpreting the data. Select an environment in which you can unobtrusively observe a young child (twelve to eighteen months of age) or a baby animal (kitten or puppy, for example). Observe for a total of twenty minutes and jot down activities for later analysis. Concentrate on how your subject explores the environment and establishes contact with others, if others are present.

Date_____Time_____Setting/Location _____

Subject (species, age, sex) _____

Others Present in Setting _____

Attach your transcribed notes to this lab sheet.

1. Summarize your observation notes in a manner that provides a concise description of the young child's or animal's behavior. Be sure to include enough information about the setting so that the reader can visualize it.

2. If you have used subjective words or phrases in your summary, go back and circle them in red for easy identification. Rewrite the subjective words or phrases to make each one a descriptive statement.

3. List the inferences you feel are justified by your observational notes. For each inference listed, identify the data that support the inference.

Inference   *Supporting Data*

1.

2.

3.

4.

5.

6.

7.

8.

9.

10.

4. Some inferences serve as hunches or hypotheses about what is going on. These hunches usually need to be tested out by either observing the same kind of situation several times, observing at different times of the day or in different settings, or observing the subject with different people (animals). Identify those inferences that need further observation, in order to confirm your hunch. How many instances or settings or whatever would be necessary to confirm or disprove the inference?

Inferential Hypotheses   *Criteria for Confirmation*

1.

2.

3.

4.

5.

The Child's Eye View

One of the guidelines offered by William Stern is to observe from the child's viewpoint—to take the child's perspective and put aside one's own perspective. This sounds easy but it is not. To do this well we must know something about how children develop—how they think, feel, and behave at different ages. Some of you will have had a course in child development and others will not. If you have not, your task is more difficult. You must rely more on your own good judgment and must be particularly able to read cues from the child's verbal and nonverbal behavior and from the situation itself.

Another important factor in being able to write your notes from the child's perspective is your role-taking ability, which quite literally means taking the role of someone else, being able to think or feel or visually see things as another person would. Some of us are naturally good at this. Some of us, on the other hand, are locked into our own perceptions in a kind of adult egocentrism (if we look at it in a cognitive manner á la Piaget).

Your task in this assignment is to observe from the child's perspective, to record your observations in a manner that reports what would be most important from the child's viewpoint. You may want to physically put yourself at the child's visual level. The world does look different to someone who is three feet tall. You will also want to be careful not to assume that the child knows how to do what seems like a simple task, or that he or she has a concept well in mind. The task at hand may seem very difficult or confusing to a child.

Procedure: Select a child to observe who is between the ages of two and twelve. Observe that child for twenty minutes, taking notes that describe the environmental setting and the child's behavior. If the child is interacting with others you will need to describe the interaction as well. Pay attention to the sequence of behavior as this may be important in helping you transcribe from your notes after the observation.

1. Record your field notes here (attach additional sheets if necessary), paying special attention to what the child says, notices, and does.

2. Now write a narrative summary of your observation keeping in mind that your task is to reflect the child's behavior and understanding. Remember our earlier caution about unwarranted inferences. Describe actual conversation, events, and behavior, not what you think the child feels or sees. Let the child's verbalizations and actions speak for themselves.

3. While making notes, record those instances, if there were any, in which the lesson guidelines kept you from misinterpreting or misreporting the child's actions or perceptions. (For example, you may have thought that the child was looking at another child across the room, but found on bending down to the child's eye level that a bookcase cut off his or her visual contact with the youngster across the room.)

Chapter Four

Diary Descriptions: The Historical Background

Dear Diary! Almost all of us at one time or another have kept diaries where we recorded the important thoughts and events of our lives. In the past, writing in a diary with some regularity was as common as it is today. Some famous diaries or journals have even been published. *The Diary of Anne Frank* is one. Anne was a Jewish child whose family went into hiding in 1942 to escape the Nazis. Anne was thirteen years old at the time. During the two years before the Nazis discovered the family and sent them to concentration camps where Anne died, Anne kept a diary which critics have called a great human document.

One of the most touching records from the past is Cotton Mather's diary, which he kept from 1709 to 1724. Cotton Mather, a New England Puritan minister, fathered fifteen children; only two lived to survive him. During the measles epidemic of 1713, he lost his wife and three of his young children in less than two weeks. His diary is a personal record of his grief:

November 4, 1713: In my poor Family, now, first, my Wife has the Measles appearing on her . . . My Daughter Nancy is also full of them. My Daughter Lizzy, is likewise full of them . . . My Daughter Jerusha, droops and seems to have them appearing. November 8–9: . . . On Munday (Nov. 9) between three and four in the Afternoon, my dear, dear, dear Friend expired.

Cotton Mather's wife gone, he turned his attention to his desperately ill children:

November 14: . . . Oh! the Trial, which I am this Day called unto in the threatning, the dying Circumstances of my dear little Jerusha! The Resignation, with which I am to offer up that Sacrifice! Father, Lett that Cup pass from me. Nevertheless—The Two Newborns, are languishing in the Arms of Death.
November 17–18: . . . About midnight, little Eleazar died.
November 20: Little Martha died, about ten o'clock A.M. I am again called unto the Sacrifice of my dear, dear, Jerusha. I begg'd, I begg'd, that such a bitter Cup, as the Death of that lovely child, might pass from me.
November 21: . . . Betwixt 9 h. and 10 h. at night, my lovely Jerusha Expired. She was two years, and about seven Months, old.
November 22: . . . My poor Family is now left without any Infant in it, or any under seven Years of Age (Bremner, 1970, pp. 46–48).

With the infant mortality rate as high as it was,[1] it is a wonder that anyone had the heart to attempt to record the growth and development of an infant whose life could be snuffed out at any time by any one of many causes. And yet, this was the period of time in which the first baby biographies were written by interested and thoughtful parents. Unlike the personal diary, these baby biographies were written by one individual about another. They were records of an infant's growth and development, usually kept by a parent who had a special interest in child study.

As a child study technique, the diary method of recording information about the growth and development of children was at its peak at the turn of the

[1]Even as late as 1925, Arnold Gesell wrote: "One-third of all the deaths in the nation occur below six years. There are ten times as many deaths during the half decade of pre-school life as during the following full decade of school life" (p. 10). Earlier estimates indicated that as many as 25 percent of children born died before their first birthday.

century. It can be argued that the diary description, or baby biography as it was more popularly called, was the first method used to study children. As mentioned in Chapter 2, Darwin's journal of his son Doddy's first three years drew public and scientific attention to the baby biography and it quickly became an important method of research in the new field of child study.

The popularity of baby biographies mushroomed during the 1890s in this country and in Europe. A bibliography of baby biographies compiled by Wayne Dennis in 1936 listed seventy-five such studies. Of the seventy-five, more than half are in English and the bulk of the publications date from 1890 to 1920. Many of the examples in this chapter used to illustrate the diary descriptions method of observation will be drawn from the baby biographies of this period. They will serve to illustrate both the development of the method and also to indicate the interests and findings of the early pioneers in child development.

The Early Baby Biographies

Although Pestalozzi had authored *A Father's Diary* in 1774, the first published diary description of an infant was by a German philosopher, Dietrich Tiedemann, in 1787. Milicent W. Shinn, author of the classic work of this kind (*The Biography of a Baby* published in 1900), gives credit to Tiedemann:

It was the Germans who first thought baby life worth recording, and the most complete and scientific of all the records is a German one. The first record known was published in the last century by a Professor Tiedemann—a mere slip of an essay, long completely forgotten, but resuscitated about the middle of this century, translated into French (and lately into English), and used by all students of the subject. Some of its observations we must, with our present knowledge, set down as erroneous; but it is on the whole exact and valuable, and a remarkable thing for a man to have done more than a hundred years ago (1900, pp. 12–13).

This study of infants attracted scientists as well as philosophers and educators. Charles Darwin's *The Origin of Species* (1859) suggested that the child was the link between animals and man, and that by observing the development of the infant, one could catch a glimpse of the development of the species itself.

Darwin, as a good scientist-father, kept notes on his infant son, William Erasmus (Doddy), born in 1840 when Darwin was thirty-one years old. This diary was not published until 1877. Although we do not have the benefit of Darwin's notes, we do have his synthesizing and speculating based on these notes. As might be expected, most of his comments and conclusions are accurate and useful ones. But there are also times when he generalizes from his data and arrives at a naive conclusion:

When two years and three months old, he became a great adept at throwing books or sticks, etc. at anyone who offended him; and so it was with some of my other sons. On the other hand, I could never see a trace of such aptitude in my infant daughters; and this makes me think that a tendency to throw objects is inherited by boys (Kessen, 1965, p. 121).

Darwin's statement points up one of the main weaknesses in the diary descriptions: with a sample of one, it is dangerous to generalize to the population. We cannot assume that what is observed in one infant is representative or characteristic of how all infants behave or develop.

Most baby biographers are not content merely to describe what they observe. They try out little experiments and note the results. So Charles Darwin did such things as touch the sole of the baby's foot, approach him backward to see what the baby would do, and test his reactions to loud noises.

Darwin was also interested, of course, in comparing his observations of an infant with his observations of other species. He comments that human infants are smarter than adult dogs:

The facility with which associated ideas due to instruction and others spontaneously arising were acquired, seemed to me by far the most strongly marked of all the distinctions between the mind of an infant and that of the cleverest full-grown dog that I have ever known (Kessen, 1965, p. 124).

Other observers were less interested in comparing human and animal species than Darwin was. A Frenchman, Gabriel Compayré (1896), was interested in the child because he believed that information on those early years would illuminate later development. He stated in the Introduction to his *Intellectual and Moral Development of the Child:* "If childhood is the cradle of humanity, the study of childhood is the natural and necessary introduction to all future psychology" (p. 3).

Compayré, and others, felt that the people who could best observe infants were parents who would follow the development of their own children with care. Compayré also admitted that "the psychology of the child is a complicated work, whose success cannot be attained unless many workers take hold of the subject" (p. 15).

Another early baby biographer who worked hard to enlist parents' aid in keeping records was Wilhelm Preyer, a German physiologist whose influential *Die Seele des Kindes (The Mind of the Child)* was published in 1881 (1888–1889 in English). His later book, *Mental Development in the Child,* published in 1893 in an English translation, has an Editor's Preface by William T. Harris, U.S. Commissioner of Education at the time. Harris reported that:

The special object of this book, as announced by Dr. Preyer in his preface, is to initiate mothers into this complicated science of psychogenesis. . . . He desires to evoke a widespread interest in the development of the infant mind (1893, p. v).

Preyer cautioned:

Of course it is not for everyone to confirm by his own observation all my statements of fact; for it is no easy thing in the case of an individual child who is in active movement, changing every instant the direction of his attention, altering his expression, and babbling unintelligible sounds, to ascertain what is in accordance with law. He only can reach the goal who, with the greatest patience and after preliminary studies in physiology and psychology, occupies himself persistently and impartially with several children (1893, p. xvii).

Not only does Preyer advocate looking at more than a sample of one, but he also shows himself to be an early ethologist, looking at the nonhuman species as well:

. . . the observation of untrained animals, especially young ones, and the comparison of the observations made upon them with those made upon little children, have often been found by me very helpful toward an understanding of children (1893, pp. xvii–xviii).

Preyer's books draw heavily upon the notes he took while observing his young son's first three years. Preyer, like Darwin, experimented to elicit response, and interpreted what he saw. In some cases he was correct and in other situations he misinterpreted what he had seen. Preyer, who is called by Compayré "a diligent and eager" observer, tested out the infant's sucking impulse at birth:

In December, 1870, three minutes after the appearance of the head—the child cried weakly as soon as the mouth was free—I touched the child's tongue; I passed the end of my finger back and forth over the surface of the organ; the child stopped crying immediately and began to suck my finger with great energy (Compayré, 1896, p. 83).

Yet this same diligent and eager observer wrote in his *Mental Development in the Child:* "Every child when just born is completely deaf. . . . no child is able to hear, out of the many thousand loving words its mother speaks in the first weeks of its life, more than single, loudly uttered ones" (Preyer, 1893, pp. 5–6).

Preyer conjures up an image of the well-read, well-intentioned new mother shouting loving monosyllables at her startled infant!

Despite his occasional inaccuracies, Preyer became the key source for most writers of diary descriptions. One of the first Americans to do an extensive record of an infant was Milicent Washburn Shinn. Shinn, like Preyer, was interested in enlisting mothers as observers. In the 1890s she persuaded the Association of Collegiate Alumni (later renamed the American Association of University Women) to become involved in child study. This had two important side benefits: The first was Preyer's enthusiastic response to this endeavor and his own offer to examine and return all diaries kept for at least six months. The second was that "College graduates kept diaries, filled in the record sheets published by Dr. Shinn, answered numerous questionnaires, corresponded with child-study leaders, read and studied the wealth of child-study literature which was being published" (Whipple, 1929, pp. 22–23). This greatly promoted public interest in the new field of child study and in the findings of the early researchers.

Shinn's own observations and diary recordings of her niece's first three years were published as part of her doctoral dissertation at the University of California (Berkeley). Her work came out in several documents published between 1893 and 1899, culminating in the publication in 1900 of her popular book, *The Biography of a Baby: The First Year of Life.*

In doing her own work, Shinn, like Preyer, kept a consecutive record of one child. She called this the *biographical method,* which she differentiated from what she called the *comparative method*, obtaining parallel data from a number of cases. She argued:

Conclusions cannot be securely drawn, it is felt, from observations on a single child: individual peculiarities might be mistaken for general traits of infancy. On the other hand, it is evident that the ontogenetic process, the unfolding of one stage of growth out of another, the evolution, in short, of the human being, cannot be traced except by watching the successive steps as they actually take place in one and the same child (1908, pp. 3–4).

Shinn points out that most of the studies of school-age children were comparative and statistical, while those of infants and very young children were biographical. She opted for a combination: the biographical method thoroughly checked and corrected by comparison with the work of other writers in the same field.

Like Darwin and Preyer, Shinn experimented to determine how the baby responded to specific stimuli. She did it carefully, however, arguing that if the aim were to follow the spontaneous process of development, experimenting needed to be done cautiously so as not to interfere with that spontaneity.

As is the case with other observers, Shinn's notes themselves are not readily available to us, but we do have the material she wrote based on those notes. Shinn clearly describes the baby's response to light in *The Biography of a Baby*:

Close on this came another great advance in vision. This was on the twenty-fifth day, toward evening, when the baby was lying on her grandmother's knee by the fire, in a condition of high well-being and content, gazing at her grandmother's face with an expression of attention. I came and sat down close by, leaning over the baby, so that my face must have come within the indirect range of her vision. At that she turned her eyes to my face and gazed at it with the same appearance of attention, and even of some effort, shown by a slight tension of brows and lips, then turned her eyes back to her grandmother's face, and again to mine, and so several times. The last time she seemed to catch sight of my shoulder, on which a high light struck from the lamp, and not only moved her eyes, but threw her head far back to see it better, and gazed for some time, with a new expression on her face—"a sort of dim and rudimentary eagerness," says my note. She no longer stared, but really looked (1900, pp. 65–66).

This brief passage epitomizes the best in the diary description method. Shinn identifies the age of the subject: 25th day; time of day: toward evening; setting: by the fire in the home; physical position of the baby: lying on grandmother's knee; emotional state of baby: content; activity of baby: gazing at grandmother's face. The observer then describes her own actions and the baby's reactions, identifying the expression on the baby's face (slight tension of brows and lips). And Shinn ends with a direct quote from her notes and a summarizing statement.

Shinn and other diarists presented a synthesis of their notes. Another kind of diary both noted the observation itself and gave comment, so that the reader had the benefit of the diary note and the perceptions resulting from it on the same page. The outstanding example of this is *Moto-Sensory Development: Observations on the First Three Years of a Child* by George V. N. Dearborn, a professor of physiology at Tufts College in the early 1900s. The book, published in 1910, was based on notes Dr. Dearborn took as he watched his infant daughter. For example, Dearborn notes the following on the thirteenth day:

So far, with but one momentary exception yesterday, I have never noticed any lack of perfect coordination in the eyes; the exception was a momentary internal stabismus of the right eye. No reaction occurred when a fist was suddenly approached to the eyes . . . Her eyes followed a slowly moved desk-candle flame held about 18 inches away from them; the eyes turned as far as was comfortable and then the head slowly turned. (This has not been tried before.) This light seemed to cause her to sneeze twice (1910, p. 11).

That was Dearborn's direct observation when his daughter was thirteen days old. His comments on it follow and put his own observation into what Shinn called the "comparative" framework:

Preyer was surprised to see his child's gaze thus following a moving object on Day 23 and says that "other children do not do this until after many months," while Miss Shinn's case showed it first on the thirtieth day. One child's eyes followed in the second week, another at the beginning of the fourth week (Tracy), while Major first noticed that his R's vision followed a person about the room on day thirty-seventh. As already noted, Mrs. Moore reports the second day. . . . Considering the completeness of the psychophysical unity with which we are born, it is not easy to understand why such typically reflex adaptations should not occur at any time when the requisite stimuli reach an adequately complete reflex mechanism. It is probably, then, wholly a matter of the degree of neural (or neuromuscular?) development. The normal variation in the gestation-period doubtless accounts for the observed wide variation in this capability, as in that of many others. L's eye-coordination was perfect from the first—an unusual condition, certainly, and perhaps in part explanatory of the earliness of this following reaction (1910, pp. 11–12).

Dearborn's little book adds two other features to the diary description literature: He includes an alphabetical list or index of "firsts" at the end of the book, and he provides a weekly summary as an appendix.

Like Dearborn, the Danish writer Vilhelm Rasmussen wrote about his daughter in his *Diary of a Child's Life*. But, unlike Dearborn, Rasmussen covered the first fifteen years of his dauther's life in a brief 187 pages. Clearly he practiced a great deal of selectivity in this published collection of notes. Rasmussen's book was published some time after 1927 (the date of the last entry); the book itself carries no date, but Dennis gives it a 1931 publication date in his 1936 bibliography of baby biographies.

William Stern and his wife, Clara, for years kept diaries on their children. Their notes became examples to help Stern illustrate points made in the body of a large college textbook, *Psychology of Early Childhood: Up to the Sixth Year of Age* (1924, first English translation).

Charlotte Bühler made the first attempt to develop information on a larger group of infants. Her team of observers worked around the clock in fatiguing eight-hour shifts. Sixty-nine babies were observed during the first four months of 1926, with at least five babies observed at each month's age level. Her report on this project, *The First Year of Life*, was translated from the German and published in this country in 1930. By this time, the diary description method was little used, and other observation techniques had begun to emerge.

Advantages and Disadvantages
of the Diary Description
Method of Observation

One hundred fifty years had elapsed between Pestalozzi's first introduction of the baby biography in 1774 and William Stern's use of the baby biography in the 1924 English publication of his German textbook on child psychology. The baby biography started as parental records of the first few years of their children's lives. Most of the parents who kept these early records were professional people: educators, physicians, biologists. At the urging first of Preyer and then of Shinn, others began to record baby biographies. Among the new league of observers were college graduates interested in helping advance knowledge about children; others were mothers with far less education. Many of these diaries found their way to Preyer, who collated, analyzed, and then published the information gleaned from the hundreds of reports sent to him.

William Stern felt that the use of untrained observers was unscientific and argued that this practice only encouraged informal, random records:

Child-psychology records can be made with two distinct aims in view. Either the observer undertakes them for his personal joy and instruction, to get a thorough knowledge of a child, near and dear to him, to have later on, for his own, a lasting remembrance of the child's tender early years. . . . Or he aims at contributing something to the general child-psychological knowledge, wishes himself to work up the collected observations and to offer them, at any rate, as raw material for the cause of science. It is an error, pure and simple, to imagine that the capacity and wish to make observations of the first kind are, in themselves, sufficient to give such observations any scientific value (1930, p. 37).

Stern was not alone in his criticism of the baby biographies. Experimental psychology was growing by leaps and bounds in the 1920s. As experimental research became a more popular method of child study, the diary description lost favor as a research technique. The criticisms of the diary descriptions were almost always these, among others:

1. *biased selection:* They lacked representativeness by virtue of the fact that the observer was usually a well-educated individual whose child was bound to be advantaged.
2. *biased observations:* The observer was usually a loving and attentive parent. This meant that the recordings were not always reliable and the interpretations were not always objective.
3. *too few cases for meaningful generalization:* Even though valiant efforts were made by advocates of baby biography research to enlist the help of educated mothers, the amount of available, and comparable, data was meager. In 1937, Wayne Dennis and Marsena Galbreath Dennis studied all available baby biographies and found only forty that gave them enough data to provide a comparative chart on behavioral development in the first year of life.
4. *too costly in time and resources:* Parents had the luxury to observe the infant daily. Any researcher with a need to earn enough to keep self and studies together could not afford the time needed to watch one infant for a year or so.

Despite these difficulties, the Dennises defended the baby biography method of study, saying that these biographies are "repositories of data which the more recent normative studies do not possess." According to them,

The incompleteness of recent studies of infant development became apparent when we attempted recently to use their data as comparison material for an investigation in which two infants were observed day by day. The current norms fail to include a great many ordinary items of behavior known to every parent. Turning to the biographies, we found that taken in the aggregate they presented a fuller picture of the course of development during the first year (1937, p. 349).

Earlier, Milicent Shinn had championed the advantage of diary descriptions for longitudinal study, investigations in which the same subject is studied across time:

. . . the biographical method of child study has the inestimable advantage of showing the process of evolution going on, the actual unfolding of one stage out of another, and the steps by which the changes come about. No amount of comparative statistics could give this. If I should find out that a thousand babies learned to stand at an average age of forty-six weeks and two days, I should not know as much that is important about standing, as a stage in human progress, as I should after watching a single baby carefully through the whole process of achieving balance on his little soles (1900, p. 11).

Current Uses of Diary Descriptions

With the advent of experimental child study and with the support for university-based research at newly established laboratory preschools in the 1920s, child development researchers became more interested in measurement than in simple description of behavior. The baby biography or diary description method became a rarely used research tool. New observation techniques were developed. But the technique of prolonged and careful observation continued on in two strands:

1. *As Case Study*—used more and more by child psychologists to record information on the "different" child. Examples include such books as Dorothy Baruch's *One Little Boy* (1952) or Virginia Axline's *Dibbs–in Search of Self* (1964). As with the nonverbal or preverbal infant, so the "damaged" child often does not communicate directly or easily. An observer must record a great deal of material before discovering what is actually going on in the child's mind. Another kind of case study involves groups of children, rather than individual children. Kohl's *36 Children* (1967) or Kozol's *Death at an Early Age* (1967) or O'Gorman's *The Wilderness and the Laurel Tree* (1972) are examples. As in the diary descriptions, in each case the observer's attention focuses on noting new behaviors and new perceptions for later analysis and synthesis.
2. *As an Ethological Tool*—used to record observations of animals (both two- and four-legged) in an attempt to discover what their behavior is all about. Like human infants, four-legged animals cannot communicate directly or easily in language understood by the observer. It is up to the observer to note down

actions and reactions which, over time, supply clues for further investigation. Examples of this form of diary description include Mowatt's *Never Cry Wolf* (1963) or Van Lawick-Goodall's *In the Shadow of Man* (1971). It is interesting to discover how similar Goodall's statements about the process of observing chimpanzees are to statements made by early baby biographers:

Without doubt the most exciting thing that year was being able to record on paper and on film the week-by-week development of a wild chimpanzee infant—Flint. . . . We learned a great deal about their behavior by means of objective recording of fact, but we also became increasingly aware of them as individual beings (p. 109).

The recent surge of interest in ethological studies, with human ethology gaining in popularity, finds researchers once more using some of the observation techniques used by baby biographers more than half a century ago.

In his Foreword to the *Ethological Studies of Child Behavior* (1972), Tinbergen describes the volume's editor, N. Blurton-Jones, as "an animal ethologist of standing who has . . . spent a number of years applying ethological methods to the study of child behavior" (p. vii). Tinbergen feels that what is happening today in human ethology parallels what happened fifty years ago in the study of animal behavior:

. . . a new type of research worker is busy building the foundations of a science, by returning with renewed attention and interest in detail, to the basic task of observation and description of the natural phenomena that have to be understood . . . Rather than extrapolating interpretations from animals to man, a growing number of young ethologists have themselves begun to collect factual information about Man's behavior, using ethological methods (1972, vii, viii).

The tools of the observer today are broader and far more sophisticated than the paper, pencil, and occasional cameras of the early diarists. Tape recorders, video cameras, and electronic recording devices assist the observer in literally recording an event and preserving it for reviewing and reanalysis later.

Summary

A diary description is defined as an observational technique involving recording changes or new developments or new behaviors in the subject being observed, usually an infant or young child. The observer takes notes on a regular, almost daily, basis. Because the observer must be in close or constant contact with the child, the role was originally filled by a parent or close relative. Darwin and Preyer watched their sons; Shinn watched her niece; Dearborn and Rasmussen watched their daughters.

Diary writers observed babies for their own purposes, which can be differentiated by examining their stated aims. Scientists like Darwin were looking for "missing links" in the development of a species. Physiologists like Preyer and Dearborn were cataloging the development of an individual within a species, hoping to gain insight into the group. Interested parents or relatives like Shinn believed in the importance of contributing observations to the work of the scientists beginning to accumulate useful data on the growth and development of the human being.

Diary descriptions have been criticized for biased selection, biased observations, limited cases, costliness in time and resources, unreliable recording, inefficient gathering and processing of data, and unwarranted interpretations. The advantages of diary descriptions are that they provide detailed permanent records, portray the full sequence of development, take into account the continuity of behavior, and give a multifaceted picture of the behavior and development of a child in relation to his or her environment.

While the number of baby biographies written today is limited, diary descriptions have found a new application through case studies and ethological records.

Suggestions for Further Reading

For the historically minded, the following early baby biographies should be of particular interest:

Compayré, G. *The Intellectual and Moral Development of the Child*. Translated from the French by M.E. Wilson. New York: Appleton, 1896. Part I contains the chapters on perception, emotion, memory, imagination, and consciousness. The Introduction (pp. 1–27) argues that the study of the child is a "natural and necessary introduction to all future psychology."

Dearborn, G.V.N. *Moto-Sensory Development: Observations on the First Three Years of a Child*. Baltimore: Warwick & York, 1910. One of the first medically oriented baby biographies, this diary is an excellent example of reporting in an easily readable manner, immediately useful to other investigators.

Preyer, W. *The Mind of the Child: Part I: The senses and the will*, 3d ed. Translated by H.W. Brown. New York: Appleton, 1890. The "bible" of the early biographers, Preyer's work served as both an inspiration and an instruction manual for other baby biographers.

Shinn, M.W. *The Biography of a Baby: The First Year of Life*. Boston: Houghton-Mifflin, 1900. One of the most popular of the American baby biographies, Shinn's book also sets a standard for comparative reporting by discussing how her observations related to the findings of other investigators.

Recent diary descriptions include:

Van Lawick-Goodall, J. *In the shadow of man*. New York: Dell, 1971, pp. 111–121, "Flo and her family." Field study observations of a chimpanzee family.

Mowat, F. *Never Cry Wolf*. New York: Dell, 1963. A highly entertaining and most interesting diary of a biologist's year among the Canadian wolves. Diary description at its popular best.

Peterson, C.C. *A Child Grows Up*. New York: Alfred, 1974. A modern diary description kept by the author's father from the time she was ten months old through age seven. The author uses the diary entries to illustrate the basic course of a child's development.

Diary Descriptions

The baby biographers did not sit hovered over their subjects with pen poised ready to write down each new behavior exhibited by the infant. They were, however, observant, carefully attentive. They noted new behaviors because they were alert to them. When the baby biographers noticed something different they recorded it in their diary. As mentioned in the text, some of the baby biographers also did small experiments and then recorded the results.

In a short space of time, it is hard to get a feeling for the task involved in keeping a diary of the growth and development of another individual. Some of you will be doing case histories and will gain good diary description experience as a part of that undertaking. Assignment number 10 is designed to give you a sampling of what it is like to keep a diary about another person.

Procedure: This observation will extend across a full week so you will need to select a person (child or adult) to observe who will be with you on a daily basis. You may select anyone you want and observe anything you like. The only restriction is that you have to enter notes in your diary or journal each day. You may do this at the end of the day thinking back on what you have seen and heard during the day or you may want to write down some notes as you see a behavior or an event happening. You can simply observe the person in general or you may want to select a specific aspect of his or her behavior to focus on. For example, you may have a friend or spouse who is trying to quit smoking and decide to record his or her behavior related to smoking during the week. Your diary might include information about how many cigarettes were smoked each day and when (after dinner, during meetings, and so on), any behavioral changes that you notice during the week, comments that he or she makes relating to smoking, responses of others to the process of trying to quit, and so on. If you are observing a child you may want to describe how the child explores a new toy, approaches a new event, responds to a new routine or responsibility.

Date(s)_____ Subject_____Subject's Age _____

1. Describe the general setting(s) in which the observations occurred.

2. Attach the diary description you made for each day of the observation. Indicate time of day for each separate activity or entry.

3. Review your diary entries and write a brief summary of your week's observation.

Observer Experimentation

Baby biographers frequently set up miniature experiments for the children they were observing. Piaget gave his daughter a match box with an object hidden inside; Dearborn placed a penny on his daughter's foot three times to see if she could succeed in picking it up; Shinn placed a candle on the stairs as a lure to her niece just learning to climb stairs.

Such experiments are helpful in eliciting behaviors that the observer might otherwise have to wait days to see happen or might miss altogether if he or she weren't there at the right time. Some biographers, like Piaget, repeated the same experiments over time to note changes in the subject's response. Your task in this assignment is to create a miniature experiment and observe results.

Procedure: Observe a child you can interact with directly. (If you are not in a situation that gives you everyday access to children and have no friends or family with children nearby, go to a public place where there are children, preferably with their parents, and, in an unobtrusive and nonthreatening manner, set up an interaction. Be sure you get permission from the parent before carrying out your experiment.) Take along something novel for the child you will observe and let the child explore it. (For example, if you are observing a preschool child you might want to take along a magnet and a variety of magnetic and nonmagnetic objects.) You can either record your observation while the child is exploring the object(s) or as soon afterward as possible. Note how the child responds from the time he or she first notices the object until he or she finishes playing with it or you terminate the exploration.

Date_____ Time_____ Setting/Location _____

Child Observed_____ Age _____

1. Briefly describe the child and the setting.

2. Describe the object that you have brought for the child to explore.

3. Write a description of the child's exploration of the object in as complete detail as possible.

4. Some of the baby biographers identified key word markers in the margins of their notes—words to identify the topic or developmental accomplishment or important happenings. This made it easier to review their notes later on. If this were going to be one in a long series of observations on this child, what descriptors or key word identifiers would you want to note in the margin to help you classify this observation later on?

Lab Assignment 12   *Observer* _____

The Problem of Generalizing

One of the criticisms of diary descriptions is that there are too few cases to allow for adequate generalization of the findings. For example, it is not safe to predict the age that children start to walk based on observing one or two children. This assignment is designed to help you become familiar with a range of individual differences and to learn some of the risks of generalizing from a small sample to a larger population.

Procedure: Select a physical activity (like sliding, climbing, or swimming) in which a small group of children who are the same age are involved. Select one child to observe and record the procedure that child carries out in performing the activity.

Date_____ Time_____ Activity _____

Age of Children_____ Setting/Location _____

1. Briefly describe the activity and any information relevant to understanding the setting.

2. Describe the child and how he or she performs the activity.

3. If you had to generalize to the population of all children this age on the basis of this individual child's performance what statement would you make?

After recording the child's behavior, select two other children of the same age and record their performance and the procedures they use in doing that same activity.

4. Description of how child #2 performs the activity.

5. Description of how child #3 performs the activity.

6. What kind of individual differences did you encounter in how different children performed the same activity?

7. What similarities did your observations reveal?

8. What kinds of generalizations would you make now that you have observed three children?

Chapter Five

Anecdotal Records, Running Records, and Specimen Descriptions

The diary description was an observational strategy that involved recording new developments or new behaviors in the subject(s) being observed. The record was a longitudinal one in that it involved repeated observations of the same child or group over an extended period of time. Most of the early diaries were kept to help expand our knowledge about the growth and development of the child, in the service of science. As the amount of information about the development of children grew, so did the interest in applying that information to home and school settings.

At the same time that the diary description was moving toward more and more scientific rigor, another observation technique was developing different kinds of information. The anecdotal description or anecdotal record was this second early technique.

Anecdotal Records

G. Stanley Hall suggested that the students at the Normal School at Worcester, Massachusetts, an early center for training teachers, should keep records on systematic observations of children as a regular part of their studies. Writing in *The Pedagogical Seminary*, an education journal edited by Dr. Hall, William H. Burnham (1892) reports on the keeping of anecdotal records by teachers in training at Worcester Normal School: "The prime motive for such study has generally been the training of teachers in the observation of children. It has been done directly for the sake of teachers; indirectly for the sake of the child, and incidentally for the sake of science" (p. 198).

The principal of the normal school, E. Harlow Russell, in an article in the next issue of *The Pedagogical Seminary*, credited Dr. Hall with suggesting and encouraging their efforts. Russell also emphasized the value of the work to the teacher in training: "No one, however, can prize the method more highly than I do, as a means of normal training, for its efficacy, which has been abundantly proved, in bringing our prospective teachers into the right attitude of mind towards children as children, not as mere material for the teacher's art" (1892, p. 348).

Burnham and Russell both felt that direct observation of children by teachers in training contributed greatly to their knowledge and understanding of children. By the time these articles were written, over nineteen thousand anecdotes, both observed and recollected incidents, had been recorded by Worcester students. Russell (1892) reported that the collection of anecdotes was growing at the rate of three thousand per year. Twelve hundred and eight of them covering children from one to sixteen years of age were put together into a book entitled *Child Observations, First Series: Imitation and Allied Activities*, edited by Ellen M. Haskell and published in 1896. Typical anecdotes are these:

#232 Charlie. Age, 3 years. Charlie was playing house with his little sister. He said he was the father. As he passed through the kitchen, his elder sister offered him some cakes which she knew he liked much. He refused them, saying, "What do I want with cakes? Men eat only at mealtimes." About ten minutes afterwards he came in and said, "Sarah, may I have those cakes now? I ain't the father any more; I'm Charlie" (p. 39).

#334 Harlan. Age, 4 years. Harlan was afraid his little sister would touch his clay spheres and cylinders while he went to the other side of the room. He said to me, "You keep saying 'no, no, no,' to the baby till I come back" (pp. 56–57).

Anecdotal descriptions are less concerned with recording the continuity of experience for a single child than they are with recording behavioral and verbal responses in general. Like diary descriptions, anecdotal reports are narrative in style. Unlike diary descriptions, they need not focus on a single child or group and are not limited to highlighting new behaviors. Anecdotal descriptions report whatever seems noteworthy to the observer, whenever that behavior occurs.

Some anecdotal records are topical. The observer is interested in studying a particular area of development and notes down only observations relating to that area. For example, the observer may be interested in studying imitation. His or her interest might be in finding out what adult behaviors are imitated by children and how they imitate or reproduce those behaviors. Several anecdotal records from our own files illustrate how children imitate adult behaviors. Both of these examples were reported by friends who had observed the incidents:

Two-and-a-half-year old Cynthia, seeing her mother nurse the new baby, said to her mother, "I'll feed the baby." Then looking down at her chest and seeming to sense that something was missing, said, "She can eat my leg." Cynthia's comment tells us what she thinks is happening when the baby nurses and also her recognition that she doesn't have the same food to offer.

The four-year-old group had spent most of the afternoon outdoors and David had been in high gear the entire time. He was exhausted when his mother came to get him. Noticing this, she said, "You need something to help pick you up when you get home. What would you like?" David's response was, "What I really need is a good stiff chocolate brownie."

It is not hard to imagine what David's father says when he gets home from work.

Not all anecdotal records are topical. Some are collected over a period of time without having any focus in mind. Still other observers may develop anecdotal records on an individual child to provide an accumulation of behavioral incidents to analyze later.

Anecdotal records are perhaps the easiest to do of all the forms of direct observation. They require no specific time frame but can be done whenever there is something of interest to record. They need no special setting or environment but can be done anywhere. They rely on no special codes or categories or charts but can simply be written on a note pad and tucked away for later use.

Anecdotal records serve a wide variety of purposes. They are a valuable aid to understanding more about children's thinking and conceptualization: how they view the world and what they understand of what goes on around them.

Anecdotal records also help teachers get to know children at the beginning of the year. If the teacher continues to record impressions and incidents throughout the year, he or she has a means of assessing progress, identifying changes in levels of understanding, and noting areas of continuing difficulty.

Guidelines for Recording Anecdotal Observations

Anecdotal records can help teachers do three things:

1. test out hunches about reasons for a child's behavior or learning style
2. identify what conditions may be reinforcing behavior
3. gain feedback about what children have learned from a particular curriculum unit or presentation

Anecdotal records have been used by researchers for the same purposes—to gather information, to test out ideas, and to measure or evaluate progress. Brandt (1972, pp. 84–85) offers the following guidelines for researchers using anecdotal records. They serve as useful reminders for teachers as well:

1. *Write down the anecdote as soon as possible after it occurs.* When Dorothy H. Cohen and Virginia Stern (1958) wrote their book, *Observing and Recording the Behavior of Young Children,* they clearly expected many classroom observations to be carried out by the teachers themselves and advised them as follows:

Since your primary responsibility is to be the teacher of the group, your times for record-ing will literally have to be snatched. Children's needs come first, and you may have to drop your pencil to race to someone's rescue. It helps to have pads, cards, or a small notebook in all your smock pockets, on shelves around the room, and up your sleeve too. Never miss out on a choice bit because no pencil is handy! (p. 7)

For Cohen and Stern, the primary purpose for keeping these records is to help the teacher analyze a child's growth and development by encouraging the teacher to attend to behavior during independent play and interaction with other children and with adults, and by attending to a child's selection and use of materials. The end result is a summary report on each child—a case study of sorts.

In her book, *Ways of Studying Children* (1959), Millie Almy, too, aimed at helping teachers use the methods of scientific research to solve educational problems in their classrooms. Almy gives an example of how a teacher's neces-sarily brief recorded notes can later be expanded into a more complete record: "Clarence 3/18/56. With Thomas at clay jar. Getting good and dirty. Completed third little dog. Painted brown and white" (p. 51). These notes are the bare bones of the observation the teacher later on expanded into this more complete report (parentheses indicate the teacher's interpretations or tentative hypotheses as separated from the factual description of behavior):

(Clarence, who has been "watching" people do things and retiring to a corner to read during periods which gave him a chance to work with other children, has begun to show some interest in working with others.) Clarence and Thomas were both working at the clay jar, and Clarence was really getting good and dirty during our art period today. He has made three little dogs which are graduated in size and which he has painted brown and white. (I think he likes Thomas, and this association is helping him get into the swing of group activities.) (p. 52).

2. *Identify the basic action of the key person and what was said.*

3. *Include a statement that identifies the setting, time of day, and basic activity.* Examples: "In the car on the way home from school . . ." or "Running toward the sandbox after snack-time. . . ." Brandt also advises the observer to identify what activity was supposed to be happening if the subject is doing something different from what would be expected. For example, "When the children were all supposed to be down for their naps . . ." or "While everyone else was working on the math assignment, Peter was . . ."

4. *In describing the central character's actions or verbalizations, include the responses or reactions of other people in the situation.* For example: "I'll be the driver," Toby declared. "No, I will," Sandy said firmly. It is also important to include comments by children peripherally involved if the comments relate to the central character. For example: "I'll be the driver," Toby declared. Melissa remarked to one of the teachers, "Why does Toby always have to be the driver?" As with guideline number three, it is also important to note the lack of response if one would normally be expected.

5. *Whenever possible note exact words used to preserve the precise flavor of the conversation.* When it is not possible to write down or remember everything that was said, note key phrases and set them off with quotation marks to make clear what was actually said by the child and what was paraphrased by the observer.

6. *Preserve the sequence of the episode.* The anecdote should have a beginning, middle, and end. The beginning should include the setting and the end should describe the conclusion of the episode.

7. Brandt describes *three levels of action that should be included in the anecdote.* The first is the major unit of behavior known as *molar behavior.* For example: "Ellen and Mollie were doing puzzles together at the manipulatives table." The molar unit describes the main action, or activity of the anecdotes. The second level of action, called the *subordinate molar unit,* identifies smaller units of action within the larger action. For example: "Ellen was putting the hospital puzzle together for the third time while Mollie was finishing one puzzle and then taking a different one." The subordinate molar unit gives additional information about the main activity. The third level of action, called *molecular units,* describes how the main action is carried out. For example: "Ellen carefully put each piece in place accompanying the action with a sing-song 'This one goes here and this one goes here and . . .' " The molecular unit is a qualitative addition to the anecdote.

8. *Be objective, accurate, and complete.* Brandt advises observers to err on the side of recording too much rather than too little: you can always cut information more easily than you can add it, especially after an interval of time has passed and you have forgotten parts of the initial observation. Keep your own interpretations to a bare minimum and be sure you have the facts straight.

Running Records

The process of writing diary descriptions and anecdotal records seems natural. All of us are familiar with the idea that we can record a significant happening in a diary or a journal and, over time, have a respectable amount of important information to study, analyze, or enjoy. The next two observational strategies, the running record and its close relative, the specimen description, present us with a more arduous and challenging task: that of picturing situations in words that are precise enough and complete enough that we, or anyone else, can use our records for later analysis. As if that were not enough of a challenge, the observer usually makes these notes over an extended period of time, rather than simply recording an incident and then not recording for minutes, hours, or days as is the case with diary descriptions and anecdotal records. The endurance record goes to Charlotte Bühler and her two observer-colleagues who kept twenty-four hour records of first occurrences of behavior on sixty-nine infant subjects (all under one year of age) by working in eight-hour shifts. We cannot help but wonder how they would have fared had they been doing running records (no pun intended) on two-year-olds instead!

The running record is best described in Dorothy Cohen's and Virginia Stern's *Observing and Recording the Behavior of Young Children*, originally published in 1958 and revised in 1978. Cohen and Stern describe the running record as a classroom observational technique for teachers. For them, the running record involves "taking on-the-spot records of behavior as it is occurring" (1958, p. 7). The main task is to record the situation in a manner that lets someone else read the description later and visualize the scene or event as it occurred.

In order to appreciate their development as early research tools we need to remember that running records evolved out of diary descriptions and anecdotal records. Fletcher B. Dresslar (a contemporary of Milicent Washburn Shinn at the University of California, Berkeley) is usually credited with giving us the first example of this technique at the turn of the century. His "A Morning's Observation of a Baby" appeared in the December 1901 issue of *The Pedagogical Seminary*. Dresslar's article records his observations of his own child at age thirteen months nineteen days during a four-hour period on January 19, 1895. It is interesting to read through Dresslar's report of his child's morning, recorded more than eighty years ago; it could as easily be an observation done just yesterday.

. . . drops a bottle which he had picked up, exactly imitates his mother who says "bad boy"; picks up the bottle, sits down and bites at it; crawls to the left with the bottle in his right hand; gets up, leaving the bottle, and walks twelve feet to his mamma, gets his food bottle, turns to the left, walks back twelve feet to the other bottle; tries to fit a cork into a tin box, crawls under the piano cover, and strikes the piano with a bottle; is pulled out, and accepts the discipline good humoredly; lies on his back taking his food; gets up, walks eight feet, tries to blow out the oil stove, turns to the left, walks eight feet to the piano, crawls under the cover, comes out when bidden, gets his doll, makes it squeal; gets the cork and the tin box and again tries to fit them together, chattering all of the time, ending with dentals; gets up, plays the piano with his right hand; sits down, gets up, sits down. (It is now 10:40 o'clock.) (p. 476).

Two of the most extensive studies utilizing running records were done by Louise Woodcock and Susan Isaacs. Both studies involved observations of children in school settings.

Louise Woodcock was a teacher of two-year-olds at the Bank Street Bureau of Educational Experiments Nursery School in New York City. She was greatly influenced by Harriet Johnson, a nurse who, with Caroline Pratt and Lucy

Sprague Mitchell, had organized the Bureau in 1917. These organizers were interested in studying the sequence of growth in terms of maturity levels rather than in terms of the age norms that were so popular in the 1920s and 1930s. Johnson and her associates believed that the best way to conduct this kind of study was to do it in the child's natural setting and so the Bureau Nursery School was begun. Harriet Johnson directed the nursery school from 1919 until her death in 1934.

Johnson strongly believed in the value of education for young children. Her nursery school originally accepted children between fourteen months and four years of age. In 1925, the age range was changed to two-to-six years of age. Louise Woodcock taught the two-year-old group for nine years and kept observational records on the children throughout that time. Through her work with student teachers she continued to collect observations of two-year-olds after her own active preschool teaching ended. Little was known of what "twoness" was about outside of what the norms cited as the average age for the emergence of various skills between the second and third birthdays. In 1941, Woodcock published the *Life and Ways of the Two-Year-Old: A Teacher's Study* to fill that void. Hers was a field study rather than a laboratory or clinic study. Although it was published nearly forty years ago, it remains the most comprehensive description we have of two-year-old behavior in a nursery school environment. In the Foreword to the book, Barbara Biber describes the work as follows:

Children are different. Ten two-year-olds are ten different people. Yet their teacher, if she is sensitive to the nuances of behavior, knows and feels their two-year-oldness. When she compares notes, no matter how informally, with the teacher of the four-year-olds she is more than ever convinced of the reality, complex though it is, of their two-year-oldness. It is this reality which the present study attempts to describe. It offers the reader no tables of average ages of first appearance of certain skills, no outlined inventory of skills accomplished, no scheme for measuring relative maturity. In fact, if there is a thesis implicit in the book as a whole it is something like this: if the changes that take place between one stage of maturity and another are to be understood, each maturity level must be described comprehensively not only in terms of accomplishments but with full attention to the qualitative aspects of the behavior described and to the directional trends of the period of growth being studied (p. 13).

In her chapter on "Meeting Problems," Woodcock describes such situations as Building a Climbing Device, Repetition of a Learned Pattern, Immature Judgment of Distance, and Arranging a Chair at Table. She uses her recorded examples to illustrate the stages of development in each of these areas as she has defined them from her observations. The following example is taken from notes about Polly's progress in learning to arrange a chair at the snack table:

Polly (2:0) went to her own table where the chair stood in proper position except that it was shoved under the table a little too far. She took it by the corner of the back and drew it toward her, which opened a space, but not on her side of the chair. She pulled and stopped to look and pulled again, all the time widening the space at the far side of the chair but not helping her with her problem unless she should let go of the back and go around to that side. Did not solve the problem. Adult bibbed her and seated her for dinner.

Polly (2:1) was asked to put the chair at the table. She pulled it an inch or two toward the table and seated herself. Not satisfied. Rose a little and lifted the chair, her hands under the seat as she sat in it. Worked it with great effort a few inches toward the table. Did not straighten up but kept her buttocks in the seat. Encouraged by adult, she rose and pushed the chair up, this time in much better position. Said, "Fis it dis way. Fis it dis way." Finally seated herself too far from the table, making no effort to pull the table toward her (p. 149).

Like Woodcock, Susan Isaacs was a teacher (in Cambridge, England) gathering information while she taught. She used the running record to collect observations that she used in writing her books, *Intellectual Growth of Young Children* and *Social Development in Young Children*. She says: ". . . the material was gathered in a school, not in a laboratory. But the records themselves are direct and dispassionate observations, recorded as fully as possible under the conditions; and as free as possible from evaluations and interpretations" (1930, p.1). The observations are taken from material written down by the staff on notebooks they carried with them. "We noted things as fully as we could at the actual moment, and then dictated a fuller record from these notes, on the same day" (1930, pp. 1-2).

Isaacs and her teachers did not have a plan when they started taking their notes, but simply noted down as much as they could of conversation and interaction for later sorting, synthesizing, and theorizing. In her section on four sample weeks, Isaacs gives us a day-by-day summary of events as recorded at the rate of about 1500 words per day. Here's a sample paragraph:

There is a gate in the railing at the back of the platform, with steps leading down to the cloakroom. The children sometimes swing on this gate, and this morning Dan, Priscilla and Christopher were doing this, and the rivalry of the two boys for Priscilla's favour gave rise to some difficulty. Dan was accidentally bumped on the foot with the gate, and the other two were unsympathetic. Priscilla said, "You stupid thing—why did you get in the way?" Dan cried very bitterly. Presently Mrs. I. said she was going to fasten the gates, as they were leading to quarrels, and asked the children to do something else. Dan was very cross about this; but presently he became interested in what the others were doing, and joined in. (He was in a generally domineering mood to-day, and easily got angry at anybody's interference with his wishes.) (1930, pp. 232-233).

Running records are generally more complete than anecdotal reports. They try to capture the most important elements of a behavior or an event in as much detail as possible. Because they are relatively easy to do and require no preplanning or extensive training, they are widely used by classroom teachers. Like anecdotal records, they are useful in testing out ideas, recording behavior for later analysis, and measuring progress. They form the backbone of most case study files and as such are probably more widely used by practitioners than any other observational strategy.

Specimen Descriptions

Specimen descriptions are the researchers' counterpart to running records. Like running records, they are narrative descriptions of behavior or events. They differ in that they require more rigorous detail and predetermined criteria. They also require that the observer be uninvolved in the action. This means that a classroom teacher who wants to use specimen descriptions rather than running records cannot just jot down a few brief notes and then expand on them after the children have gone home for the day. He or she must find a short period of time (five to thirty minutes) when he or she can observe and record at the same time without interruption.

If your task is to observe, not to interact with the children, it is important that you be both unobtrusive and uninviting to the children. Cohen and Stern advise that "Should the children ask you what you are doing, don't let them in on the secret because they may become self-conscious. Be nonchalant and say something noncommittal, like 'It's teacher's work,' or 'It's writing I have to do' " (1958, pp. 7–8).

It was Roger Barker who first introduced the term *specimen description* in the 1940s. He used it to define a detailed, continuous or sequential narrative account of behavior and of its immediate environmental context; Barker put it to use in his study of *Midwest and Its Children* (1955) with Herbert Wright. The task of the observer doing specimen descriptions is to record all that he or she can about what is happening and the context within which it is happening according to some predetermined criteria (time of day, person, setting, and so on). Specimen description is an eye-witness account *par excellence*. The following example is taken from specimen descriptions collected by Barker and Wright:

Subject: Margaret Reid (Midwest, Female, Social Group 4, Age 4.6)
Episode: Hitting Bradley
Setting: Reid Home, Outdoors
Associate: Bradley, 18 month-old brother
Time: June 2, 1949, 1:03 P.M.
Margaret has been teasing her mother to go to the neighbors' to play; but Mrs. Reid goes into the house, having firmly refused Margaret's pleas. Bradley is wandering about the yard while Margaret and her mother argue.

Bradley picked up a tin bucket that Mrs. Reid had taken from Margaret. He swung it, rattling a stone in the bottom of the bucket.

Margaret went over and started pounding on Bradley's legs, his back, and the back of his head. Bradley seemed to expect this. When she came toward him, he knew what was coming. He cowered as if it were rather a regular occurrence for her to hit him.

Margaret hit Bradley again and again.

He cried a little each time she hit him and, finally, started crying seriously.

Seeing that Bradley was really going to cry in earnest, Margaret let him alone. But she taunted, "I can hit you and I can throw you" (Wright, 1967, pp. 176–177).

This example has less of the narrative, story-telling quality of Isaacs's observations but reads more like the script for a play; positions and actions are identified in proper order. We can expect to have more detailed raw material from the noninvolved observer, which means that the data allows others to make judgments for themselves. The involved observer must, of necessity, do more interpreting along the way and be more selective about what is recorded.

The Question of Detail

If the goal of specimen descriptions and running records is to record behavior and its context in sufficient detail so that the record can be preserved for later use, and so that a naive reader can picture the scene, the question naturally arises as to how much detail is enough. One valuable exercise in determining whether or not you, the observer, have described a scene in a way that communicates precise action to a stranger is to have a friend act out what you have observed. In attempting to act out the examples we have read so far in this chapter, we need to ask several questions:

**How does Dresslar's son walk to his mother? Quickly? Haltingly? Sure-footedly? On his toes?

**How did Dan's foot get bumped in Isaacs's observation? Did someone push the gate open onto his foot? Did the wind blow it? Did he pull the gate himself?

**How did Margaret hit Bradley in Barker and Wright's observation? With closed fist? Bare palm? Back of her hand?

**What does "good and dirty" mean in Almy's report of Clarence at the art table? Are his hands full of paint? Paint up to his elbows? Paint all over his clothes?

Obviously, if three different people were to act out or role play the observations, we might have three different versions of what occurred.

The question of how much detail we need is best answered by asking the purpose of the observation. Dresslar was recording the activities of his young son: how he spent his morning. Detail as fine as how he walked was not central to the observation. Isaacs was interested in children's reasoning and how Dan hurt his foot was important only in that it was accidental, not in how the accident happened. Barker and Wright were attempting to describe the stream of behavior and concentrated more on actions and reactions in the environmental setting than on qualitative descriptions of each movement. Almy's concern was how teachers could use observation to help them solve classroom problems. In the case of Clarence, the teacher was more concerned with Clarence's participation than with his degree of messiness. It is important to keep your mind on the purpose of your observation when you are taking notes.

A good rule of thumb is that it is better to note too much information than too little. The advantage of having as much detail as possible is that it allows you to analyze behaviors or gestures or responses that could be important to the final interpretations at a later date, even though they did not seem relevant at the time you were taking notes.

Louise Woodcock's observations contain more detail than most of the examples we have cited. This was in keeping with her purpose which was to describe the two-year-old in all his or her aspects—movement, language, reasoning, and social relations. Every detail contributed to forming a total picture of the two-year-old child.

If your purpose is to record the event as completely and as accurately as possible, you will want to use some form of technological assistance to capture more of the event and to preserve it for later analysis. Researchers who study kinesics—body movement or body language—need to be able to analyze movement and behavior in almost microscopic detail. To do so, they use a sound camera, a slow-motion analyzer, and a tape recorder. This allows the observer to go beyond capturing the sequence of behavior and recording conversation. Through stop-action, frame-by-frame analysis of movie film, the observer can analyze position of hands and feet, expression of the mouth, position of eyebrows, and width of eyes, coding the results into a symbolic photograph of the participants and events within a sequence.

Ray L. Birdwhistell (1970) of the University of Pennsylvania has been a pioneer in kinesic research. An example of Birdwhistell's own coding system follows:

USUAL OBSERVER'S REPORT: Just west of Albuquerque on Highway 66 two soldiers stood astride their duffle bags thumbing a ride. A large car sped by them and the driver jerked his head back, signifying refusal. The two soldiers wheeled and one Italian saluted him while the other thumbed his nose after the retreating car (p. 173).

Now look at the "macrokinesic translation" of just the first sentence of that paragraph:

The two soldiers stood in parallel, legs akimbo with an intrafemoral index of 45 degrees. In unison, each raised his right upper arm to about an 80-degree angle with his body and, with the lower arm at approximately a 100-degree angle, moved the arm in an anterior-posterior sweep with a double pivot at shoulder and elbow; the four fingers of the right hand were curled and the thumb was posteriorly hooked; the right palm faced the body. Their left arms were held closer to the body with an elbow bend of about 90 degrees. The left four fingers were curled and the thumb was partially hidden as it crooked into their respective belts (p. 176).

The coding of that same *first sentence* looks like this:*

Soldier No. 1:

Head	$H > 1°$	●	●
Forehead-brows	Hfb-b	●	●
Eyes	00		
	driver	●	●
Nose	Mz	●	●
Cheeks			
Mouth	L-L	●	●
Chin			
Neck			
Shoulders	$11 \geqslant 1°$	●	●
Trunk	TpTp	●	●
Hips			
Right arm	RAN[RA2:45 $\leq \geq$ 3:45n		
Hand and fingers	R/1?4P	●	●
Left arm	LAn-15'3u\[A;TA]	●	
Hand and fingers	L/lc2C3C4C5Cbelt	●	
Right leg	Y45Y	● ● ●	
Foot			
Left leg	Y45Y	● ● ●	
Foot			

Soldier No. 2:

Head	$H > 1°$	●	●
Forehead-brows	Hfb-b	●	●
Eyes	00		
	driver	●	●
Nose	Mz	●	●
Cheeks			
Mouth	L-L	● ●	●
Chin			
Neck			
Shoulders	$| \geq 1°$	●	●
Trunk	TpTp	●	●
Hips			
Right arm	RAN[RA2:45 $\leq \geq$ 3:45n		
Hand and fingers	R/1?4P		
Left arm	LAn-15'3ul A;TA	●	
Hand and fingers	L/lc2C̄3C̄4C5Cbelt		
Right leg	Y45Y	● ● ●	
Foot			
Left leg	Y45Y	● ● ●	
Foot	●	● ● ●	

*(pp. 174–175)

While it is interesting to know that such coding procedures exist and are used by some researchers, few observers will be concerned with anything as elaborate as a Birdwhistell kind of system. Most researcher-teacher-observers making use of the specimen description or running record technique will do something closer to the Dressler-Woodcock-Isaacs-Wright tradition. As interacting observers, they will record data on individuals or groups of children; they will use the observational situation to test existing theory, to collect the raw data from which theories develop, or to gather information for case studies, curriculum planning, or problem solving. The purpose of the observation will serve as a guide for how detailed the observational records need to be.

Guidelines for Recording Running Records and Specimen Descriptions

The guidelines for anecdotal records also apply to running records and specimen descriptions. In addition, Wright (1960, 1967) offers the following guidelines gleaned from the pooled directives of the various researchers and teachers using this technique:

1. Describe the scene as it is when the observer begins the description.
2. Focus on the subject's behavior and whatever in the situation itself affects this behavior. Wright defines two cases in which events or conditions removed from the subject need to be considered:
   a. an action or circumstance that would normally impinge on the subject but does not do so in this case.
   b. an action or circumstance that leads to a change in the subject's situation, even though the subject is not initially aware of the change.
3. Be as accurate and complete as you can about what the subject says, does, and responds to within the situation.
4. Put brackets around all interpretive material generated by the observer so that the description itself stands out clearly and completely.
5. Include the "how" for whatever the subject does.
6. Give the "how" for everything done by anyone interacting with the subject.
7. For every action report all the main steps in their proper order.
8. Describe behavior positively, rather than in terms of what was NOT done.
9. Put no more than one unit of molar behavior in one sentence.
10. Put no more than one thing done by a person other than the subject into a single sentence.
11. Do not report observations in terms of the time an event happened, but do mark off predetermined time intervals (one-minute intervals, for example).
12. Write in everyday language.
13. Use observational tools whenever possible (tape recorders, cameras, or video tape) and transcribe notes on the typewriter. Barker and Wright (1955) used a system of observe-dictate-interrogate-revise in making their observations for *Midwest and Its Children*. This procedure calls for an initial observation period followed by dictation of the observation. A colleague then listens to the dictated narration of the observation and asks questions or interrogates the observer to correct inconsistencies, ambiguities, unclear or incom-

plete information, and so on. The observer then transcribes the dictation and revises the observation. Barker and Wright find it helpful to have the interrogator look at the revised transcription once more before it is submitted for final typing. Time, purpose, and budget will determine what, if any, observational tools you will be able to use and what steps you will take in preparing a final copy of your anecdotal observations (1967, pp. 47–53).

Wright further suggests that an observer work for no more than thirty minutes at a single sitting. The reason for this is that fatigue sets in after thirty minutes of continuous observing and recording, and the observer is more likely to miss things that are important to the observation.

Advantages and Disadvantages of the Specimen Description and the Running Record

The uses of the specimen description technique and running record are broad and varied. Because of the details these records provide, they are especially helpful to teachers and other professionals who deal directly with children. Observations using these methods are written in everyday language. They describe behavior as it occurs within its environment, and the record can be reviewed again and again. These advantages make the specimen description and the running record especially valuable as information tools for planning, evaluating, and problem solving. Specimen descriptions and running records can be used to gather information about a child or to assess group processes. These techniques can be used to evaluate the curriculum or use of materials. Because the records they generate are permanent, they can be reviewed, added to, rearranged, or cross-referenced as other information becomes available. In some ways, their value increases with time as more information is collected. Comparisons can be made, progress charted, and changes evaluated.

The beauty of specimen descriptions and running records for professionals who work directly with children is that they can be done with a minimum of equipment. A pad and pencil suffice. Data can be collected whenever the situation warrants it. On the other hand, if the purpose of the observation demands that you gather as much information as possible, you can use more technical data-gathering equipment.

Given all the advantages, plus the simplicity of doing the observations, it is not surprising that specimen descriptions and running records, along with anecdotal records, are the observation techniques most frequently used by classroom teachers and teachers in training. The same does not hold true for researchers, however. While researchers appreciate the advantages of comprehensive data that can be reread and reanalyzed years later, they must face the realities of time, manpower, and funding.

Specimen descriptions and running records are costly in all of these areas. They take a long time to record, transcribe, and code. All the hours needed for the task increase the cost of the project. Also they often require a larger team of observers than do some of the other methods.

Blurton-Jones's recommendation (1972) about the value of a preliminary phase of observation before pursuing a research question seems to have been written with specimen descriptions and running records in mind. If time and money do not permit you to collect such extensive records as part of a study, you can certainly collect some preliminary data to help define both the problem and the proper methodology for studying it. Specimen descriptions and running records are particularly appropriate for this important preliminary work.

The researcher faces an additional problem that is usually of less concern to the teacher: what to do with the data—with the specimen descriptions and running records—once they have been collected and transcribed. Researchers need to develop coding categories and divide the observations into manageable units for statistical analysis. Wright deals with this problem in his 1960 review chapter and in his 1967 book on recording and analyzing children's behavior. Fred Kerlinger's book, *Foundations of Behavioral Research* (1973), is also an excellent source of information on research design, methodology, and data reduction.

Sometimes methodology decisions are based on efficiency. Other times the decision is based on what the available funds can support. The methods that we will study in the following chapters on time sampling, event sampling, and rating scales are all more efficient in terms of time and manpower and therefore less costly. However, they do not produce as comprehensive data as do running records and specimen descriptions. In addition, they do not offer the advantage of a permanent record of the observation for future reference.

Summary

G. Stanley Hall first suggested that teachers in training do systematic observations of children as a regular part of their studies. Brief notes, or anecdotes, were written down by students at the Worcester, Massachusetts Normal School. These anecdotes accumulated at the rate of three thousand per year.

Anecdotal records do not usually involve descriptions of prolonged actions or events. Two observational strategies, the running record and specimen description, attempt to describe every action within an extended time frame. Fletcher B. Dresslar is credited with first using the technique, in 1901, in "A Morning's Observation of a Baby."

The specimen description was originally developed by Roger Barker as a research method of direct observation that provided a detailed, narrative account of behavior and its immediate environmental context. Both the running record and specimen description had been used from the turn of the century, but were not formally given their present names until the middle of this century.

The early use of these observational techniques was in gathering information about the course of development in infants and children. Louise Woodcock and Susan Isaacs were collecting observational records of child development in the 1920s and 1930s. Their reports contain detailed descriptions of children's intellectual and social development (Isaacs) and the integration of skills in the life and ways of the two-year-old (Woodcock).

Because the running record became such a popular observational tool for classroom teachers, certain guidelines needed to be developed. Cohen and Stern and Millie Almy offer sage advice to the teacher-observer who must steal minutes away from his or her duties with children to jot down important notes.

The amount of detail needed in specimen descriptions and running records is largely determined by the purpose of the observation. The most important consideration is to have enough detail about the central observational focus and then to provide the fullest possible detail about peripheral areas. Where complete and exact detail is required, technological aids can be employed to record the event for later playback and analysis.

Over the years, researchers and teachers using specimen descriptions and running records have offered their own suggestions or guidelines for others who wish to use the methods. Herbert Wright synthesized these suggestions in two different publications; his synthesis has been paraphrased in this chapter for easy reference.

There are many advantages of specimen descriptions and running records. They are easy to record and offer detailed accounts of behavior which preserve the sequence of behavior, the environmental influences, and the responses of others in the setting. The observation is also a permanent record of the event. This allows reanalysis at a future date when the observer has collected other information or has generated new theories. It also makes it possible to chart the process of development over time. The main disadvantages are that these techniques are costly in terms of time, people involved, and money.

The problem of data reduction was not discussed directly in the chapter. Instead the reader was referred to Wright (1967) and Kerlinger (1973) for their excellent discussions on this topic.

Suggested Further Readings

Cohen, D. H., and V. Stern. *Observing and Recording the Behavior of Young Children.* New York: Teachers College Press, 1958. By far the most comprehensive guide on running records for classroom teachers. The book discusses observations of five aspects of child behavior: behavior during routines, children's use of materials, interactions with other children, with adults, and in a group. It also outlines how to use and interpret running records. The authors offer excellent guides on what details to look for in recording various behaviors, how to identify patterns of behavior, and questions to consider in summarizing the behavioral areas. A quick, easy-to-read must.

Haskell, E. M., ed. *Child Observations: First Series: Imitation and Allied Activities.* Boston: Heath, 1896. A collection of 1208 anecdotes on children from ages one to sixteen, compiled from notes recorded by students at the Worcester, Massachusetts Normal School in the 1890s. The collection is topical, focusing on imitation and modeling.

Russell, E. H. The study of children at the state Normal School, Worcester, Mass., *The Pedagogical Seminary,* 1892, 2, 343–357. The first extensive collection of anecdotal records about children were collected at the Normal School in Worcester, at the prompting of G. Stanley Hall. In this interesting historical article Russell, principal of the school, describes the method and its use in teacher training.

Wright, H. F. *Recording and Analyzing Child Behavior.* New York: Harper & Row, 1967. This book is taken largely from sections of *Midwest and Its Children* by Barker and Wright, a book now out of print. Written by the originators of the specimen description method of direct observation, it is a researcher's bible of how to record, analyze, and present the findings of specimen description observation.

Visualizing the Situation

One of the goals in writing specimen descriptions or running records is to provide enough detail so that a naive reader can visualize the situation as it actually occurred. This assignment is designed to help you learn to record observations so that others can accurately visualize what occurred.

Procedure: Select a child who is playing or working alone or who is not actively interacting with other children; observe him or her for five minutes. Record your observations using the specimen description method of observation.

Date_____Time_____Setting/Location _____

Subject _____

1. Record your transcribed observation here.

2. Select a partner who did not observe in the same setting and time you did your observation (someone who could have had no way of seeing the events recorded in your observation). Read your observation out loud and, as you read, have your partner act out the behaviors of the child you observed. Do not offer any comments, guidelines, or directions. Let your transcribed observation do all the talking. Write down all of the things that your partner acts out that are different from the child's actions. When you have finished listing the differing actions, go back and use a colored marking pen to circle those parts of your transcribed observation that were obviously incomplete or unclear.

3. Rewrite the unclear sections so that there is less opportunity for misinterpreting the behavior recorded.

Children's Thoughts and Reasoning

Anecdotal records have frequently been collected by teachers and researchers to provide raw data for studying particular areas of child development. An area of study that has captured investigators' interest from the beginning of child study to the present day is children's reasoning. In 1885, G. Stanley Hall encouraged the faculty of the Normal School at Worcester, Massachusetts to record anecdotes about child development (Russell, 1892). Under the leadership of the school's principal, E. Harlow Russell, over nineteen thousand anecdotes had been collected by 1892. H. W. Brown wrote an article for *Pedagogical Seminary* in that year in which 375 anecdotes about the thoughts and reasonings of children were reported. Brown arranged the anecdotes under the headings of: Misunderstandings of Words, Applications of Sayings, Explanations of Things, False Reasonings, and Thoughts and Reasonings about God, Christ, and Heaven.

In 1926, Jean Piaget published his observations and interpretations of children's reasoning in a book richly illustrated with anecdotes. His theory of cognitive development captured the interest of many child psychologists and started a wave of research that still continues over fifty years later.

Susan Isaacs was collecting anecdotes about children's reasoning when Piaget's book was published. In 1930, she published her findings of work carried on at Cambridge, England from 1924–1927. The anecdotal records collected by Isaacs and her teachers focus on discovery, reasoning, and thought. Isaacs was well aware of Piaget's work and commented on it, comparing it to her own observations throughout the book.

One of the most recent studies of children's reasoning based on anecdotal records is the 1962 study of Kenneth Wann, Miriam Dorn, and Elizabeth Ann Liddle. Their study was done out of "a concern that the education of young children was not keeping pace with the changing social scene and the consequent changes in the educational needs of young children . . . (The) study was launched to test the growing belief that children could know more at this early period than many educators believed possible" (pp. 1–2).

Your task in this assignment is to collect your own anecdotal records of children's reasoning.

Part I: Anecdotal Records

Procedure: In the course of a day, record as many examples of children's reasoning as possible. Be sure to identify the setting, age, and sex of the child(ren) involved in each anecdote. Transcribe the anecdotes that you collected below; attach additional sheets if necessary.

In the left margin of your transcribed anecdotes, list key descriptions to identify the specific content area of the observation: e.g., *why* questions, concepts of time, concepts of friendship, etc.

Part II: *Specimen Record*

Your task in this part of the assignment is to do a specimen description that focuses on children's thoughts and reasoning. Observe a child or group of children until you can isolate an example of children's thinking or reasoning. When you do, record that episode for as long as it lasts, keeping Wright's guidelines for writing specimen descriptions in mind.

1. Transcribe your observation here (attach additional sheets if necessary).

2. Using your own experience, compare and contrast the anecdotal and specimen description methods of observation. How do they compare in ease of recording? Information generated? Value to other readers? What purpose do you feel each method is best suited for?

Part III (optional): Comparative Analysis

Use the studies of children's reasoning reported in one of the following references as a basis for comparing and evaluating your own findings.

Brown, H. W. Some records of the thoughts and reasonings of children. *The Pedagogical Seminary*, 1892, 2, pp. 358–396.

Isaacs, S. *Intellectual Growth of Young Children.* New York: Harcourt, Brace Jovanovich, 1930.

Piaget, J. *The Language and Thought of the Child.* Translated by M. Gabain. New York: World, 1955.

Wann, K. D., M. S. Dorn, and E. A. Liddle. *Fostering Intellectual Development in Young Children.* New York: Teachers College, 1962.

1. How do your observations compare with the age findings given in the comparison study?

2. What, if any, sex differences do you see in your study of children's reasoning or thinking? How does this compare to earlier findings?

3. The world has changed considerably since the observations reported in the four studies were collected. Identify and discuss any changes in children's reasoning reflected by the examples that you observed and recorded. What factors in modern society do you feel might account for or contribute to these changes?

Observing the Guidelines

The guidelines for anecdotal records and specimen descriptions summarized by Brandt and Wright are designed to help you become more alert, accurate, complete, and objective when you observe. This assignment will help you apply those guidelines to your own work and the work of others.

Part I: Applying the Guidelines

Procedure: Two student observations are reproduced below. Evaluate each against the guidelines outlined in the chapter.

ANECDOTAL REPORT: One of the teachers had a birthday today and the four-year-olds sat in a circle to clap for each year, as they always do for a birthday. The teacher was 38 years old and the children clapped and clapped. Finally, on reaching 38, Michael said, "You're even older than my father. He's only 43."

	Present	Absent	Not Relevant	Comments
1. Identifies the primary action and speech of the key person.	_____	_____	_____	_____
2. Includes a statement that identifies the setting, the time of day, and the basic activity.	_____	_____	_____	_____
3. Includes responses of other people in the situation.	_____	_____	_____	_____
4. Uses exact words in recording the conversation.	_____	_____	_____	_____
5. Preserves the sequence of the episode.	_____	_____	_____	_____
6. Includes three levels of action in the episode:				
a. molar unit	_____	_____	_____	_____
b. subordinate molar unit	_____	_____	_____	_____
c. molecular unit	_____	_____	_____	_____
7. Is objective and complete.	_____	_____	_____	_____

TOTALS:
Not relevant _____
Relevant
  #Present _____
  #Absent _____
% of total
Present to total
Relevant _____

FIVE-MINUTE SPECIMEN DESCRIPTION: It is after dinner in the observer's home. David is a seven-year-old boy who has hastily eaten his supper in order to return to the block-building project he had begun before he and his family had dined. He is so engrossed in his project that he forgets that his favorite TV program is on. The racetrack under construction is situated on a tiled portion of the floor adjoining the dining room and the entrance to the living room. The subject is in the area alone. The track is circular and fairly large. Situated near the track and the subject is a deep orange-colored milk crate containing many hardwood blocks. The observer (his mother) is seated on the couch behind David. The subject is unaware that he is being observed since it is usual for the observer to sit and read in the living room after supper.

7:14 David sits on the uncarpeted dining room floor with his legs stretched out, extending diagonally from his torso. His eyebrows slightly raised, he methodically glances toward the orange-colored block crate. With a rhythmic left arm extension, he lowers his hand into the crate, grasps a rectangular-shaped block from the top and lifts it out. Placing his right palm flat on the floor, his arm automatically stiffens vertically above his hand.

7:15 Shifting his body weight onto the straightened arm, he lifts his body up and forward. With his left arm he reaches to the opposite side of his racetrack and gently lowers the rectangular block on top of a cylindrical one, while muttering to himself, "The obstacle course, we have to do it with barrels."

7:16 He quickly turns his head to the left, glancing at the crate. As he returns his head toward the center of his body, he lowers and presses his chin against his chest. Rolling his head toward his spread legs, he lifts his right hand up slowly as his torso gradually straightens to a standing position.

7:17 Taking a few quick steps back to balance, he mutters, "Yup, we have to do it with barrels," and quickly drops to a crossed-legged sitting position near the crate. Slightly twisting his body to the right, David grasps the rim of the crate with his left hand and glances down into the heap of blocks. In rapid succession he balloons his right cheek a few times, then reaches with right hand into the crate.

7:18 With rapid brush-like motion he pushes blocks aside digging deeper into the container. Stopping, he grasps a cylindrical block, mutters, "Ah, there you are; now one more," lifts it out, and places it on the floor in the space between his body and folded legs. Again, his right hand swings up and into the crate. He repeats the digging motion while muttering, "Come on, I know you're down there—oh, there." Lifting the second block out he holds it in his right hand as he dislodges his left hand from the rim. Reaching down between his folded legs,

7:19 he picks up the first retrieved block, rapidly claps the two together and (with an air of satisfaction) mutters, "Now we can do it."

Wright's Guidelines for Specimen Descriptions

	Present	Absent	Not Relevant	Comments
1. Focuses on behavior and situation				
a. remote/related action or circumstance	_____	_____	_____	_____
b. exterior force changing situation	_____	_____	_____	_____
2. Accurate and complete report of what subject says and does	_____	_____	_____	_____
3. Brackets interpretive material	_____	_____	_____	_____
4. Includes "how" for actions	_____	_____	_____	_____
5. "How" for interacting persons	_____	_____	_____	_____
6. All steps recorded in proper order	_____	_____	_____	_____
7. Describes behavior in terms of what was done, rather than not done	_____	_____	_____	_____
8. Describes scene as observer finds it	_____	_____	_____	_____
9. No more than one unit of molar behavior per sentence	_____	_____	_____	_____
10. No more than one action done by another per sentence	_____	_____	_____	_____
11. Marks off predetermined intervals	_____	_____	_____	_____

TOTAL:
Not relevant   _____
Relevant   _____
  #Present   _____
  #Absent   _____
% of total
Present to total
Relevant   _____

Part II: *Critiquing Your Own Records*

>   **Procedure:**   Analyze one of your own anecdotal reports (identify which one you are using) and your own specimen description against the guidelines for each.

Brandt's Guidelines for Anecdotal Records

	Present	Absent	Not Relevant	Comments
1. Identifies the basic action of the key person and what was said.	_____	_____	_____	_____
2. Includes a statement that identifies the setting, the time of day, and the basic activity.	_____	_____	_____	_____
3. Includes responses of other people in the situation.	_____	_____	_____	_____
4. Uses exact words in recording the conversation.	_____	_____	_____	_____
5. Preserves the sequence of the episode.	_____	_____	_____	_____
6. Includes three levels of action in the episode:				
a. molar unit	_____	_____	_____	_____
b. subordinate molar unit	_____	_____	_____	_____
c. molecular unit	_____	_____	_____	_____
7. Is objective and complete.	_____	_____	_____	_____

TOTALS:

Not relevant _____
Relevant _____
  #Present _____
  #Absent _____
% of total
Present to total
Relevant _____

Lab Assignment 15 (cont.)

Wright's Guidelines for Specimen Descriptions

	Present	Absent	Not Relevant	Comments
1. Focuses on behavior and situation				
a. remote, related action or circumstance	_____	_____	_____	_____
b. exterior force changing situation	_____	_____	_____	_____
2. Accurate and complete report of what subject says and does	_____	_____	_____	_____
3. Brackets interpretive material	_____	_____	_____	_____
4. Includes "how" for actions	_____	_____	_____	_____
5. "How" for interacting persons	_____	_____	_____	_____
6. All steps recorded in proper order	_____	_____	_____	_____
7. Describes behavior in terms of what was done, rather than not done	_____	_____	_____	_____
8. Describes scene as observer finds it	_____	_____	_____	_____
9. No more than one unit of molar behavior per sentence	_____	_____	_____	_____
10. No more than one action done by another per sentence	_____	_____	_____	_____
11. Marks off predetermined intervals	_____	_____	_____	_____

TOTALS:
Not relevant _____
Relevant _____
  #Present _____
  #Absent _____
% of total
Present to total
Relevant _____

Observer _____

Part III: Correcting the Omissions

    1. Look at the components of your own anecdotal record that you checked as absent. Rewrite your anecdotal record to correct those omissions. Underline the changes or additions to your original anecdote.

    2. How would you change your specimen description to correct the components that you marked absent?

Chapter Six

Case Studies and
Field Studies

Two methods of study that draw heavily on narrative observations—diary descriptions, anecdotal and running records, and specimen descriptions—are case studies and field studies. Case studies are frequently used by educators and people in the helping professions. Field studies are more commonly used in anthropological, ethological, and biological studies.

Case Studies

A course on observation of children can be organized in many different ways. One common organization is known as the case-study approach. Each student in the class selects a child who can be observed over an extended period of time and does a case study or in-depth study of that child. Class sessions usually focus on topical areas of child development (e.g. language development, physical development, intellectual development, and so on) or on education. The information gathered from the total number of case studies done by the class provides living examples for class analysis and discussion.

The case studies section of this chapter is designed primarily for students who will be doing case studies as a major part of their observational work. The case study is an assessment or evaluation technique, rather than an observational technique. Observational records frequently form the nucleus of case study data, however. Students doing case studies will find many of the assignments in other chapters valuable in collecting case-study information. A wide range of observational techniques is particularly helpful in providing a well-rounded picture of a child; by using a variety of techniques, the observer can avoid introducing the kind of bias that might slip into the record through the use of only one observational technique. At the same time, the observer will gain experience in determining which techniques are best for gathering specific kinds of information and how reliable that information is under various circumstances.

Case studies serve two broad purposes: to gather basic information about a subject and to gather information for problem solving. Students of child development, teachers, psychologists, medical students in training, and administrators in both the educational and business worlds are among those who can learn a great deal from participating in such exercises as part of their training. The main benefit of doing a case study is that it makes the subject matter "come alive." If the subject is a child, for example, that child is no longer a disjointed collection of unrelated bits, but becomes an intact individual emitting a thousand examples of language, perceptual, motor, social, emotional, and cognitive development.

Analysts and therapists routinely use case studies as part of their means of accumulating a portfolio of information on an individual with some manifest problem. Teachers and administrators can also benefit from a case-study approach to problem solving as it helps them to look at information gathered on behavior in a variety of settings, across an extended period of time, and from a variety of perspectives.

The method used to gather information for a case study may be as simple as collecting anecdotal records about a child's behavior throughout the year or as complex as amassing a full work-up including tests, interviews, observations, and other records. In both cases, the accumulated information is organized, analyzed, and written up for a final report. In reality, most teachers compile a case study of sorts on each child by gathering information throughout the year for use in curriculum planning, behavior management, and parent conferences.

It is hard to identify the first case study ever written on a child. For centuries the child simply was not important enough to warrant much attention, and biographies of famous people spent no more than a few paragraphs, if that, on a person's childhood and adolescence. One child who did warrant considerable attention was the wild boy of Aveyron. In 1799, a French physician named J. M. Itard discovered an adolescent boy running wild in the woods of Aveyron. The boy, whom Itard named Victor, did not speak intelligibly and walked and behaved like an animal. Itard spent five years trying to teach him language and appropriate human behavior, with minimal success. This case study of *The Wild Boy of Aveyron* (Itard, 1962) is a classic in therapeutic literature.

Characters from fiction have provided the raw material for case-study analysis in many college courses. Mark Twain's Huck Finn, Charles Dickens's Oliver Twist and David Copperfield, Betty Smith's Francie (*A Tree Grows in Brooklyn*), J. D. Salinger's Holden Caulfield (*The Catcher in the Rye*), and Carson McCullers's Frankie (*A Member of the Wedding*) are all children in literature who can serve as subjects for case studies. After reading these books, we feel that we know these children well and have many clues to help us interpret their behavior.

We also know the children of the diary descriptions fairly well. Shinn's niece and Dearborn's daughter are individuals we have come to know by the time we have finished reading details about their early years.

Children described in individual anecdotal records are less people than incidents. It is a rare anecdote that gives us much insight into a child's individuality. But an extensive collection of anecdotes, covering behavioral episodes over a period of time, can be analyzed and strung together into a well-ordered whole. The insightful teacher or researcher can, given enough time and enough raw material, make some definitive statements about an individual child's self and style.

Katherine Read writes: "Notes taken during observations are the 'raw material' out of which understanding grows." Written up for a child's file, such notes "can be reviewed and summarized at intervals and can be used in evaluating a child's progress and in making plans for him." Read also suggests that such notes can be used in parent conferences (Read, 1976, pp. 125–126).

There are a number of reasons to do a case study:

1. To aid in analyzing the problems of a child having physical, intellectual, or emotional difficulties.
2. To develop information on any child for occasional reports or interviews involving parents.
3. To assess growth, development, or change in an individual.
4. To enable us to know an individual's learning style and coping style well enough that we can plan appropriate guidance.
5. To provide records that can be useful to other educators or specialists as background data in future years.
6. To accumulate examples that can be used to illustrate lectures, articles, workshops, and classes designed to train professionals.

In developing a case study, it is important that all the information in the file be accurate and objective, and that as many real-life examples as possible be included. When an incident occurs, it is not enough simply to report the events as they happened, but it is also important to include as much of the actual verbalization as possible. Often the material collected at the time seems to have no significance. Only after a certain number of incidents are accumulated is it possible to examine them and see patterns of behavior or reactions that are consistent across time. Case studies allow for an accumulation of evidence about a child which can eventually lead to insights to guide future action or interpretation.

If you will be doing a case study on one particular child during this course, you will want to note the following kinds of information:

1. physical description of the child
2. family background
3. school environment
4. activity pattern; how he or she spends the day
5. skill in the various developmental areas: language, motor, cognitive development
6. interaction with others: peers, teachers, parents
7. behavior in school
8. television viewing habits and other use of leisure time
9. indicators of self-concept
10. coping style and response to frustration
11. approach to routines, new activities, and unexpected events
12. use of materials

You will want to observe the child in as many different situations as possible: in different activity areas, indoors and outdoors, large groups and small groups, individual activities, with different materials, on different days of the week, even away from the school environment if that is possible. If you are observing a child with special needs, you may want to get the following information in addition:

1. reports from doctors or specialists who have examined or treated the child in the past
2. results of tests or assessment inventories done on the child
3. opinions of other individuals who have spent time with the child—other teachers, for example
4. notes taken during interviews with parents and others relating to the child (eating and sleeping habits, favorite activities, family patterns affecting the child, fears, and so on)

In some cases, the decision to do a case study on an individual is deliberate and the process is carefully planned. In other situations, notes kept occasionally may suggest that a particular child is having difficulty and that a case study might be helpful. At other times, the need for a case study will be generated by a difference of opinion about whether a child's behavior is really cause for concern. Let us consider one such example and the different kinds of information that might be collected in a routine case study in the classroom setting.

John Oliver Lynn

For seven years, Mrs. Walters and Mrs. Clark met at the end of the school year to discuss the children in Mrs. Walter's four-year-old group who would be in Mrs. Clark's five-year-old group the next year. Mrs. Clark liked to be well prepared for her young students and found that knowing something about them helped her make plans for them as individuals and as a group. She was particularly interested in Mrs. Walters's report of John Oliver Lynn: "a neat, orderly little boy, very well socialized, a natural leader with a great sense of fun." She counted on Jack (as he was called by his family) to help the group work together happily and productively, and she selected him to play a key role in special projects she had planned for the beginning of the year. The group did not come together as she had hoped, however, and she decided to do a series of observations to see if she could pinpoint the problem.

The first thing she did was an activity check to see how the children were spending free time: how the various areas of the room were being used, what the flow of activity was, what materials were most popular, and so on. She discovered that the block corner was used less often than in past years and that there were not enough of the more difficult puzzles available, but she did not feel that this was the root of the problem. Her next step was to look at the sociometric status of the group. What kind of interpersonal relationships had developed? In doing so, she began to get some unexpected information on John Oliver Lynn. Because Jack was gregarious and outgoing and interacted with many children quite easily, he appeared in her observations often. The picture she began to see added another dimension to the glowing picture painted by Mrs. Walters. Jack was indeed neat and orderly, and he seemed to be well-socialized. He met other children, especially the girls, easily and quickly, putting them immediately at ease. He had become a leader in the class but there seemed to be some dissembling in his leadership. Mrs. Clark felt that behind his facade of goodwill and merriment she saw some rather disturbing behavior patterns. He seemed to be adept at pitting children against each other by subtly encouraging situations that created competition and jealousy within the group. She asked Mrs. Walters if she had noticed any of this behavior the previous year and Mrs. Walters said she had not. "Jack was a delightful child to have in the group and hardly ever got into any sort of trouble. He was very popular and well-liked by most of the children in the group," Mrs. Walters reported. The only negative comment Mrs. Walters could make was that Jack had trouble admitting errors or accepting the fact that he was in the wrong when he was in need of correction, which was rare. Mrs. Clark decided to do a short case study on Jack to see if there were anything to her suspicion, and enlisted the help of her student teacher, Rebecca Jardine.

First Mrs. Clark got permission to look through Jack's file. It contained a developmental history that Jack's mother had filled out when she enrolled him at Tiny Tots Nursery School at age two and a half, the report of two home visits (one for each year that he was at nursery school), some anecdotal records, and the results of Mrs. Walters's kindergarten readiness test given in March of the previous year.

The developmental history indicated that Mrs. Lynn's pregnancy was uneventful and that Jack's birth was normal. Jack was toilet trained somewhat earlier than most boys, and his mother reported that he is fastidious about keeping his hands and his clothes clean. He has never been a messy eater. Jack's favorite foods are fried chicken and carrot sticks. Because he does not like to get his hands greasy, his mother has to cut the chicken off the bone so he can eat it with his fork. She was pleased that he seems to be orderly by nature. He usually goes to bed at 8 P.M. and sleeps until 7 A.M. He has not napped since he was twenty-two months old.

In describing his emotional behavior, Mrs. Lynn mentioned that Jack becomes upset when he is told "no." He feels bad if he is caught doing something wrong. "This bothers him so much that he usually tries to pretend that he didn't do it." To the question, how does the child comfort himself, she answered, "When he is a bit upset or insecure, he takes his blocks off the shelf in his room and stacks them first in one pile and then in another and then puts them back on their shelf very neatly."

Mrs. Lynn indicated that they do not leave him with a baby sitter very often, but have had no trouble doing so. He does not seem to mind. "He seems to be very self-sufficient; even as a toddler, he did not cling to me the way so many children do to their mothers."

Under "play interests," Jack's mother indicated that he prefers playing with his blocks and likes to color in coloring books and is already trying to stay inside the lines. His language development is normal; he speaks clearly with very little baby talk.

The information about Jack's parents indicated that the father, Max, worked for a local animal shelter. His mother, Nel, had been a secretary before her marriage. She is expecting their second child shortly. Jack's medical record indicated that he has a slight allergy to dust and mold.

It was the custom for teachers to make home visits before school started so that the children would know their teachers and the teachers would be able to observe children in the home environment. Miss Fischer, Jack's first teacher, made the following report on her home visit.

Jack seemed somewhat shy for the first few minutes, but soon was the center of attention. He is very responsive, and smiles easily and readily. His room is exceptionally neat and clean. His favorite play activity is blocks; Nel reports that he will spend hours straightening them. Max is an outgoing and friendly father, who seems to let his wife make the child-rearing decisions. He did ask me, however, if I felt that a 2½ year old should be at school instead of home with the mother. We talked about the animals we have in the classroom and Max indicated that he would be glad to help out with them any time. Nel is less outgoing than Max; she is soft-spoken, with a well-modulated voice. She is very reflective about questions asked her and pauses a long time before answering—quite different from Max's ready answers.

Her main expectation of nursery school is that Jack will have a chance to play with other children his own age. The pets in the house are a pet snake kept in a case in the family room, an ant farm in Jack's room, and a Myna bird in a cage in the kitchen. The bird, who was once owned by a carnival shooting gallery owner, has only two phrases which it repeats with great regularity: "Who's next?" and "Too bad!" Jack enjoys the ant farm and Nel reports that he is intrigued by the efficient scurrying that goes on there.

Another entry was made at the end of the first week of school (Jack had started going five mornings a week from the very beginning):

Nel Lynn is in the last month of pregnancy; Max brings Jack to school each morning. They plan to car-pool with two other parents in the neighborhood, but felt that Max should bring Jack the first week. Jack showed the same initial shyness at school that I had noticed on the home visit. I asked Max to stay for a few minutes just to be sure that Jack was comfortable in the new environment. I showed Jack the block corner knowing that this was an important activity for him at home and he immediately began taking the blocks off the shelf and piling them in straight neat towers. He seemed to divide his attention between the blocks, which he played with almost mechanically, and watching the other children. Occasionally he checked to see if his father was still there. After about 15 minutes, Max told Jack he was leaving. Jack said, "No. I want you to watch me." Max said he would only be gone a few minutes, which seemed to satisfy Jack. Max did not return until the end of the morning; this pattern persisted all week. When I commented that it might be better to tell Jack that he would be back at the end of the morning instead of letting him think he would return sooner, Max became defensive and tried to change the subject. He did not seem to like having his behavior or his judgment questioned.

Jack fell into the routine of nursery school very quickly and by the third morning loved to announce to other children what came next. He would march around the room, saying "clean-up time," or "snack time," or "story time," rounding up followers as he went. He likes puzzles, coloring, blocks, and books and stays away from the messier areas like paint, gluing, and water play.

There were three other anecdotal entries about Jack that fall. Mrs. Clark felt that the most significant one concerned the birth of his new baby brother—a redhead they called Sandy.

Nel Lynn reported how surprised she was that there were no problems of resentment when the baby was born. (Jack was 2.7 at the time of the baby's birth.) With obvious pride, she reported how generous Jack was about sharing his toys with the new baby the day she brought him home from the hospital. The baby was in the crib, located in the parents' bedroom. Jack went to his room and brought back one of his stuffed animals, which he dropped over the side of the baby's crib. Nel reported that she and Max both praised Jack for sharing the toy. Jack then went back to his room and returned with another stuffed toy—a snake—and dropped it over the side of the crib. Again he was praised. Then he went to his room and returned with a large plastic ball which he rolled over the side of the crib onto the baby. Nel cautioned him to be careful not to hurt the baby. This time when Jack returned from his room, he brought his most prized toys—several of his large blocks which he was about to drop onto the baby when his mother intervened, saying the baby was too little to play with Jack's blocks yet. Nel explained to me that in his obvious eagerness to share, he did not understand that the baby could get hurt.

The record for the rest of the year indicated that Jack had had measles in February (along with three other children in class); Nel didn't believe in preventive vaccinations but rather that children should have these diseases when they are young so that they wouldn't have them when they are older. Jack had visited his grandmother in Ohio in March, an exciting event because it was his first plane ride, but somewhat complicated by the fact that he got too excited and threw up on the airplane. The end-of-year report summarized information reported in anecdotes, checklists, and other observations and information across the year. The end-of-year summary described Jack as an interesting child with a sparkling personality.

He displays a rather vivid imagination and tells elaborate stories about his brother, Sandy, both making fun of him in what seems to be a very accepting way, and reporting events in great humor. He is an entertaining child. He is easy to work with on projects and often is found showing others how to do things—a real teacher's helper. The only occasional problem with his peer teaching is that sometimes in his eagerness to be sure he doesn't forget something, his directions become so long and complicated that no one can follow him. He likes blocks, lotto games and puzzles the best and art or any messy activities the least. He is a quick learner and enjoys mastering new tasks. He is always first to help clean up. If there is any trait worth watching as a possible trouble spot, it is his almost compulsive need to organize, often with no reason to do so. Perhaps this is the comfort behavior mentioned by his mother on the developmental history form. Jack is soft-spoken and has a well-modulated voice like his mother's but his laughter is surprisingly hearty like his father's.

The records from the second year read much the same. In fact, the only notes that shed any new light were one about his father and another note written by Mrs. Walters's student teacher named Betsy Gordon.

I feel that under the guise of being an animal lover, Max Lynn may take pleasure in brutalizing them. In a recent incident, one of the baby rabbits had a foot caught in the wire mesh of the cage. Max had just come in with Jack when we discovered the bunny's plight and he offered to help. He didn't take the time to work slowly and carefully and consequently the animal was hurt in the process. In a previous situation, one of the adult rabbits had dug its way out of the pen and was loose in the yard. Max was helping us catch it, but when it went under the fence into the street, Max advised us to let it go—that it would probably get hit by a car before we could get it anyhow, and he could always get us a new one at the animal shelter.

Mrs. Clark asked Mrs. Walters about these anecdotes. In the conversation that followed it was clear that Mrs. Walters did not have a very favorable impression of Max Lynn. She felt that he was openly critical of everyone and everything and had a need to put people down. The entry reported on two incidents involving classroom animals. When Mrs. Clark asked about Jack's mother, Mrs. Walters said that she was a very sweet person—nice to everyone and with a reputation for being a very honorable person. She also felt that Jack was quite attached to her and that he imitated many of her mannerisms.

The incident reported by Betsy Gordon occurred one day when she was unobtrusively stationed in the play yard. Jack had begun to spend more time with younger children in his class (which was a family-age grouping class of two-and-a-half to five-year-olds). Her notes indicated that he spent more time helping the younger ones than he did interacting with his peers. Betsy's observation reported several incidents and then queried whether Jack was trying to influence the younger children in their selection of friends. The last incident and her query are as follows:

Jack (age 4.3) was playing in the big block area with Marcia (3.0) and Sean (3.3). They were building a zoo, under Jack's direction, when Tom (4.6) joined them. Tom and Sean had been playing together for the past several days and seemed to be striking up a new friendship. Jack told Tom that there was not enough room for him. Sean quickly moved over and said, "There's room now, Jack." Then Jack said there weren't enough animals and Sean said he would share his. A minute later Jack told Tom to "find some grass to feed the animals in the zoo." Tom went outside to pick the grass and as soon as he left, Jack turned to Sean and said, "You shouldn't play with Tom. He likes to hit little children. If he tries to hit you, just come over to me." When Tom returned, Sean said he couldn't play in their zoo.

My impression is that Jack's motives may be self-serving ones. His alliance with the younger children puzzles me. Is it related to the fact that he has, for several months, selected the easy rather than the challenging table activities? When there is a choice of indoor activities, Jack invariably selects the kind of project that makes minimal demands (e.g., easy puzzles). When I have occasionally tried to switch him to a more age-appropriate activity, he has resisted quietly and firmly. Last week, I gave him two rather complicated puzzles to substitute for an easier one. As long as I was there, he worked on one I had given him—long enough for me to know that it was a good challenge but not an impossible one by any means. As soon as I left the table, he set the puzzle aside and went back to the easier 5-piece one. Is it something in his confidence in himself, perhaps?

When Mrs. Clark asked Mrs. Walters about Betsy's report, Mrs. Walters indicated that Betsy was a perceptive young lady, but that she (like many other students) tended to project motivation at times rather than simply describe a child's behavior, and perhaps she has read too much into the incident. She felt Jack's playing with younger children was just part of his wanting to be helpful to everyone.

The kindergarten readiness inventory given to Jack by Mrs. Walters in March added information about his ability in school-related areas. It indicated that Jack's small muscle motor coordination was very good but that he was less sure of himself in large muscle motor skills and somewhat below his age mates in skill level. She noted that this might be related to the fact that he was small for his age and a bit fearful of heights, an emotional rather than a physical coordination response. His language development was close to the top. He could say in order all of the numbers from one to twenty and could sort nine blocks but could not deal with concepts of *more* or *less*. He knew all the shapes and colors that she asked him to identify and could correctly demonstrate understanding of relational concepts like *under, over, behind, on top of*. Perceptual tasks such as finding similarities and differences were harder for him. He could pick out pictures that were the same when they dealt with whole objects (two cats, a sheep, and a lion) but had trouble when it was only part of the object that he had to discriminate (the number of wheels on a wagon). He could cut and could draw a circle and did a person in the draw-a-man section of the test complete with eyelashes and belly button. In comparison to the rest of the class, Jack was at the eighty-third percentile. Mrs. Walters told Mrs. Clark that she was a little surprised that he didn't score higher because he seemed so capable in everything he did.

Armed with this information, Mrs. Clark and Rebecca felt that a short-term case study was in order. If, in fact, Jack were causing friction in the group, he was doing so very quietly for all appearances suggested the opposite. If Mrs.

Clark were wrong in her suspicion, it was important to correct her perception of Jack quickly as it would influence her interactions with him. If she were right, they had to try to find out what was at the base of Jack's behavior. Perhaps his cheerful facade masked an unhappy little boy. They had some clues, and some real concern. It was enough to start on.

A Word of Caution

Teachers need to be cautious about what they say in written reports destined for a child's file. As a result of the Family Educational Rights and Privacy Act of 1974, a federal statute, "a parent or student has the right to inspect student records. If it appears they contain inaccurate material, a hearing must be held within a reasonable time before an impartial hearing officer to present the student's side of the story. An explanation may be inserted into the file by the student or parent. Second, written permission must be secured from the parent or student before information in the file is released to others" (Hollander, 1978, p. 24).

Analyzing the Data

In the case of John Oliver Lynn, or any other child, once the raw data has been collected, the task of analysis begins. One method of analysis is to note key descriptors in the margin to the left of each entry. Those entries that focus on the same descriptive feature can then be grouped together and scanned for patterns of similarity or for changes over the year.

Brandt (1972) suggested a second method of listing all the recurring patterns of behavior that can be found in both the subject's behavior and in the behavior of others toward the subject. Each entry also includes the date on which it happened. The entries are then grouped by area (relationship with adults, relationship with children, and so on). When the recurring pattern list is complete, it is scanned for overall interpretation. The interpretation is made by identifying the developmental tasks that the subject seemed to be working on during the course of the case study. It is also possible to identify the positive and negative strategies a child has developed as coping strategies.

While it is important to gather case-study data accurately and carefully, the data is lifeless until it is put to use for the good of children. Without an accumulation of information, no analysis can be made, and without perceptive analysis, no action can be planned. One step grows out of another. Each step has the same goal: understanding children in order to better help them.

Case studies serve an important function in child study in that they make principles of growth and development "come alive." They serve another very important function for professionals who use them in the course of their work. This can best be described as a problem-solving function. The teacher or medical or social worker identifies a problem behavior or a question for observation and then sets out to gather information that—hopefully—will contribute a to a greater understanding of that individual.

Field studies, on the other hand, are discovery oriented. The researcher or observer sets out to add to our understanding of a group or a behavior for the purpose of increasing our knowledge about the subject rather than in a direct attempt to help the subject.

Field Studies

Field studies require a great deal of commitment in both time and people resources. Researchers must go into the field, the natural environment of the subject, and live among their subjects long enough to be able to describe the growth, behavior, or major characteristics of subjects under study.

As early as 1891, researchers were advocating field studies that focused on children. Franz Boas, one of the leading anthropologists of his day, wrote that ". . . we must conclude that a study of the anthropology of children is of the greatest importance for a knowledge of the conditions of laws of growth" (1891, p. 225). In the 1940s, John Whiting, an anthropologist, and Irving Child, a developmental psychologist, teamed up to review the observations on children recorded in field studies and reported their work in *Child Training and Personality* (1953), a classic book in child development literature.

Most of the field studies on people (as opposed to plants and animals) have come from anthropology. Margaret Mead, one of Franz Boas's bright young students in the 1920s, helped bring the knowledge gained from these studies to the attention of the general public. Mead used the observation and recording skills of her field to expand our understanding of other cultures, as well as our own. She described her research technique as one that involves constant observation and voluminous notes. These notes then serve as raw material for later thinking and theorizing and finally result in coherent presentations in book form, put together into a smooth narrative, usually organized by topic rather than chronologically. In her 1930 book, *Growing Up in New Guinea,* Mead described a situation concerning one of the rites of passage (transitions from childhood to adolescence) she had observed and noted in detail:

The house is full of visitors, all the relatives of Pwisio's wife are there, with laden canoes to celebrate the ear piercing of Pwisio's sixteen-year-old son, Manuwai. In the front of the house all is formal. Manuwai, in a choker of dog's teeth, painted and greased, sits up very straight. His father's two sisters are waiting to lead him down the ladder. But his mother is not there. From the curtained back of the house come sounds of weeping and the low-voiced expostulation of many women. In the front sits Pwisio, facing his guests but pausing to hurl insult after insult at his wife whom he had caught sleeping naked. (There were strangers in the house, and during the night an unwedded youth, a friend of her son's, had stirred the house fire into a blaze.) So Pwisio overwhelms his wife with obloquy, fearful to beat her while so many of her kin are in the house, and she packs her belongings, tearfully protesting her innocence and angrily enumerating the valuables she's taking with her. "This is mine. I made it, and my sister gave me these shell beads. This belt is mine; I got it in return for sago at the birth feast last week." Her little adopted daughter Ngalowen, aged four, stands aside in shame from her mother whom her father brands thus publicly as a criminal. When her mother gathers up her boxes and marches out the back door, Ngalowen makes no move to follow. Instead, she slips into the front room and cuddles down beside her self-righteous and muttering father. After the long confusion, the ceremony is resumed; the absence of the mother who would have had no official part in it receives no further comment (Reprinted in *New Lives for Old,* 1956, p. 36).

Margaret Mead, like Susan Isaacs, used her material to generate theories. She took extensive notes as a present, but noninvolved observer. Because she could not know ahead of time what behaviors would be important for later analysis, she wrote down as much detail as possible about every event she observed. Only then could she expect to have the raw material she might need later.

Ethologists have also used narrative observation strategies to record field notes of animal behavior. In 1960 Jane Goodall set out to extend our knowledge of chimpanzee behavior. Prior to that time, most of the studies had focused on chimpanzees in captivity. Goodall felt that these laboratory studies might not reflect the behavior of chimps in the wild, their natural environment, and set out to study them in their habitat.

Goodall's work, still in progress nineteen years later, covers four generations of chimpanzees. In her 1971 book, *In the Shadow of Man,* she reported on one chimp family consisting of Flo and her children, Faben, Figan, Fifi, and Flint. The following passage is an observation made when Flint was an infant:

When Flint was thirteen weeks old we saw Fifi succeed in pulling him away from his mother. Flo was grooming Figan when Fifi, with infinite caution and many quick glances toward her mother's face, began to pull at Flint's foot. Inch by inch she drew the infant toward her, and all at once was in her arms. Fifi lay on her back and cuddled Flint to her tummy with her arms and legs. She lay very still (1971, p. 113).

Most chimps leave the mother's nest at about three years of age, but Flint, born when Flo was in her forties, became the proverbial spoiled child and refused to leave even after the birth of his sister, Flame, four years his junior. When Flint was eight years old, Flo died of old age and Goodall recorded Flint's reactions:

Weary with age, Flo died. Flint, then 8 years old, seemed to lose the will to live, and was unresponsive to his sister Fifi's attentions. Three weeks after Flo's death, Flint returned to the spot where she had breathed her last. And he, too, lay down and died (1979, p. 605).

Goodall's field studies have not only dramatically expanded our knowledge of the behavior of chimpanzees, but have also demonstrated the value of continued observation. Seventeen years after she began her study, Goodall realized that the chimpanzees practiced their own form of warfare, including cannibalism; neither behavior had been observed previously.

The late Dr. Louis S. B. Leakey predicted, when I set off to Gombe in 1960, that I was starting a study that would take ten years; I was young, and that seemed a lifetime. Now I realize that the first ten years were just a beginning. Certainly our picture of chimpanzee behavior would be very different if the work had ended in 1970. We had no notion then that chimpanzees might, deliberately and systematically, kill one another. It is sobering that our new awareness of chimpanzee violence compels us to acknowledge that these ape cousins of ours are even *more* similar to humans than we thought before (1979, p. 620).

One of the best known field studies in child development is the series of studies on group formation and intergroup relations by Carolyn and Muzafer Sherif. They first began their experiments in 1948 and their work spanned the next 20 years. Sherif and Sherif depart from the strict naturalistic observations of Mead and Goodall and adopt an experimental field study approach. Experimental field studies involve research that combines a setting that is viewed as naturalistic to the subject while still affording some control over the situation to the researcher.

The first stage of the Sherif and Sherif studies was devoted to observation of group formation among previously unacquainted individuals. Sherif (1967) describes the experimental field setting as follows:

To control subject selection and ensure that backgrounds of subjects be homogeneous in crucial respects and to control conditions of interaction during the experiments, the location of facilities, and the timing of events, summer camps for boys in isolated sites were established as the experimental settings. (p. 94)

Subsequent studies, all involving summer camps, investigated other aspects of group formation such as the conditions of interactions between groups which would promote hostility and the conditions which would reduce intergroup hostility. The researchers structured the camp activities to increase the likelihood of intergroup tension and hostility. For example, a tournament of team games was developed with prizes awarded to the winning group.

As a result of successive win-or-lose encounters of this sort, readily identifiable unfavorable attitudes and consistently hostile actions developed between the groups. Operationally, unfavorable attitudes were measured by the frequency and stabilization of negative stereotypes of the out-group and its members, the "social distance" maintained between the groups, and manifest attempts toward hostile encounters. (Sherif, 1967, p. 95)

Likewise, conditions were structured to help reduce intergroup hostility.

. . . a series of goals which were compelling and highly desired by both groups was introduced in apparently natural situations. The goal was attainable only through the joint efforts of the two groups. Examples: A threatened water shortage owing to dysfunction of the supply system; preparations for a much-desired outing which required greater efforts and resources than either group could provide separately. (Sherif, 1967, p. 95)

The camp situations were viewed as naturalistic by the boys attending them but were, in fact, controlled in ways important to the experimental design. The researchers were able to specify the ecological and sociological setting and to observe how individuals responded to what happened in that setting. By using a combination of research methods, researchers have a better cross-check on their findings and are more confident about the validity of their generalizations. Sherif explains the advantages gained by integrating field and laboratory approaches as follows:

1. By painstaking efforts, the naturalness of real life situations in the eyes of individual participants can be attained. In the group experiments mentioned above, the subjects perceived the experimental situation as a summer camp and did not suspect that from the beginning the conditions and activities in which they interacted were being controlled and manipulated. They were not aware that their behavior was constantly observed and rated. Every effort was made to make measurement techniques a natural part of the situation by presenting them in the form of activities appropriate in the situation.

2. Because experimental control extends to choice of subjects in accordance with specified criteria and to location of the experiment and activities engaged in, the precision of laboratory manipulation of variables need not be sacrificed.

3. Because subject background and experimental conditions and their alteration are controlled, it becomes possible to specify crucial stimulus variables in the formation of social attitudes and to assess the psychological effects of these attitudes as a function of developing group membership through precise laboratory techniques suitably adapted to the phenomenally natural situations of the subjects (Sherif, 1967, pp. 96–97).

Whether it is Jane Goodall watching chimpanzees or Margaret Mead watching the people of New Guinea or Carolyn and Muzafer Sherif watching adolescent boys in a summer camp, there is observer impact. Peter K. Smith and Linda Daglish, in their study "Sex Differences in Parent and Infant Behavior in the Home," asked parents to go about their business, ignoring the presence of the observer. They stated that "None of the parents seemed disturbed by her (the observer's) presence, but in eight of the 64 visits (four to boys, four to girls) it was judged from the child's behavior or subsequent parental comment that the child had been noticeably affected" (1977, p. 1251). Thus, one of the observer's challenges in doing field work is to become a familiar part of the subject's environment in order that the behavior being observed is, in fact, the same as would occur without the observer's presence. It is this need to become a familiar part of the environment that contributes to the time needed to do useful field study.

Field notes, like other narrative methods, preserve the sequence of action and interaction. They differ in that they are more likely to include interpretation, perhaps because the observer is trying to make sense of what is going on while it is happening, rather than simply trying to record without comment for later analysis.

Summary

Two methods of study that draw heavily on narrative observations are case studies and field studies. Case studies are done by a wide variety of people in helping professions—teachers, counselors, therapists, doctors, and so on. The case study is a useful means of learning about behavior and of analyzing patterns in behavior. It is an especially valuable aid for classroom teachers who want to plan for the needs of individual children. Case studies make use of a wide variety of information. Some of the most important categories of information to consider in doing a case study of a single child were outlined in the chapter.

One of the problems of observational research is that the data generated is only as objective as the observer is. Sensitivity of the observer, acuity of the observer, and awareness or perceptiveness of the observer all influence what is noticed and recorded. Case studies have these same limitations plus an additional drawback: It is left to the teacher to decide what information to include and is, therefore, open to another form of bias.

Field studies involve observational research in the subject's natural habitat. They are extremely costly in time and people resources, but provide some of the most comprehensive information that can be gathered.

Suggestions for Further Reading

Axline, V. *Dibs—In Search of Self*. Boston: Houghton Mifflin, 1964.

Baruch, D. W. *One Little Boy*. New York: Dell, 1952. These two books are classics in case studies of emotionally disturbed children. Written more for parents and teachers than for psychologists or psychiatrists, they relate the unraveling of the inner world of two children in search of themselves.

Brandt, R. M. "Four naturalistic cases." In *Studying Behavior in Natural Settings*. New York: Holt, Rinehart and Winston, 1972, pp. 215—284. Brandt is interested in observation as a research tool which can be applied to a wide variety of settings and problems. In this chapter, he outlines four case studies: one of a ninth-grade student by his teacher (an individual); one of children's recreational groups (group process); one of the management practices of an institution undergoing change (organizational analysis); and one of a mass demonstration (public event). Each case study includes an introduction to case-study methods appropriate to the question under investigation.

Cohen, D. H., and V. Stern. *Observing and Recording the Behavior of Young Children*. New York: Teachers College, 1958. This book was written for classroom teachers in early childhood education as a guide in how to observe, report, and summarize anecdotal observations. It is richly illustrated with observational examples and identifies many questions to help focus the observer's attention on important details of behavior.

Mead, Margaret. *New Lives for Old*. New York: New American Library, 1956. A study of the culture of the Manus in 1928 and again in 1953 recording this primitive people's transition from their traditional ways to modern ways. Mead's thoughtful observations "then" and "now" reflect a wealth of field notes and detailed records.

Sherif, Muzafer. *Social Interaction: Process and Products*. Chicago: Aldine, 1967. The book of selected essays describes two decades of work on social interaction. Sherif and his associates draw on a wide variety of methods to study social interaction. Chapters 3 and 14 offer particularly good discussions of experimental field research.

Van Lawick-Goodall, Jane. *In the Shadow of Man*. New York: Dell, 1971. Observations of wild chimpanzees in their natural habitat—after the author's first ten years in the forests of East Africa. A fascinating pioneer study.

Planning a Case Study

This assignment is designed to help you identify information important to structuring a case study. It is based on the example of John Oliver Lynn used in the text.

Procedure: You have been given some basic information about John Oliver Lynn and told that other information exists in his school file. Your task is to outline the questions you want to answer through the case study and the information that you would gather in trying to answer those questions.

1. List below the questions that you would want to answer in trying to understand Jack's behavior.

2. What clues do you have about his behavior from the existing records?

3. What information would you gather to assist you in answering the questions you identified in #1? Star the items that could be gathered from observational data.

4. Look at the items you starred above. What kind of observations (settings, focus, and so on) would you do to answer these questions?

5. How many observations, and for how long, would you need in order to have enough reliable information to begin to interpret Jack's behavior?

Identifying Questions

You had a lot of information about John Oliver Lynn to get you started in planning your case study. This assignment demands more from you. You are given only a snapshot description of each child and then asked to generate appropriate questions to guide the case study for each.

Procedure: Four situations are presented in which a child's behavior suggests that further attention might be beneficial. After reading each paragraph, note down four or five important questions to pursue in developing a case study on the child described.

1. SAM: (age 5.6) Sam is a Down's Syndrome (mongoloid) child who has been in nursery school for two years. Although the oldest children in his class are a year younger than he is in this prekindergarten facility, the parents and the school have felt he was doing well and should stay there rather than move into the public school kindergarten. Now that he is older and larger, it is time to reevaluate plans for the following year. What questions should you ask to get the data you need for this decision?

2. SHARON: (age 3.9) Sharon is a quiet child, with an unusually well-developed artistic talent for a child her age. Over the past few months, her teachers have begun to notice that she wanders off, almost unconsciously, when the group goes on a field trip. In the classroom, she tends to stand apart and simply gaze into space. At other times, she is happily, though quietly, involved in the activities around her. She rarely smiles and never shows that she is upset. One of her teachers has suggested that there might be some psychological or neurological damage. What questions should you ask to get the data you need for this assessment?

3. MRS. B. AND GWEN: (age 3.5) Gwen is a new child in this preschool. Her mother brings her to school every morning. It is now six weeks after the opening of school and the mother still has to stay with Gwen or she cries hysterically. All teachers are familiar with separation problems, but this one seems a bit different. One of the teachers remarked at a recent staff meeting that she has heard Mrs. B. say on several occasions: "Gwen, you know I love you very much and will not leave you." The teacher feels that this pseudo-reassurance may be interpreted by the child as a threat. The child might reason that if the mother leaves, her mother must not love her. Another teacher feels that the mother is the one with the separation problem, not the daughter, and the daughter is behaving the way the mother wants her to. What questions should you ask to get the data you need in order to analyze this situation?

4. LEOTA: (age 7.3) Leota has always been an active, fairly aggressive child in her peer interactions, but the intensity of her reactions seems to have increased in the past month. Children she formerly spent time with very happily are now reluctant to play with her. She has become verbally abusive and snatches things she wants out of other children's hands. Something must be done before her hostility has totally isolated her from everyone in class. No one can identify the beginnings of the behavior but everyone agrees that it is something that occurred within the past four to six weeks. What questions do you need to ask to get the data you need to get at the problem?

Observer _____

The Vocabulary of Observation

In 1936, Gordon Allport and H. S. Odbert did a psycholexical study of trait names and found that there were 17,953 words in the English language describing as many different types of behavior. A good observer needs to have a ready reserve of words to adequately and accurately describe different behaviors. You don't need to know 17,953 words but you do need to be able to describe common actions like *walk,* for example, in various ways. Shuffle, saunter, scurry, stroll, amble, stride, and march all convey different images of someone walking along.

Procedure: Observe a person in a public place for ten minutes and list all of his or her large motor actions and movements. Observe for another ten minutes and list all of his or her body positions and postures. For each descriptive word you list, find two others that can define a different quality of the same action. (For example, large-toothed grin could also be described as a flashy grin, or a grin from ear to ear; each has a slightly different image.)

Date_____Time _____ Setting/Location _____

Subject_____Age_____

1. List all large motor actions and behaviors and identify two alternative descriptors for each.

   ACTIONS/BEHAVIORS   *ALTERNATIVE 1   ALTERNATIVE 2*
   a.

   b.

   c.

   d.

   e.

   f.

   g.

   h.

   i.

   j.

2. List all facial expressions and identify two alternative descriptors for each.

FACIAL EXPRESSIONS   *ALTERNATIVE 1*   *ALTERNATIVE 2*

a.

b.

c.

d.

e.

f.

g.

3. List all body positions and postures and identify two alternative descriptors for each.

BODY POSITIONS AND POSTURES   *ALTERNATIVE 1*   *ALTERNATIVE 2*

a.

b.

c.

d.

e.

f.

g.

4. Identify as many words describing vocalization as you can think of, grouping them by similar characteristics (e.g., *scream, yell,* and *holler* are part of the same category of loud vocalizations).

Chapter Seven

Time Sampling

The observational strategies we have studied so far all involve narrative records. The great advantage of these methods is that the resulting data describe behavior in context and in enough detail to provide a permanent record of actions and happenings. The records also maintain the original sequence of events. Their major disadvantage is the time needed to record the information in the first place and the time needed to reduce and analyze the data once it has been gathered.

One way to minimize both recording time and coding time (data reduction) is to select observational strategies that use predetermined categories which allow the observer to count or to time behavior or events. Time sampling and event sampling are both methods that "sample" behavior rather than attempt to describe it in detail. They do not provide the richness of information that narrative records do, nor do they provide a permanent record of actions and events. They do, however, allow the observer to sample a larger number of subjects in a greater variety of situations within a reasonable time frame. This is important if researchers or educators want to generalize their findings to a larger population. You will remember, for example, that this inability to generalize findings from the one subject to many is a weakness of the diary description method.

Time sampling developed as a major new observational strategy shortly after the first laboratory nursery schools were established (thanks to the Laura Spelman Rockefeller funds and Larry Frank's efforts) in the mid 1920s. The laboratory nursery schools provided groups of young children, and the institutions that administered the schools provided an increasing number of researchers interested in child study. The combination hastened the growth of information about children. Time sampling and event sampling became popular new tools for dealing with these larger populations of children.

The Development of Time Sampling

Unlike the narrative observational methods, which were borrowed from the natural sciences, time sampling was developed within the framework of child study and "appears to be indigenous to research in child development" (Wright, 1960, p. 93).

The first time sampling study focused on the nervous habits of normal children. Willard C. Olson of the newly established Institute of Child Development at the University of Minnesota devised the technique in 1926-27. In her 1934 textbook, *Developmental Psychology*, Florence L. Goodenough, a colleague of Olson's, stated that "in the time-sampling procedure, children or adults are observed for definite short periods of time and their behavior during each period is looked upon as a 'sample' of their usual behavior" (p. 450).

Using observation to sample, rather than to describe behavior, made it necessary to place some restrictions on what would be observed. First of all, if behavior would be observed only for short periods of time, it was important that the behavior occur frequently enough that the observer could be reasonably sure of being able to see it. Ruth Arrington (1943) stated that if the behavior to be observed occurs less than once in fifteen minutes on the average, time sampling should not be used. For example, Lois Murphy's (1937) work on social behavior and child personality indicated that sympathy was a behavior that occurred too infrequently to be measured by time-sampling techniques. In 1954, Phil Schoggen analyzed the specimen day records of sixteen children ranging in age from two to ten. He identified success, failure, and frustration as behaviors that also occurred infrequently.

One could easily generate a list of other behaviors that occur with great irregularity: patriotism, hysteria, grief, and tree climbing, to name a few. It would also be easy to generate a list of frequently or regularly occurring behaviors: talking, smiling, playing, and eating, for example. If, however, observers are not sure that a behavior occurs regularly or frequently enough for time sampling, they may need to do some preliminary work to test it out.

Another limitation of time sampling is that it is best suited to overt behaviors. Behaviors that occur within the subject's mind—thinking, day-dreaming, scheming—cannot be studied by time-sampling techniques.

When Olson developed the time-sampling method, he looked at it as a way to measure behavior; in fact, he called his method "a natural history approach to the problem of measurement" (Olson and Cunningham, 1934, p. 43). Time sampling is closely tied to measurement because it allows the observer to tally behaviors, noting how frequently they occur, or to measure the length or duration of behavior.

In some time-sampling studies, the observer notes each time a behavior occurs within a time frame. For example, Glen Heathers (1955) used three-minute intervals to study dependency in preschool children and recorded every dependent, independent, or solitary play bid as it occurred within the three-minute interval. Thus, if a child sought affection from the teacher four times within the three-minute interval, the child would receive four checks for that category. This yielded a measure of how frequently the behavior occurred. Willard Olson (1929), on the other hand, gave each child only one check per behavior for each five-minute interval in his study of the nervous habits of school children. Thus, if one child bit his nails seven times during a five-minute period and another bit his only once, both received one checkmark. In some studies, presence or absence of a behavior is all that is needed. In others, the observer wants to know how frequently or how long the behavior is exhibited.

If Olson had been interested in how long a child persisted with a nervous habit (duration), he would have measured the length of time the child exhibited the behavior within each time frame. If he had done this he would have been able to state whether the children he studied spent more time biting their nails or twisting their hair. The purpose of the study determines whether or not frequency or duration are important factors.

Within the first decade of its use, time-sampling studies had focused on thirty-eight behavior areas ranging from *aggressiveness* to *whispering* (Olson and Cunningham, 1934, p. 45). Each of these studies focused on a specific behavior or constellation of behaviors (as opposed to running records and specimen descriptions which describe all of the behavior that occurs).

One of the most famous early studies using the time-sampling technique was Mildred B. Parten's study of children's play (1932-33). From October 1926 to June

1927 Parten observed children who ranged in age from under two years of age to five years of age. She was interested in children's social participation and developed six categories of participation to guide her observations: unoccupied behavior, onlooker, solitary independent play, parallel activity, associative play, and cooperative or organized supplementary play. These terms have become a familiar part of child development vocabulary. Parten was aware of the factors that could influence social participation and chose to observe children only during their free-play period (9:30-10:30 A.M.) when they were free to act and interact without adult interference or guidance. Parten found that there was a developmental sequence to children's social behavior. Younger children were more apt to engage first in solitary and then in parallel play activity while older preschoolers spent more time in associative or cooperative play.

Parten's study is a good example of the need to define clearly the terms that you use to describe the behaviors or events that you are studying. You want to be sure that others reading your work or assisting you in your observations will have no trouble understanding how you used a defined term. This kind of definition of meaning and use is called an *operational definition* because it assists others in being able to "operate" from the same basis of understanding. Kerlinger (1973) defines an operational definition as a "sort of manual of instructions to the investigator."

An *operational definition* assigns meaning to a construct or a variable by specifying the activities or "operations" necessary to measure it. Alternatively, an operational definition is a specification of the activities of the researcher in measuring a variable or manipulating it (Kerlinger, 1973, p. 31).

Operationally defining terms is doubly important if several different observers are working on the same project. If solitary play were labeled but not defined, different people might give it different meanings or interpretations. Parten defines solitary play as follows: "The child plays alone and independently with toys that are different from those used by the children within speaking distance and makes no effort to get close to other children. He pursues his own activity without reference to what others are doing" (1932, p. 250).

During the second decade of time-sampling use, researchers focused on refining the method with particular attention to the guidelines governing the length, spacing, and number of time intervals. The fruits of that effort are best summarized in Ruth E. Arrington's classic monographs published in 1939 and 1943. She reviewed all of the time-sampling studies conducted to that date.

The most recent developments in time-sampling techniques have focused on technological advances that allow observers to record observations directly onto magnetic tape that can be run through a computer for data organization, reduction, and analysis.

In fifty years, time sampling, "indigenous to research in child development," has become a major tool for both naturalistic and experimentally based studies. Just as anecdotal records are the most frequently used observational strategy for classroom teachers, so time sampling and its close cousin, event sampling, are among the most frequently used observational strategies for child development researchers.

Guidelines for Time Sampling

1. *Time sampling is appropriate only for behaviors that occur fairly frequently*—once every fifteen minutes on the average. If there is any doubt, the observer should spend time in preliminary observations to determine whether the behaviors or events occur often enough and also to identify any special personal or situational factors that might influence the occurrence of the behavior. It would be unwise, for example, to pin one's analysis of an individual child's social partners on one day's observation. Perhaps the child's favorite playmate is out ill that day. Perhaps the child is feeling out of sorts and is not relating as he or she would another day. It would be better to observe a child over a period of time to make sure that results are not distorted by temporary peculiarities. On the other hand, in observing a group of children for socialization patterns by sex, it is likely that observations made periodically throughout one school morning might give fairly representative information.

2. *Time sampling should be used only for behaviors that are easily observable.* Time sampling is not appropriate for covert (hidden) behaviors, whether those covert behaviors are mental behaviors or private behaviors.

3. *It is important that observers state their operational definitions so that all terms are clearly understood by others.* In observations for classroom use, this means clearly defining the behavior or event to be observed. In research studies it has the additional meaning of defining what the researcher must do to measure the behavior or event being observed.

4. *It is important to state the purpose of the observation so that you can determine exactly how a time-sampling study should be structured.* The purpose will help determine the following:

   a. *the number of subjects needed in the observations.* Studies that focus on behaviors largely governed by maturation—natural development—may require fewer subjects than behaviors that have a wide range of individual differences and levels of response. Most children go through the same stages of language development as they move from babbling to speaking. Aggressive behavior, on the other hand, has many variations and more subjects would be needed for a meaningful study.

   b. *whether the observations will focus on individual or group results.* If you are interested in changing the behavior of a specific child in your classroom, you may want to use time sampling to gather baseline data (how often or for how long the behavior occurs) before you try to change it so that you can measure the effects of your intervention. In this case, you would study a single child. If, on the other hand, you were interested in fathers' responses to newborn infants, you would need to study a larger number of subjects before you could predict how fathers respond—with any degree of accuracy.

   c. *how often you need to observe to provide a representative sample.* Mildred Parten observed an hour a day for nine months to gather her data on the nature of children's play. Teachers interested in using behavior modification techniques to alter undesirable behaviors often observe for several days to a week to establish "base line" data (normal level or frequency of occurrence).

The guidelines listed above all help in defining the purpose of the observation, providing operational definitions for behaviors to be studied, and deciding if time sampling is an appropriate observational strategy to use for the need or problem identified. Once you decide that time sampling is the best method to use, another whole set of guidelines becomes important. The definition of time sampling that we gave at the beginning of the chapter (Goodenough, 1934) focused on two important features of time sampling:

1. Children are observed for definite short periods of time.
2. The behavior observed is regarded as a "sample" of usual behavior.

Hutt and Hutt's (1970) definition reflects a third component of time sampling: "Those methods which sample preselected categories of behavior at regular (and usually brief) time intervals for a specified observational period are collectively called time-sampling procedures; in such procedures all behavior categories occurring in any one time interval are recorded and measures of frequency and duration are approximate and relative" (p. 67).

This definition focuses more on the method of recording and states that the observer selects categories of behavior to observe before the observation begins. Once the categories of behavior are selected, the observer does not simply go out and write narrative descriptions of these behaviors, but records them on a specially prepared record sheet. This record sheet allows the observer to check the occurrence of the preselected behaviors, to tally the frequency of behaviors, or to measure their duration—in essence, to code the data rather than describe it. This coding is done within specified, uniform time limits; thus the behavior is sampled with a specified time frame (hence the term *time sampling*). The following guidelines relate to developing the record sheet for coding time-sampling observations.

1. *Determine what kind of information you need to record.* According to Medley and Mitzel (1963) most behaviors are recorded by either checkmarks, which tell whether or not a particular behavior occurred, or by tally marks, which tell how often the behavior occurred during the observation period. If the observer only needs to know if the behavior was present or absent, he or she will use checkmarks (Olson's study of nervous mannerisms in school children, for example). If frequency of occurrence is important, tally marks will have to be used (Heathers's study of dependency in preschool children, for example).

   Sometimes it is also important to note the duration of the behavior(s) within each time interval. If, for example, in a study of infant crying you select one minute as a time interval, you may want to know whether or not the infant cries (presence or absence of behavior) and, if he or she does cry, how long the crying persists (duration of behavior). Three short whimpers of four seconds each across three one-minute intervals is not the same as three full minutes of crying. Both would receive three checkmarks (one for each minute of observation) to indicate presence of crying behavior. Thus, if you just record presence or absence of the behavior, the short whimpers and the continuous cry would look the same on the record sheet. If you add duration, however, the two would appear quite different.

2. *Once you have determined what kind of information to record (presence/absence,*

frequency and/or duration) you will need to decide what kind of time interval to use. The optimum time interval will be governed by the purpose for your observation. According to Herbert Wright (1960), time sampling "fixes attention of observer and analyst upon selected aspects of the behavior stream as they occur within uniform and short time intervals. The length, spacing, and number of intervals are intended to secure representative *time samples* of the target phenomena" (pp. 92-93). The decisions of what length, what spacing, and what number of time intervals to use will depend upon the needs and purpose of the observer and will have to be carefully worked out in a preliminary phase.

a. When Arrington reviewed the first dozen years of time-sampling studies, she concluded that the length of the time interval should be regulated by the frequency of the behavior and that the time interval should approximate the minimum length of a single instance of behavior (1939, p. 152). Wright (1960) says that periods of five minutes or less are most common. Many time-sampling studies use intervals of less than a minute. Hutt and Hutt (1970) offer a caution for observers who use intervals measured in seconds rather than minutes. They feel that ten seconds to one minute is needed by an observer using a checklist *with more than three categories to watch* (p. 68). The time factor selected is a product of behavior duration and ease or complexity of the recordkeeping needed, plus observer fatigue.

b. The spacing of time intervals will depend upon several factors—the length of time interval selected, the number of individuals that you need to observe within that time interval, and the amount of detail that you need to record.

Ann Frodi and Michael Lamb (1978) used time sampling to study sex differences in adults' responsiveness to infants. The time interval they used was six seconds, the number of individuals they observed per interval was two adults, and the amount of detail required was a checkmark in one of three categories of behavioral responsiveness (what the adult actually did in the presence of the baby). Because the recording procedure was a very simple one, the time intervals could be consecutively spaced without a break for six full minutes of observation for a total of sixty time intervals.

Beverly Fagot (1978) used time sampling to study what effect the amount of teaching experience has on how teachers reinforce sex role behaviors. The time interval used was five seconds and the observer watched one child at a time—so far not very different from the Frodi and Lamb study. Simple checkmarks were used, but instead of three categories of behavior to keep in mind, Fagot's observers had to keep track of thirty child behaviors, five reactor categories, and fourteen consequences—forty-nine items in all. It would have been extremely difficult to score consecutive time intervals with this kind of detail. Fagot had her observers watch for five seconds, score the child behaviors first, then the reactor behaviors, and finally the consequences. The only restriction was that each of the twelve children in the play group be observed for one five-second interval every five minutes—in other words, a total of one minute of observing to four minutes of scoring for each five-minute period.

c. The number of time intervals needed for each subject will depend on how long you need to observe to obtain a representative sample of the behavior you are studying. Frodi and Lamb (1978) observed each adult for a total of six minutes. Parten (1932) observed most of her children for sixty to a hundred minutes. Fagot (1978) observed each child for a minimum of twenty hours. In general, more total observation time is required for behavior that varies a great deal or for behaviors that we know little about (and, therefore, are unable to predict).

If a classroom teacher is interested in gathering some specific information about a child with behavior problems, she may decide to observe the child for the first five minutes of every hour and focus on the child's on-task and off-task behavior.

She could do the observation in several different ways. First, she could observe the first five minutes of every hour. This would provide information across the day but would not take into account the fact that the child would be engaged in different activities and would probably even be at different points in completing those activities.

A second way to observe would be to select the first five minutes of each activity. This would allow her to compare on-off-task behavior across activities (as long as the definitions were appropriate for all of the activities involved).

A third strategy would be to select one or more activities and observe for ten to fifteen minutes to gather representative on-task and off-task behavior data.

Regardless of the strategy she will need to keep the format fairly simple so that she can easily turn from her active teaching duties to her observation task. One way for her to proceed would be to use a checkmark for every ten-second interval to indicate whether the child was on- or off-task. She would have thirty checkmarks at the end of five minutes and could easily calculate the percentage of on-task or off-task behaviors. This kind of classroom use of time sampling would provide concrete data to use in planning and she would have gained it with a minimum of effort and disruption.

After determining the kind of information important to record and the length, number, and space of time intervals, the next step is to plan the layout of the observation sheet itself. The first guideline to use in laying out the record sheet is to keep it simple. It should be as visually uncluttered as possible so that the observer can easily record whatever information (checkmarks, tallies, time duration) is required.

1. *Many time-sampling observations will require the observer to use some sort of coding system in recording the data.* This allows the observer to break a larger behavior unit into component behaviors. Hyperactivity is a large behavior unit. Teachers interested in what kinds of hyperactive behaviors are exhibited by children in their classrooms will want to look at discrete components of hyperactivity like inability to refrain from calling out, inability to inhibit touching others, inability to stay in his or her seat, and so on.

Medley and Mitzel (1963) discuss two methods of breaking a larger behavior unit into component behaviors. The first method is called a *sign system* and requires that the categories of behavior developed be mutually exclusive, meaning that a subject cannot be involved in two of these activities at the same time. If you wanted to study children's laughter, for example, you might develop a sign system with the following components:

quick, vanishing smile
slow, expansive smile
silly giggle
warm chuckle
brief, quiet laughter
genuine, hearty laughter
excited laughter with shouts of glee

Each of the categories is separate and discrete. A child cannot engage in two categories at the same time; they are mutually exclusive. If the researcher has confused the issue by including a competing category, the record would be inaccurate and incomplete. For example, if, in addition to the categories listed above, one were to add "throws head back," the observer would need to decide which of the two actions to record when two actions occurred together. It is likely that a child might throw his or her head back while smiling, giggling, or laughing.

The second method outlined by Medley and Mitzel is called the *category system*. Category systems also require mutually exclusive categories of behavior but, in addition, the categories must be *"exhaustive"*: They must include the total range of behavior so that anything the child does can be tallied. Parten's system was a *category system* because all observed behavior could fit into one of the six categories. If she had omitted "unoccupied behavior" she would have had a *sign system* instead. The remaining five would be mutually exclusive, but not exhaustive, as there would be no way to code children who were not engaged in any one of the five play arrangements.

The purpose of your observation will dictate whether you need to use a sign or category system. If you want to account for all behavior, you will want a category system. If you are interested only in what occurs within the target behavior, a sign system will suffice.

2. *The record sheet will seldom have room for the operational definitions and full-word descriptions of the category or sign system used. This means that you will need to develop some sort of code to identify the different behaviors.* Researchers Lisa A. Serbin, Illene J. Tonick, and Sarah H. Sternglanz (1977) were interested in how to encourage cross-sex cooperative play among preschoolers. Four male and four female undergraduate students were trained to use a specially developed observational code to record preschoolers' play during ten-second time samples at free-play time. The code itself is a modification of Parten's categories:

S = solitary behavior
PS = parallel play, same sex
PO = parallel play, opposite sex
CS = cooperative play, same sex
CO = cooperative play, opposite sex

The Serbin et al. code illustrates another point; it is easier to remember the code if it is an abbreviation of the words it stands for. PO in the above code gives you a memory aid. If the same behaviors were simply labeled 1, 2, 3, 4,

5, or a, b, c, d, e, the number 3 or letter c would offer little help if you forgot what the code stood for.

It is essential, of course, that the observer be thoroughly familiar with the coding system and understand the operational definitions before actually doing the work. Boehm and Weinberg (1977) state that the coding system must always be memorized before sampling begins. The easier and more logical the system is, the quicker and more reliable the results will be. If, in addition, the code offers a memory jog, it is less likely that errors will occur due to observer confusion. It is a good idea to keep a "definition sheet" handy in case your memory does fail you and the abbreviations don't jog your memory immediately. The definition sheet simply outlines the operational definitions and the code being used.

3. *It is helpful to provide space for noting what seem to be irrelevant but important interferences or distractions that occur during the observation unit.* These could provide valuable clues for later analysis. Arrington (1939) indicates that Goodenough points out that "a change in the situation . . . not only brings about a change in the pattern of behavior most typical of the entire group but also changes the rank-order of the individuals composing the group" (p. 32). Having space to note such changes makes it possible to identify these shifts in behavior and provides clues that otherwise would be absent. It might be that a child doesn't feel well, that an exciting event has just occurred in the classroom (like the birth of baby rabbits), or that a focal person (like the teacher) is absent that day. Such events will affect what occurs during a given observation. It is important to have space to note those comments for later reference.

What To Do with the Data

The problem of data reduction is not nearly as difficult with time sampling as with narrative methods of observation because it is already "reduced" when it is recorded. The observer does not need to read paragraphs and decide how to code them; the coding system is predetermined and behavioral categories established before the observer begins to collect data.

The observer can use a wide variety of tabulation techniques. Selecting which one to use will depend upon the needs, purposes, and resources of the observer. Willard Olson (1929) merely counted checkmarks to get a measure of each individual's range of nervous habits. Total frequencies or total time is often the only information a classroom teacher needs from a time-sampling observation. But, as Jersild and Meigs (1939) pointed out, "gross frequencies alone may fail to tell the whole story" (p. 5).

If additional information is desired, you may want to compute percentages or calculate the average (mean, $\bar{x}$) amount of time spent on an activity or the average number of children that engaged in the behavior or activity under study. Simple charts or bar graphs allow you to display your data visually. Charts are somewhat easier to prepare than bar graphs and have the added advantage of allowing you to put several different phases of your observation on the same graph.

Suppose, for example, that the teacher who gathered baseline data on her student's off-task and on-task behavior found that the child spent 69 percent of the time observed off-task on day 1, 75 percent on day 2, 84 percent on day 3, 72 percent on day 4, and 86 percent on day 5. Your baseline graph would look like this:

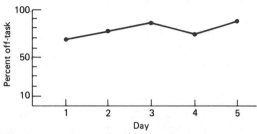

If the teacher decides to use a little behavior modification in an attempt to reduce the amount of off-task behavior during the second week, she might find the following results: 65 percent on day 1, 60 percent on day 2, 47 percent on day 3, 56 percent on day 4, and 52 percent on day 5. She could plot those findings on the same chart using a broken line to indicate that it was a different time frame:

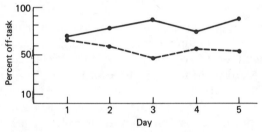

If the teacher wanted to follow the child's progress in succeeding weeks, it would be best to use additional charts to avoid intersecting lines that would be difficult to read. A summary chart plotting the first and last week of the intervention would provide a quick visual scan of how effective the behavior modification had been.

Researchers usually need to be concerned about how significant their findings are—whether or not (statistically speaking) their findings could have occurred by chance. Kerlinger (1973) offers excellent advice for the most appropriate statistics to use in data analysis. Such a discussion is beyond the scope of this book, but we would like to cite one brief example of how recent technological advances can assist data reduction and statistical analysis.

In a recent study by Robert L. Burgess and Rand D. Conger (1978) family interaction was observed in abusive, neglectful, and normal families. Each family was observed during four 15 to 20 minute tasks in which all family members participated. Time intervals of 1½ to 2 minutes were used, and each family member was the focus of observation for 2 time intervals for each task. Burgess and Conger describe the time-sampling recording procedure used as follows:

The observational code used was recorded through the Behavioral Observation Scoring System (BOSS). BOSS consists of a 10-digit keyboard, a stopwatch, and an especially modified cassette tape recorder. When a particular behavior occurs, the observer depresses a key and an electrical impulse is transmitted onto a magnetic tape inside the attached recorder. Special computer programs decipher the impulse from the magnetic tape . . . Once a family has been observed, the cassette tapes are played through a special electronic interface which notes the events as they occurred as well as the passage of time between the data entries (pp. 1165-1166).

The 10-digit keyboard allows the observer to record more data more efficiently than he or she could with a recording sheet and pencil. The computer hook-up also stores, sorts, and analyzes the data, saving hours of work and guaranteeing greater accuracy.

Data treatment can be as simple as totaling the tally or checkmarks on the recording sheet, or as sophisticated as computer technology will allow. The purpose of the observation and the time and resources available to the observer will determine how to process the data once it is collected.

Advantages and Disadvantages of Time Sampling

Time sampling introduces a new approach to observation. The observer must do a great deal of planning *before* observing. He or she must develop operational definitions, decide on what kind of time intervals to use, and select categories and a recording format for the record sheet. The time spent in planning before observing has its rewards, however, for the observation task itself is made easier as a result, and data reduction and analysis are done more efficiently.

This shorthand version of observation has a number of decided advantages as well as some disadvantages. The advantages are:

1. It allows for greater control of what is to be observed by focusing on specific behaviors or problems to be observed and studied.
2. It is useful for determining the frequency of occurrences of behaviors or events. This serves two purposes: (a) it is useful for collecting information in situations where frequency is important to monitor—behavior modification and precision teaching, for example; and (b) the information gained from frequency counts can be used to develop other measures like checklists and rating scales.
3. It allows the teacher or researcher to collect a larger number of observations in a shorter period of time. This is particularly useful when the observer wants to collect information about groups of children, and it also makes it easier to gather a more representative sample of behavior within a specified time frame—a task that is very difficult to do with narrative methods without an army of observers.
4. It is an efficient means of observation that takes less time and effort than narrative methods. The record sheet guides the observer and codes the data at the same time. The behavioral descriptors also encourage accuracy and objectivity.

5. It permits recording and scoring without interfering with the subject's normal activities and does not require establishing rapport with the subjects in advance.
6. It provides quantitative results capable of statistical analysis for both individual and group data.

Disadvantages usually include some of the following:

1. It is limited to problems or behaviors that occur with high frequency (at least once every 15 minutes).
2. Unless it is specifically coded into the recording system, the data from time sampling studies tell us little of the *how* or the *quality* of actions.
3. It is difficult to identify the interrelations among a number of behaviors since the observation focuses only on specified behaviors (usually one larger behavior broken into component behaviors).
4. The method does not maintain behavior units intact. The time interval rather than the behavior episode dictates the framework. This can cause some distortion, because the time frame promotes dealing with fragments of behavior rather than with whole behavioral episodes.
5. Unless specifically built into the coding system, there is no information about the environment or the situation.
6. Using predetermined categories in a checklist observation format can bias what you see (you look for things to fit the categories rather than describe what is occurring), and can cause you to overlook behaviors that might be important in helping understand the behavior or pattern under study.
7. The data seldom reveal cause-and-effect relationships because of the limitations of the stated focus and the fact that the behavior sequence is not preserved. A notable exception to this is in cases of behavior modification where time sampling is used to gather initial base-line data and to monitor progress throughout the intervention. The time-sampling data is then used to demonstrate the effect of the behavior modification, i.e., that the intervention is the cause of the change in behavior.

Perhaps Kerlinger, (1973) summarized it best when he wrote, "Time samples suffer from lack of continuity, lack of adequate context, and perhaps naturalness. This is particularly true when small units of time and behavior are used" (p. 546). Yet, as Brandt points out, ". . . they seem absolutely necessary if one is to be able to generalize about a larger universe of behavior and provide observational norms" (1972, p. 140).

Summary

The time-sampling technique provided a new research tool in the 1920s for use in the study of behavior that occurs often enough (once every 15 minutes on the average) and is reliably regular over time and, therefore, a valid sample of the behavior. It gave the observer access to a great deal more information a great deal faster than had been possible with the cumbersome narrative records that preceded it.

The newly established laboratory nursery schools provided large numbers of young children and the institutions that administered them provided an increasing number of researchers interested in child study.

Early studies using the time-sampling technique include Willard Olson's (1929) study of nervous mannerisms in school children and Mildred Parten's (1932-1933) study of social participation among school children.

Guidelines are given for defining the purpose of the observation, providing operational definitions for behaviors to be studied, and deciding if time sampling is appropriate for a particular study.

Once time sampling is selected, other considerations are important: selecting behavioral categories; preparing a recording form; coding the data in terms of the presence or absence of behavior, its frequency and its duration; and determining length, spacing, and number of time intervals needed to get representative results.

Two methods of breaking a larger behavior unit into component behavior units are discussed: *category system* and *sign system*. Both provide mutually exclusive categories (a subject cannot be involved in two of the behaviors at the same time). In addition, category systems are also exhaustive (the total range of behavioral possibilities is included).

In tabulating data, the observer's task is made a bit easier because data is already coded as part of the recording task. A wide variety of tabulation techniques can be used ranging from a simple counting of checkmarks or tallies to a sophisticated computer analysis.

A number of advantages and disadvantages need to be considered in selecting or rejecting time sampling as a viable technique for a particular study. Among the advantages are the fact that time sampling delimits the time involved, focuses the observation on particular behaviors, and provides quantitative results. Key disadvantages are that it can be used only with behaviors that occur with high frequency, and that it isolates the behavior being observed from its context.

Suggestions for Further Reading

Arrington, Ruth E. Time-sampling studies of child behavior. *Psychological Monographs*, 1939, 51 (2), entire issue. Part One of the monograph is concerned with the background, development, assumptions and status of the time-sampling method in the child behavior field. A good historical analysis of the development of the technique with a summary of a number of early studies. Part Two presents the results of a five-year program of time-sampling studies of young children done by Parten and her associates at the Columbia Child Development Institute (involving nursery school children, 1930-31) and in the New Haven Public Schools (involving kindergarten, first and third grade children from 1931-1935). These studies focused on the overt responses of children to the social and material stimuli of their environment.

Arrington, Ruth E. Time sampling in studies of social behavior: A critical review of techniques and results with research suggestions. *Psychological Bulletin*, 1943, 40 (2), 81-124. Aims to show by a critical review of time sampling and related studies available at the time (1943) the extent to which scientific observation of social interaction "has contributed and can contribute further to understanding of the process of social development and the patterning of social behavior in the individual" (p. 81). A good review of pioneering time-sampling studies.

Medley, D. M., and H. E. Mitzel. Measuring classroom behavior by systematic observation. In N. L. Gage ed., *Handbook of Research in Teaching*. Skokie, Ill.: Rand-McNally, 1963. In the process of analyzing good and bad observational studies concerned with the behavior of teachers and pupils in classrooms, the authors do an impressive critical analysis of observational systems of research. They point out that when a study is weak, the technician—not the technique of observation—is often at fault. As a way of encouraging better present studies, they indicate how past studies might have been strengthened.

Determining Appropriateness of Time Sampling

This assignment is designed to help you focus on the first steps in planning a time-sampling observation—defining terms and determining whether or not the selected behaviors occur frequently enough to be measured by time-sampling techniques.

Part I: Operational Definitions

Procedure: We have selected six behaviors for you to consider: fear, sharing, crying, laughter, tattling, and boasting. Your first task is to operationally define each of these behaviors. Remember, the purpose of writing an operational definition is to clearly define your terms so that others can "operate" from the same basis of understanding.

Operational Definitions

1. Fear

2. Sharing

3. Crying

4. Laughter

5. Tattling

6. Boasting

Part II: Determining Frequency of Occurrence

Arrington (1943) says that if the behavior to be observed occurs less than once in 15 minutes, on the average, then time sampling is not an appropriate technique. Select six children from a larger group and spend 30 minutes watching for incidents reflecting the six behaviors identified in Part I. Spend five minutes observing each child; use the five-minute interval time-sampling format below to record the frequency of occurrence of each of the behaviors. Use one tally mark for each time the behavior occurs within a given time interval (e.g., if the child you are watching laughs four times within the five minutes, mark four tally marks //// in the time interval).

TIME	CHILD'S NAME	AGE	FEAR	SHARING	CRYING	LAUGHTER	TATTLING	BOASTING
1st 5 min.								
2nd 5 min.								
3rd 5 min.								
4th 5 min.								
5th 5 min.								
6th 5 min.								
Average per 15 minutes (divide by two)								

1. After doing the study, reexamine your operational definitions. Identify any changes you feel would make the tally task easier and more precise.

2. What is your conclusion about the appropriateness of the time-sampling method for each of these behaviors? (Arrington suggests once per 15 minutes is a minimum.) Support your comments by reference to your data.

Comparison of Recording Formats

One of the most important considerations to keep in mind when developing a recording sheet for time-sampling observations is what the purpose of your observation is. Different recording formats yield different kinds of information. You will want to be sure that you select the right format for your observation needs. This assignment is designed to help you become familiar with several different recording formats so that you can more meaningfully compare the advantages and disadvantages of each.

Part I: Presence/Absence of Behavior

On-task behavior is a relatively easy behavior to observe, especially in more structured (rather than open-education) classrooms where tasks are clearly defined. All of the observations associated with this assignment will involve on- and off-task behavior. On-task behavior is defined as attention to teacher or materials associated with assigned activities. Off-task behavior is defined as inattention, disruptive actions, or activities that are irrelevant to the task at hand.

Setting/Location_____ Date_____ Time _____

Age/Grade of Children _____

Procedure: Observe five children from the classroom. Use some random procedure to select the children (every fourth child, for example). Observe each child for one minute and simply check whether ot not the child is on- or off-task during that one-minute interval. (Note: Some children may be on-task at the beginning but off-task before the minute is over; if so, that child would receive a checkmark in each column.)

CHILD'S NAME	ON-TASK	OFF-TASK
1.		
2.		
3.		
4.		
5.		
TOTALS		

Part II: Nature and Frequency of Behavior

Observe the same children for another five one-minute time intervals. This time use a checklist to define more precisely the character of the on-task and off-task behavior.

STUDENT'S NAME	On-Task, Engrossed	On-Task, at Work but Not Engrossed	Off-Task, Quietly Disinterested	Off-Task, Disruptive
1.				
2.				
3.				
4.				
5.				
TOTALS				

Now observe the first two children on your list for three minutes each. This time, instead of simply using a checkmark to indicate presence or absence of a behavior, use tally marks to indicate frequency of each behavior.

STUDENT'S NAME	On-Task, Engrossed	On-Task, at Work but Not Engrossed	Off-Task, Quietly Disinterested	Off-Task, Disruptive
1.				
2.				
TOTALS				

Part III: Duration of Behavior   ***Observer*** _____

This time your task is to measure the duration of each of the behaviors. Observe the last three children on your list for three minutes each and record the number of seconds that each one engages in each behavior. (You will need a stop-watch or a watch or clock with a second hand or digital second recorder.)

STUDENT'S NAME	On-Task, Engrossed	On-Task, at Work but Not Engrossed	Off-Task, Quietly Disinterested	Off-Task, Disruptive
3.				
4.				
5.				
TOTALS				

1. When you have completed the observations, comment on ease of reporting, accuracy of reporting, and differences in information among the Part I, Part II, and Part III records.

   a. ease of reporting

   b. accuracy of reporting

   c. differences in information

167

2. The purpose of the observation, as has been stated, helps the observer determine which kind of recording format to use. Some questions need just a presence−absence checklist; others require that you measure frequency or duration of behavior. Think of a question you might investigate and phrase it in various ways that would be appropriate to each recording format we have discussed. Tell why that format would be best for your question:

a. presence or absence of behavior

b. checklist for presence or absence of specific characteristics of behavior

c. checklist for frequency of behavior

d. checklist for duration of behavior

Developing Sign and Category Systems

In the last assignment we introduced a short checklist that focused on two different components of on-task and off-task behavior. Often the observer needs to look at a larger range of component behaviors. For example, Mildred Parten could have looked at children playing by themselves or with others. That would have given her some limited but useful information about social participation, but not nearly as much as she learned by outlining six categories of social participation covering a broader range of play behaviors. We will use Parten's study to help illustrate how you can develop appropriate sign and category systems.

Part I: Using a Category System

The best place to start is to become familiar with Parten's categories. Parten's six categories are a category system rather than a sign system because they are both mutually exclusive and exhaustive.

Procedure: Select a group of children to observe who are engaged in free play activity—the free play portion of the indoor curriculum in nursery school or outdoor activity in nursery school or recess in elementary school. Parten observed each child for one minute, moving from child to child in a predetermined random basis. Your task in this part of the assignment is to observe 15 children, each for one minute, and check which category of social participation each child is engaged in. Parten uses the following operational definitions in her study of "Social Participation among Preschool Children," in the *Journal of Abnormal and Social Psychology,* 1932-33, 27, pp. 243-269.

Unoccupied behavior: The child apparently is not playing, but occupies himself with watching anything that happens to be of momentary interest. When there is nothing exciting taking place, he plays with his own body, gets on and off chairs, just stands around, follows the teacher, or sits in one spot glancing around the room.

Onlooker: The child spends most of his time watching the other children play. He often talks to the children whom he is observing, asks questions, or gives suggestions, but does not overtly enter into the play himself. This type differs from the unoccupied in that the onlooker is definitely observing particular groups of children rather than anything that happens to be exciting. The child stands or sits within speaking distance of the group so that he can see and hear everything that takes place.

Solitary independent play: The child plays alone and independently with toys that are different from those used by the children within speaking distance and makes no effort to get close to other children. He pursues his own activity without reference to what others are doing.

Parallel activity: The child plays independently, but the activity he chooses naturally brings him among other children. He plays with toys that are like those which the children around him are using but he plays with the toy as he sees fit, and does not try to influence or modify the activity of the children near him. He plays *beside* rather than *with* the other children. There is no attempt to control the coming or going of children in the group.

Associative play: The child plays with other children. The conversation concerns the common activity; there is a borrowing and loaning of play material; following one another with trains or wagons; mild attempts to control which children may or may not play in the group. All the members engage in similar if not identical activity; there is no division of labor, and no organization of the activity of several individuals around any material goal or product. The children do not subordinate their individual interests to that of the group; instead each child acts as he wishes. By his conversation with the other children one can tell that his interest is primarily in his associations, not in his activity. Occasionally, two or three children are engaged in no activity of any duration, but are merely doing whatever happens to draw the attention of any of them.

Cooperative or organized supplementary play: The child plays in a group that is organized for the purpose of making some material product, or of striving to attain some competitive goal, or of dramatizing situations of adult and group life, or of playing formal games. There is a marked sense of belonging or of not belonging to the group. The control of the group situation is in the hands of one or two of the members who direct the activity of the others. The goal as well as the method of attaining it necessitates a division of labor, taking of different roles by the various group members and the organization of activity so that the efforts of one child are supplemented by those of another. (pp. 249-251).

Category of Social Participation

Child	Unoccupied	Onlooker	Solitary	Parallel	Associative	Cooperative
1.						
2.						
3.						
4.						
5.						
6.						
7.						
8.						
9.						
10.						
11.						
12.						
13.						
14.						
15.						
TOTALS:						

The other side of social participation is social isolation. Some children do not interact with others. Perhaps they are too shy, or prefer to play alone, or are rejected by other children. Your task is to develop a sign system that will provide information about social isolation in children. Remember, a sign system contains mutually exclusive categories, but not exhaustive categories.

Procedure: Medley and Mitzel (1963) suggest that the observer list the specific acts or incidents of behavior which may or may not occur during a period of observation before beginning the observation. In doing a trial run, the observer will discover which of them occur and also which occur often enough to warrant being part of the study. This helps in the building of categories or signs to be used in the study. You may want to spend some time observing children who are not actively interacting with others before you develop your sign system as a way of helping you define it.

1. Identify your operational definition of social isolation:

2. List and define each of the behaviors that are part of your sign system for observing social isolation:
   a.

   b.

   c.

   d.

   e.

3. The major difference between a sign system and a category system is that while both must contain mutually exclusive categories, the latter must also contain exhaustive categories; in other words, all behavior must somehow be accounted for. What would you have to add to your sign system to make it a category system?

Part III: Evaluating Sign and Category Systems
Now that you have constructed both a sign and a category system, it is time to try them out. Decide on the type of information you want to record (presence/absence, frequency, duration) and lay out the recording sheet for your sign system. Then observe 10 children, using the recording sheet you have developed. Rotate through the ten children, observing each child for one minute. Attach your recording sheet(s) and report your findings below.

Would you change any of your categories now that you have had a chance to try them out? Why or why not?

Do the same observation as outlined on preceding page, only this time use the category system you developed. Attach your recording sheet(s) and report your findings below:

1. Would you change any of your categories now that you have had a chance to try them out? Why or why not?

2. Which system did you find easier to use—the sign system or the category system? Why?

Chapter Eight

Event Sampling

In looking at the development of observational techniques over the decades, we can trace a logical and evolutionary process at work. Early observers recorded one child's activities in a diary and attempted to note every important event whenever it occurred. It was a labor intensive system, with a sample of one. A refinement of this procedure, the specimen description, made the task more manageable by limiting it to a finite time frame: a morning in Dresslar's case (1901) and a day for Barker and Wright (1951). Even with this limitation, the amount of raw material gathered was abundant and the sample was still small. In both diary and specimen descriptions, the observer had no discrete focus or question to investigate, but rather, had a general openness and curiosity about the *what* and *how* of human development.

Bühler (1930) compounded the observer's difficulties when she attempted her round-the-clock marathon of recording on 69 babies. That certainly provided data on more subjects, but the amount of data and lack of focus proved unwieldy.

In the 1920s, some researchers decided that you could dip into the "behavior stream"—Barker's (1955) term for on-going behavior—at regular intervals and capture the essence of an activity more economically. Time sampling was developed to allow the observer to attend and record at intervals and still have a representative stream of events.

This method proved to be very efficient in reducing observation time and had the added bonus of providing data that could be summarized easily and subjected to statistical analysis. It had a drawback, however. It could only be used to study behavior that occurred at least once every fifteen minutes. This created a problem for observers who wanted a shortcut to narrative observation methods and also wanted to study infrequently occurring behavior. The answer to the problem was event sampling.

The Role of Observational Sampling Techniques in Child Study

Observational methods designed to sample rather than describe behavior met an important need during the decade from 1925 to 1935. The narrative observation methods had been criticized by experimentalists for being too costly in observation time, too limited in sample size, and too biased. Observational sampling procedures met the experimentalists' demand for objectivity, control, and efficiency. The development of these techniques also allowed the researcher to use experimental designs in the laboratory as well as in the naturalistic setting.

Thus, Mary Cover Jones used event sampling in an experimental study of the emotions of preschool children in 1925. Jones chose to present children with fearful situations involving animals, insects, faces, etc.—strange objects and sudden presentations. Using information she was able to gather from these events, she went on to test different ways of extinguishing fear responses in children.

Both naturalistic observation and experimentation provide useful information for the interested researcher. As Hutt and Hutt (1970) say, "To oppose . . . experiment and naturalistic observation as science and nonscience is conceptually unhelpful; what is important are the data for which one or the other method is the more appropriate" (p. 197).

One of the early classic studies to use the event-sampling technique in the natural setting was Helen C. Dawe's analysis (1934) of 200 quarrels of preschool children. This investigation describes quarrels as they occurred spontaneously during the free-play hour of a nursery school from October 19, 1931 to February 17, 1932. The subjects were 19 girls and 21 boys from 25 to 60 months of age.

The observer simply waited for a quarrel to occur. When it did, the stop-watch was started, the observer attended to the quarrel, stopped the stop-watch when the quarrel was settled, and then filled in the record blank which included space for name of subject(s), age and sex of involved children, duration of quarrel, what was going on when the problem arose, types of behavior (non-participator, precipitator, aggressive behavior, retaliative behavior during quarrel, motor and vocal activity, outcome, and after effects). Whenever possible, actual conversation was remembered and recorded. Although time was a factor in this study, the duration of the quarrel was just one piece of data collected. The event— quarreling—was the focus of the observer's attention.

Dawe developed a great deal of information from her study, including the following:

1. For the 58.75 hours of observation, 200 quarrels were recorded, or 3.4 per hour.
2. 68 took place outdoors; 132 were indoors.
3. Only 13 lasted longer than a minute.
4. Boys quarreled more often than girls.
5. Disagreements about possessions were leading causes of quarrels.
6. The children settled most quarrels themselves, recovered quickly, and showed no evidence of resentment.

The total amount of observation time, 58.75 hours, is relatively small when one thinks about how many hours of observation would be needed to generate data on 200 quarrels from narrative methods of observation.

Andrew Sluckin and Peter Smith (1977) used a procedure very similar to Dawe's to study dominance in preschool children. They observed three- and four-year-olds during free play and recorded incidents of aggression. Like Dawe, they scanned the group and recorded each aggressive episode they saw, but unlike her, they did not have to write out all the details. They used instead a cassette tape recorder to record details of who initiated the incident, who was involved, what it concerned, and what the outcome was.

Sluckin and Smith also demonstrate the usefulness of combining event sampling with other methods of child study—in this case, a picture-sociometric technique. The researchers showed children pictures of all the children in the group and asked each child individually to point to the toughest child. The photograph that the child pointed to was then taken away and the question was asked again. This procedure was repeated until all of the children in the group had been rank ordered by each child.

When the results of the event-sampling observations of aggressive behavior were compared with the children's perceptions of dominance (toughness), it was found that there was a relationship between children who were perceived as "tough" by their peers and the initiation of aggression. The children who were identified as the toughest in the group were the most likely to initiate aggression.

Although classroom teachers will probably not carry out a formal research project, they are apt to use event sampling to gather information for case studies or to assist them in classroom planning and evaluation. A teacher who is interested in children's dominance, for example, might do a case study on the child identified as the class bully—the one who is toughest, bossiest, and most often an aggressor against another child. The teacher would develop a recording sheet (perhaps quite similar to the one used by Sluckin and Smith). Whenever the target event occurred, he or she would check the appropriate categories and provide relevant narrative information about the child's physical or verbal aggression against another child.

A teacher interested in using event sampling for classroom planning, on the other hand, might be interested in whether there are differences in the ways boys and girls build with blocks and, if there are, what effect different teacher-planned or teacher-directed activities might have on how the blocks are used. The teacher would decide what information he or she wanted to obtain, develop an appropriate recording sheet, and then watch for the target event to occur—block building.

Wright (1960) points out that biological scientists have "built up vast stores of knowledge about such events" as the nesting habits of geese or the process of building a beaver dam "by the straightforward tactic of describing each one as it occurs repeatedly in nature" (p. 104). Wright goes on to say that event sampling is the psychological application of techniques developed for research in the natural sciences.

Use of Event Sampling versus Time Sampling

Like time sampling, event sampling "samples" behavior. Unlike time sampling, the unit of measure is the behavior itself rather than the time interval imposed on the behavior being studied. In event sampling, the observer waits for the selected behavior to occur and then records it. There are no time constraints with event sampling. The focus is on the behavior itself and time is a product of the event's normal duration. The range of behaviors that can be studied with event sampling is limitless.

Because time sampling focuses on specified intervals of time rather than waiting for selected events to occur, it is used more often by researchers than event sampling. A researcher knows exactly how much time he or she will spend collecting data with time sampling, but can only guess at the time needed in an event-sampling study.

Classroom teachers and people in other service professions, on the other hand, often find event sampling a more congenial observation strategy than time sampling because it focuses on behavior rather than on time. The child-study observer needs to be familiar with both observation strategies.

Both time and event sampling offer observational short cuts; however, they yield different kinds of information. For example, teacher verbalization is a topic—like many others—that can be studied using either event or time sampling.

A time-sampling study of teacher verbalization might focus on the frequency and duration of teacher talk versus student talk. An event-sampling study might focus on whom the teacher talks to and what the antecedent and outcome behaviors are. Time sampling is more concerned with the existence of an event and event sampling is more concerned with exploring its characteristics.

Guidelines for Event Sampling

If you have mastered the narrative methods of observation and time sampling, you will find event sampling very easy.

1. *Clearly identify and then operationally define the behavior that you want to study.*
2. *Know enough about the behavior in general that you know where and when to observe.* You will not learn much about children's fantasy play by observing a science activity, but you are apt to learn a great deal by observing children during their free-play time. Brandt states that it is important to know enough about the behaviors you want to study so that you will "be able to recognize them immediately whenever they do occur in one's presence" (1972, p. 139).
3. *Determine what kind of information you want to record.* Event sampling offers greater flexibility than time sampling because you can use both precoded categories and narrative descriptions. You are not bound to time intervals that automatically move you along, but are freer to code and describe the event in detail. Dawe was interested in six kinds of information relating to children's quarrels:
   how long the quarrel lasted
   what was happening when the quarrel started
   what kind of behavior occurred during the quarrel
   what was done and said
   what the outcome was
   what happened afterward
   Her recording sheet provided space for all six pieces of information needing to be recorded. The first (duration) could be a blank to be filled in: e.g. _____ seconds. The second (situation) might be a short narrative description of specific details, or a precoded set of categories if the general situation is all that is required. The third (quarrel behavior) would be a checklist (precoded categories). In this case, Dawe had four items on her checklist: nonparticipator, precipitator, aggressive behavior, retaliative behavior. The fourth kind of information (motor and vocal activity) would be recorded in anecdote form. The fifth kind (outcome) and sixth (after effects) would both be checklists.
4. *Make your recording sheet as easy to use as possible.* Your precoded categories should be clearly labeled and easy to scan and you should have adequate room to record narrative remarks. As with time-sampling record sheets, let-

ters or abbreviations are easier to remember and code than numbers if you do not have room for complete phrases.

Advantages and Disadvantages of Event Sampling

For Wright, the primary advantage of using event sampling is that it "structures the field of observation into natural units of behavior and situation" (1960, p. 107). The behavior is neither isolated nor interrupted as it may be in time sampling, but like the narrative observation methods, it preserves the context into which the event fits. This makes it possible to analyze causal relationships and get at the *why* as well as the *what* of behavior.

For Brandt, "a primary virtue of event sampling in naturalistic research is the economy of observer time spent collecting data. . . . Careful specification of the events to be observed and a system for recording them whenever they do occur free the observer at all other times for other duties" (1972, p. 140). In this respect, event sampling is much like anecdotal recording in that the observer is continually observant—alert to important or relevant happenings, but not continually recording. A classroom teacher interested in studying a rarely occurring behavior like sympathy can simply wait for the situation to arise and then focus on it. Event sampling differs from anecdotal recording in that the observer uses precoded categories both to help focus the observation and to help organize and reduce the data.

A third advantage of event sampling is the fact that it can be used to study any behavior or event, unlike time sampling, which is limited to frequently or regularly occurring behaviors.

Depending upon the recording format, a potential disadvantage for event sampling is that the data may not be as readily quantified as time-sampling data. Recording sheets that are designed to record frequency of behavior are easily quantified, and while event sampling can be used to count frequency of behavior, it usually records qualitative data (*how* and *why* data) also, which is not as easily quantified.

The only disadvantage of the event-sampling method Wright identifies is that, despite its focus on the entire behavioral episode, it still separates that episode from conditions or situations in the past that may have led up to the event. Wright states: "The natural history researchers in biology characteristically describe things, from births to migrations and life cycles, in process as well as in context. Child psychology needs such descriptions" (1960, p. 108).

The Technology of Sampling

In sampling and recording behavior and events, scientists have long made use of observational aids that extend the power of the senses. For example, a stethoscope registers the existence of a heartbeat and tells the skilled listener more about the characteristics of the heart than can be learned without the aid of this instrument. A seismograph not only registers the existence of an earthquake, but also tells the scientist how long the earthquake lasted, how strong it was, and what its pattern of recurrence was. In similar fashion, an EKG reading gives a "print-out" of the behavior of the heart. Both the seismograph and the electrocardiogram record the event or behavior by printing out an image for later reference and analysis.

A variety of technical aids are also available for use in sampling behavior and events in child study. These aids range from the simplest pen and paper technique to highly sophisticated equipment. In the last chapter, for example, we described a study by Burgess and Conger (1978) in which observations were recorded through BOSS, a 10-digit keyboard which transmitted electrical impulses onto a cassette tape which could later be fed directly into a computer. The counterpart of the BOSS in event sampling is the event recorder.

The name *event recorder* refers to any automated device which registers the occurrence of a selected event. Most commercial event recorders consist of a stylus, or pen. The more complex ones can have as many as 66 pens which record portions of an event, its duration, and perhaps its intensity on graph paper as the event is occurring. This type of event recorder is used to record physiological or behavioral activity—usually within a laboratory setting. One of the best known event recorders is the polygraph or lie detector.

Event recorders, 10-digit keyboards and computers, may be readily available to researchers but are not yet standard equipment for classroom teachers. Teachers must use other aids for sampling behavior.

The kind of record we want to make—as teachers or as researchers—guides us in our choice of recording aid. We may try to capture the look of the event by taking a picture or series of pictures. If we can do so, we may choose to use a movie or video camera so that the sequence of events is properly preserved. If it is important for us to know who said what when, we may decide to tape record the event for later playback and analysis.

And there are special techniques and equipment for even more precise analysis. If we are interested in studying separation behavior when parents bring children to school, we would simply film the first 15 or 20 minutes of the session. We could then analyze it in slow motion to catch those nonverbal clues that are so subtle that we might otherwise miss them. For example, Paul and Happie Byers (1972) reported on an analysis of techniques used by preschoolers to gain a teacher's attention. They examined a film of a 33-minute session involving two white and two black four-year-old girls with their white teacher. By slowing the film and stopping frames for analysis, they discovered a subtle body language system at work that seemed to favor the white children. In the first 10 minutes of a table activity, the more active black child looked or glanced at the teacher 35 times and caught her eye four of these times. The more active white child was successful in 8 out of 14 tries during the same time interval. Thus, the white child's success rate was 57 percent and the black child's was only 11 percent. The film analysis showed a difference between the white and black children in how and when they made their bids for attention. The white children and teacher had a compatible sense of timing that worked for the child, but the black children's timing was off—out of tune with the teacher's rhythm of interaction. The researchers call it a "mismatching or difference in communication systems" (p. 24). These clues were only visible through slow motion and stop-action analysis. They were subtle, nonverbal clues that would have escaped the attention of even a seasoned observer.

The use of motion picture film is a relatively expensive means of recording an event. And yet there are situations—like the one outlined above—in which the use of the movie camera is most appropriate.

If we are going to study a continuing and time-persistent event—like the use of various areas of a classroom and the traffic and behavior patterns involved—the most time-efficient method would be time-lapse photography. Obviously no observer could take complete notes over a period of time on a group of children in a specific classroom without spending a great deal of time gathering the data. To let the camera simply run for a period of hours would be of little help inasmuch as an enormous amount of time would be required to play the film back for analysis. The most economical way to gather material for an analysis of this sort is to use a time-lapse method of photography which telescopes the actions of hours into minutes and still preserves the data in sufficiently intact form that valid conclusions can be drawn.

Hutt and Hutt (1970) list five groups of investigations for which motion picture and videotaping are especially appropriate:

1. where action is so quick that it cannot be seen in its entirety by the observer (the prey killing behavior of the cat)
2. where the action is so complex that attention cannot be given to all components at once (response of human newborns to sounds)
3. where changes in the behavior are so subtle that delineation between one act and another is difficult (gaze behavior)
4. where sequential changes in fairly complex behaviors are being looked at (transition from investigation to play)
5. where one must measure specific parameters of brief or complex behavior events (gait) (pp. 97–98).

Clearly the more machinery or hardware for observing and recording behavior that intrudes into the naturalistic environment, the less natural the event will become. The person or persons being observed will be alert to any irregular element in the environment—whether it be human or machine. A subject can get used to the irregular element in time, perhaps, but the use of such elements needs to be carefully planned and closely monitored.

The Question of Reliability

An important aspect of time and event sampling is that rater reliability can be readily established for both. Reliability refers to the extent of observer agreement or consistency in recording observational information. This is important for two reasons. First, it helps to guarantee objectivity. If five observers all report the same data, it is less likely that personal biases have slanted the observation. Second, it guarantees the likelihood that other researchers (using the same procedures to study the same kind of subjects) will find the same results. This is an important consideration for researchers. Other people must be able to reproduce the findings in order to assure that the study was not just a chance occurrence.

We have repeatedly stated the need to define the purpose of an observation and to work out operational definitions for behaviors being studied. This lays the groundwork for obtaining good observer reliability. If the observer has clearly defined what the object of the study is, and if the observer has clearly defined what is to be measured, looked at, and recorded, then the findings should hold up over time and place. In other words, the same study done a day, a week, or a month later should provide essentially the same results, and the same study done in another place with comparable subjects and conditions should also yield similar results.

Reliability of behavioral observation is usually a product of measuring the amount of agreement between two or more different observations. *Inter-rater reliability* is measured when two or more researchers observe the same situation, record it independently, and then check to see how much they agreed or the extent to which their recordings match. *Intra-rater reliability* is measured when a single researcher observes a situation more than once, recording data each time, and then checks to see how consistent he or she was in recording the same behavior over time.

The degree of agreement between two observations—either from different individuals or from the same person at various times—is expressed as a correlation (or a co-relation—the degree to which one measure relates to another measure). Perfect agreement between measures, or identical results, is expressed as a +1.0. When the results do not match or there is no agreement, the correlation is 0. A perfect negative correlation—where the presence of one factor suggests the absence of a second factor—is expressed as −1.0. For example, we might expect that we would find a fairly high correlation—+.75 or above probably—between the number of books read by children and measures of reading ability. If we were to correlate the number of books read by children with measures of distance from their homes to school, we would probably find a very low correlation—+.12 or possibly even a low negative correlation like −.06. In either case, we would conclude that the two factors are unrelated.

A quick and easy method of estimating correlation when checking inter- and intra-rater reliability is to:

1. Count the total tallies in a category for both observations involved.
2. Count the number of agreements in the tallies—those instances when the two observations resulted in identical tallies—one mark for the same behavior.
3. Divide the number of agreements by the total number of tallies.
4. Multiply the result by the number of observers (or observations if it is a case of intra-rater repeat).

The resulting correlation provides the measure of reliability, or agreement between observations. For example, let us assume that two observers were researching Olson's nervous mannerism study and recorded as follows:

	Observer 1	Observer 2	Agreement
1. biting the nails	5	4	4
2. thumb/finger in mouth	16	11	11
3. picking the nose	1	3	1
TOTAL	22	18	16

Working out the correlation following the steps above would give us:

1. total tallies = 40
2. agreement = 16
3. divide agreements (16) by tallies (40) = .40
4. multiply result (.40) by number of observers (2) = .80

The resulting correlation, .80, is a high one that indicates good reliability from one observer to another in this case.

It is important that reliability be high (preferably .80 or above) in time and event sampling. If it is not, the observer must find the reason and remedy the problem.

When two observers do *not* agree in their findings, Brandt (1972) points out that several factors may be involved:

1. One of the observers may be inexperienced and need more practice.
2. One of the observers may be poor at the observation task. As is the case with most skills, ability to be a good observer is a talent some people possess and others do not.
3. The categories or characteristics being rated may be so poorly defined that they allow for differing interpretations.

If a single observer cannot come up with consistent results on a second observation, perhaps boredom or preoccupation with another problem has interfered. The other possibility, again, is that the individual is a poor observer.

Summary

The narrative observation technique gave way in the 1920s to two new methods: time sampling and event sampling. Event sampling, unlike time sampling, focuses on the behavior itself rather than on the time interval. The behavior being studied is attended to for its normal time duration. The range of behaviors that can be studied with event sampling is limitless.

Event-sampling techniques can be used in both experimental and natural settings. Mary Cover Jones (1925) studied the emotions of preschool children in an experimental study. The researcher presented children with fearful situations in order to elicit a fear reaction. Jones then attempted to develop techniques that would extinguish fear responses.

One of the early studies using the event-sampling technique in the natural setting was Helen Dawe's (1934) analysis of 200 quarrels of preschool children.

Although classroom teachers probably will not carry out a formal research project, they are apt to use event sampling to gather information for case studies or to assist them in classroom planning and evaluation.

Guidelines for using event sampling include:

1. clearly identifying and defining the behavior you want to study
2. knowing enough about the behavior to know when and where to observe
3. determining what kind of information you want to record
4. making your recording sheet as easy to use as possible

A key advantage of the event-sampling technique is that it structures the field of observation into natural behavior units, preserving the behavioral context. The only disadvantage Wright points out is that it separates the event from conditions or situations related to it but separated in time.

A variety of observational aids have been used to record events: commercial event recorders, cameras, and computers in addition to pen and paper. Careful planning needs to be done by the observer to make sure that the recording aids do not intrude into the research situation.

The chapter ends with a brief discussion of reliability—the amount of agreement between two or more different observations—and presents information on working out correlations.

Suggestions for Further Reading

Boehm, Ann E., and Richard A. Weinberg. *The Classroom Observer: A Guide for Developing Observation Skills.* New York: Teachers College, 1977. Presents components that are critical to developing good observational skills and then provides a series of graduated tasks designed to help the reader integrate those skills into his or her own professional repertoire. Chapters 4 and 5 (Labeling and Categorizing Behavior and Sampling and Recording Behavior) are particularly helpful for observers who need a simplified approach to the skills required for time and event sampling. Lots of information in a brief little book.

Dawe, Helen C. An analysis of two hundred quarrels of preschool children. *Child Development*, 1934, 5, 139–157. A classic event-sampling study, well worth reading in the original report.

Hutt, S. J., and C. Hutt. *Direct Observation and Measurement of Behavior.* Springfield, Ill: Charles C Thomas, 1970. Chapters 4, 5, and 6 give the reader information on the range of equipment and procedures available for recording an event. They include both simple and sophisticated techniques. A good introduction for the observer who is interested in doing more rigorous observational research. Chapter 4: Methods and Techniques I: Tape Recording; Chapter 5: Methods and Techniques II: Checklists and Event Recorders; Chapter 6: Methods and Techniques III: Motion Picture and Videotape.

Kerlinger, F. N. *Foundations of Behavioral Research*, 2d ed. New York: Holt, Rinehart and Winston, 1973. Chapter 31, Observations of Behavior, discusses some of the problems and processes involved in the complicated study of behavior—such things as questions of validity and reliability, developing categories, sampling of behavior by time and event methods, and rating scales. Gives examples of several behavior observation systems.

Using the Event-Sampling Technique

This assignment starts off by "walking you through" an event-sampling observation in which the operational definitions and recording format are already worked out. The second part of the assignment provides only the skeleton outline and gives you practice in making the decisions that finish it. The target behaviors in this study are adapted from David E. Barrett and Marian Radke Yarrow's study, "Prosocial Behavior, Social Inferential Ability, and Assertiveness in Children" reported in *Child Development*, 1977, *48*, 475-481.

Part I: Event Sampling of Assertiveness in Children

Procedure: Begin by familiarizing yourself with the operational definitions provided below. Note the abbreviation given with each definition as it will be used on the recording sheet.

ASSERTIVENESS: involves attempts to direct or to stop another person's activity. Assertive behavior is intended to influence or control, but is not intended to injure. Assertions include commands, acts of physical leading, and implied directives. The operational definitions for these behaviors are as follows:

COMMANDS (C): attempts to issue directions or tell other children what to do or how to do something. Examples of commands are statements such as "Get out of our Bat Cave," "Watch me go down the slide," "Give me the big blocks."
PHYSICAL LEADING (PL): behaviors in which the child makes physical contact to guide or direct the other child's behavior. Taking a child by the hand or putting an arm around a child's shoulder to physically direct him or her are examples of physical leading.
IMPLIED DIRECTIVE (ID): behaviors that suggest direction but do not make direct commands. An example of an implied directive is "We'll do that later."

OUTCOME BEHAVIORS: behaviors that follow the assertive attempt.

COMPLIANCE (COMP): The child who is the subject of the assertive attempt yields or agrees to the assertive command.
REFUSAL (REF): The child who is the subject of the assertive attempt refuses to do what is asked or demanded.
COMPROMISE/NEGOTIATION WITH POSITIVE OUTCOME (+C/N): The child who is the subject of the assertive attempt counters with a suggestion of his or her own, with the outcome being the compromise suggested.
COMPROMISE/NEGOTIATION WITH NEGATIVE OUTCOME (−C/N): The child who is the subject of the assertive attempt counters with a suggestion of his or her own, but the compromise is rejected by the assertive child.
IGNORING (IG): The child who is the subject of the assertive attempt pays no attention to the assertive bid.

Once you have the definitions well in mind and the abbreviations memorized, select an environment in which a number of children are interacting freely (playground, classroom, home). Do not select an environment where you are the primary adult available for children to turn to for help. When you see an assertive event, observe it and record the information identified on the recording sheet. *Target child* refers to the subject of the assertion. After *situation*, briefly identify what the children were doing at the time of the assertive behavior. After *action*, identify as many specific motor or verbal behaviors relating to the event as you can remember. Collect data on five assertive events.

Event #1   Setting _____ Date _____ Time _____

    Assertive Child: Age _____ Sex _____   *Assertive Behavior*
    Target Child: Age _____ Sex _____   _____ C
    Situation: _____ PL
                                           _____ ID
                                         Outcome
    Action: _____ COMP
                                         _____ REF
                                       _____ +C/N
                                       _____ −C/N
                                       _____ IG

Event #2   Setting _____ Date_____ Time _____

    Assertive Child: Age _____ Sex _____   *Assertive Behavior*
    Target Child: Age _____ Sex _____   _____ C
    Situation: _____ PL
                                           _____ ID
                                         '*Outcome*
    Action: _____ COMP
                                       _____ REF
                                       _____ +C/N
                                       _____ −C/N
                                       _____ IG

Event #3   Setting _____ Date_____ Time _____

         Assertive Child: Age _____ Sex _____   *Assertive Behavior*
         Target Child: Age _____ Sex _____   _____ C
         Situation: _____ PL
                                         _____ ID
                                       Outcome
         Action: _____ COMP
                                       _____ REF
                                     _____ +C/N
                                     _____ −C/N
                                     _____ IG

Event #4   Setting _____ Date _____ Time _____

         Assertive Child: Age _____ Sex _____   *Assertive Behavior*
         Target Child: Age _____ Sex _____   _____ C
         Situation: _____ PL
                                         _____ ID
                                       Outcome
         Action: _____ COMP
                                       _____ REF
                                     _____ +C/N
                                     _____ −C/N
                                     _____ IG

Event #5   Setting _____ Date _____ Time _____

         Assertive Child: Age _____ Sex _____   *Assertive Behavior*
         Target Child: Age _____ Sex _____   _____ C
         Situation: _____ PL
                                         _____ ID
                                       Outcome
         Action: _____ COMP
                                       _____ REF
                                     _____ +C/N
                                     _____ −C/N
                                     _____ IG

Five events are not enough to base any conclusions on, but they give you enough information that you can determine how well the behaviors are defined and how well the recording sheet works. What (if any) suggestions would you make for clarifying the definitions or improving the recording form?

Part II: Event Sampling of Aggressive Behavior

In the first part of the assignment you were asked to do an observation based on an existing set of operational definitions and a recording sheet. In this part of the assignment, you will be asked to do the background work yourself.

The target behavior is aggression, which is operationally defined as: *behaviors that are intended to injure others or make them feel bad.* You need first to identify and define the specific behaviors that are included under aggression and then develop a recording sheet that provides room for recording relevant information about the children involved, the situation, the aggressive behavior, the outcome of the event, and the after-effects. You should list your definitions on one page and the layout for your recording sheet on the second page. Attach both pages with this assignment.

Record three samples of aggressive behavior. What changes, if any, would you make in your definition or your recording sheet based on your three observations?

Technically Assisted Observations

We have discussed the use of equipment to assist the observer in collecting data. This assignment will give you some first-hand experience in using mechanical aids to assist you in your observation.

Part I: The Observation

Procedure: Select two classmates to work with. You will be doing three event-sampling observations of aggressive behavior. Your first task is to review the work that each of you did for Part II of Lab Assignment 22. You will need to agree on one common set of definitions and a common recording sheet; either select one as is or combine the best features of all three into a new set.

Your second task is to gather the equipment that will be needed. You will need 18 recording sheets to give you one sheet for each observation (three of you will do three observations each under two sets of conditions); a cassette tape recorder; and either a video or a movie camera.

The assignment involves three separate observations. Each member of the observation team will do all three observations. One observation will be done using the recording sheet; one will be done using a cassette tape recorder to narrate the information you need; the third observation will be done using a camera to film the information you need. You will need to go back and review your observation "notes" and then code the recording sheets for both the tape recorder and camera observations. Be as unobtrusive as possible in all three observations.

Observe as a team, all at the same time. Watch the children until you see an aggressive event occurring and then record that event. You will record two aggressive events for each segment of the observation—two paper and pencil, two taped, and two filmed observations per team member. You will find that you concentrate more on the equipment in the first one; the second one is to let you concentrate more on the child(ren) and the event.

When you have finished recording two events, trade equipment and record two more (you may want a short break between). Then repeat the procedure for the final set. When you have finished all three types of observation, *independently* review your own observations and complete your recording sheets. Each of you will have completed six observations when you finish, two for each of the three recording techniques. You should attach the recording sheets for all six to this assignment sheet.

Indicate the order of your own observations here:

1.

2.

3.

Part II: Comparing Methods and Data

1. Discuss the advantages and disadvantages of using a tape recorder and a camera as a "memory bank."

    Tape Recorder:

    Video or Movie Camera:

2. Which method did you prefer? Why?

3. Compare your recording sheets with those of your teammates. Circle in green any items that you have recorded that *do not appear* on one or both of your teammates' recording sheets. Circle in red items that *differ* from what one or both of your teammates recorded—i.e., items that you disagreed about. Which observations contain the most green circles? How do you explain this?

    Compare the items you have circled in red. Try to determine how much of the difference is a result of your own perceptions and what is a product of the method of recording data.

Inter-Rater and Intra-Rater Reliability

According to Herbert and Attridge (1975), the main value of inter-rater reliability is "as indicators of the clarity of the structure, focus, and procedures of the (recording) system, and as a measure of observer bias or the ambiguity of observed events" (p. 4). It is a valuable check on the observation process itself. Intra-rater reliability, on the other hand, tells you more about your own consistency as an observer across time.

Part I: Time-Sampling Reliability

Procedure: The focus of the observation will be children's bids for attention. Review the sign system outlined below and memorize the code words. Select an adult (teacher, parent) to use as the focus of the observation in a situation where three or more children could be competing for that adult's attention. Record *every attempt* made by a child to get the adult's attention, using the recording format on the next page. Observe for two five-minute intervals. You will check your own reliability by doing two time-sampling observations—separated by at least a day—for a total of 10 minutes each. The second observation should be done with a partner who will be doing the same observation at the same time, but independently; this will make it possible to complete the inter-rater reliability portion of this assignment (Part II).

Operational Definitions:

BIDS FOR ATTENTION: Verbalizations or behavior designed to make another person notice the individual making the bids for attention.

Sign System Components:
1. *Tugs:* Tugs on adult's hand, leg, or clothing.
2. *Calls:* Calls the adult's name.
3. *Object:* Holds an object in front of the adult's face.
4. *Stands:* Stands in front of the adult.
5. *"Me":* Says to the adult, "Look at me," or "Watch me," or some related focusing phrase.
6. *Asks:* Asks the adult for help or assistance.
7. *Cries:* Cries or whimpers.
8. *Yells:* Yells or screams.
9. *Teases:* Teases or pesters other children or the adult.
10. *Hugs:* Gives the adult hugs, kisses, or other loving gestures.

Observation procedure: You will need to code the children that appear in the observation in some manner that allows you to remember each child. Report them in your observation as child 1, 2, 3, etc. Identify the age and sex of each child at the bottom of the recording sheet. Record all bids for attention *in the order in which they occur*. If two bids occur together, record them on the same line. If, for example, child 2 tugs on the adult's sleeve and says, "Look at what I made," code it as child 2 Tugs, "Me."

Time-Sampling Observation # 1

Observer _____

Setting _____ Date _____ Time_____
Adult _____ Age of Children _____ Size of Group _____

ATTENTION BID #	CHILD #	TUGS	CALLS	OBJECT	STANDS	"ME"	ASKS	CRIES	YELLS	TEASES	HUGS	COMMENTS
1.												
2.												
3.												
4.												
5.												
6.												
7.												
8.												
9.												
10.												
11.												
12.												
13.												
14.												
15.												
16.												
17.												
18.												
19.												
20.												
21.												
22.												
23.												
24.												
25.												
26.												
27.												
28.												
29.												
30.												
GROUP TOTALS												

Time-Sampling Observation # 2   *Observer* _____

Setting _____ Date _____ Time_____
Adult _____ Age of Children _____ Size of Group _____

ATTENTION BID #	CHILD #	TUGS	CALLS	OBJECT	STANDS	"ME"	ASKS	CRIES	YELLS	TEASES	HUGS	COMMENTS
1.												
2.												
3.												
4.												
5.												
6.												
7.												
8.												
9.												
10.												
11.												
12.												
13.												
14.												
15.												
16.												
17.												
18.												
19.												
20.												
21.												
22.												
23.												
24.												
25.												
26.												
27.												
28.												
29.												
30.												
GROUP TOTALS												

Now that you have completed both observations, compute your intra-rater reliability and the inter-rater reliability between you and your partner on the second observation.

1. *Intra-rater reliability:* First compute your own consistency in recording group totals.

	Observation 1	Observation 2
Total # of Tallies (both observations)	_____	_____
Agreement (total for both observations)	_____	_____
Divide Agreements by Tallies	_____	_____
Multiply by Number of Observations (2)	_____	_____

2. It would be extremely unlikely that you would ever reach a 1.0 correlation for intra-rater reliability, even if you were an expert observer. Why?

3. *Inter-rater reliability:* Compute the inter-rater reliability for observation #2 using the group totals:

	Observer 1	Observer 2
Total # of tallies (both observers)	_____	_____
Agreement (total for both observers)	_____	_____
Divide Agreement by Tallies	_____	_____
Multiply by # of Observers (2)	_____	_____

4. Speculate on why you achieved the level of inter-rater reliability that you did—what accounted for your high or low correlation?

Select a partner to observe with. Observe together (at the same time and place) but independently record event samples of attention-getting behavior. Observe until you have collected ten events each. Use the definitions and code words outlined in Part I. You will need to record duration and outcome of the attention bids in addition to the other data.

OUTCOME BEHAVIORS

IA: *Immediate Attention:* Adult focuses on child within two seconds of attention bid.

DA: *Delayed Attention:* Adult focuses on child within 5 seconds of attention, but with a delay of at least 2 seconds.

I: *Ignores Bid:* Adult does not respond to attention bid.

Adult Affect

+A: *Positive Affect:* The adult's affect (the emotional tone of his or her response) is positive.

−A: *Negative Affect:* The adult's affect is negative.

Setting _____ Date_____Time _____

Adult _____ Age of Children _____ Size of Group

EVENT	CHILD	SEX	AGE	ATTENTION BID(S)	DURATION	OUTCOME BEHAVIORS	AFFECT	COMMENTS
1.								
2.								
3.								
4.								
5.								
6.								
7.								
8.								
9.								
10.								

1. Tally the total number of bids for each of the categories in the sign system, the total number of outcome behaviors, and the total number of affect behaviors:

	Observer 1	Observer 2	Agreement
TUGS			
CALLS			
OBJECT			
STANDS			
"ME"			
ASKS			
CRIES			
YELLS			
TEASES			
HUGS			
IA			
DA			
I			
+A			
−A			

Compute inter-rater reliability: _____

2. With which sampling method did you achieve the best inter-rater reliability? Speculate on why this was so.

3. What could you do to improve the inter-rater reliability in the time-sampling observation?

   In the event-sampling observation?

Chapter Nine

Checklists and Rating Scales

We are all familiar with lists. We see and use them almost every day—shopping lists, a manufacturer's list of steps to follow in assembling a toy, lists of "dumb things I gotta do." Checklists are simply lists of behaviors. Their basic purpose is to remind us to look for the presence of behaviors that we feel are important.

We used checklists in time and event sampling to remind us to observe for specified behaviors. If we saw these behaviors within the specified time interval or event we checked them off to indicate their presence. While a checklist is an efficient way of determining whether a behavior is present or absent, it tells us nothing about frequency, duration, or quality of behavior nor does it give us a description of behavior. We can tell whether the event or behavior occurred, but we know little else.

Guidelines for Developing Checklists

As with event sampling, we need to have some idea of what we want to look for before using a checklist. When we are going to have a dinner party, we plan the menu and then make out a shopping list. As we find the items in the supermarket, we cross them off our list. By the time we have reached the check-out counter, we have either found everything on the list or discovered that the item is not there. When we use a behavioral checklist we also need to do some advance planning. For example, Mr. Seymour is interested in finding out what kind of math readiness skills his five-year-olds have. He starts by identifying the skills he feels are important background or readiness skills and includes the following:

1. Recognizes a circle, triangle, square, and rectangle.
2. Knows the names of a circle, triangle, square, and rectangle.
3. Can rote count to 10.
4. Can do one-to-one correspondence up to ten.
5. Knows the relational concepts bigger, smaller, longer, and shorter.
6. Understands first, middle, last.
7. Understands more than and less than.

Thus, the first guideline for doing a checklist is that *the checklist itself be prepared before doing the observation.*

The second guideline is that the observer needs to *list the target behaviors separately on the checklist.* It will be easier to check for the presence or absence of math readiness skills if Mr. Seymour lists the items separately. Thus the first item would look like this on the checklist:

1. Can pick out the following shapes as the teacher names them:

	YES	NO
circle	_____	_____
square	_____	_____
triangle	_____	_____
rectangle	_____	_____

The third guideline is that *the checklist should be logically organized.* Once Mr. Seymour has developed statements for each of the readiness behaviors he has identified, he is ready to organize his checklist. It should be arranged so that it will be easy to scan in finding the behaviors he is looking for. Some people organize shopping lists according to where the item is shelved in the store. Others might arrange their list alphabetically. Mr. Seymour might decide to arrange his list according to the level of difficulty of the item. He might feel that recognizing basic shapes is the easiest skill for most five-year-olds and that the concepts of *more than* and *less than* are the most difficult. His completed checklist might look like this:

TASK	YES	NO
1. Can pick out the following shapes as they are named		
circle	____	____
square	____	____
triangle	____	____
rectangle	____	____
2. Can count from 1 to 10	____	____
3. Can name properly the following shapes		
circle	____	____
square	____	____
triangle	____	____
rectangle	____	____
4. Demonstrates understanding of the following relational concepts		
bigger	____	____
smaller	____	____
longer	____	____
shorter	____	____
5. Can do one-to-one correspondence for		
two objects	____	____
three objects	____	____
five objects	____	____
ten objects	____	____
more than ten objects	____	____
6. Can follow directions involving the following concepts		
first	____	____
middle	____	____
last	____	____
7. Demonstrates understanding of		
more than	____	____
less than	____	____

The fourth guideline is that *the organization of the checklist should meet all the stated purposes of the observation.* Mr. Seymour's stated purpose is: (1) to identify the presence or absence of specified math readiness skills at the beginning of the term (entry level); and (2) to record the chronological development (emergence) of skills not present at the beginning of the term. Mr. Seymour can easily add another column labeled DATE to his checklist. This will allow him to enter the date he first sees the child exhibit each of the behaviors checked under the NO column. At the end of the term he can then go back and look at the sequence of emergence and at the span of time between behaviors for any child or any group of children. His completed checklist might look like this:

CHILD __WALTER LEONARD_____   DATE __9/24/79__

TASK	YES	NO	IF "NO," DATE FIRST SEEN
1. Can pick out the following shapes as they are named			
circle	✓		
square	✓		
triangle	✓		
rectangle	✓		
2. Can count from 1 to 10	✓		
3. Can name properly the following shapes			
circle	✓		
square	✓		
triangle	✓		
rectangle		✓	10/2
4. Demonstrates understanding of the following relational concepts			
bigger	✓		
smaller	✓		
longer		✓	10/19
shorter		✓	10/26
5. Can do one-to-one correspondence for			
two objects	✓		
three objects	✓		
five objects	✓		
ten objects		✓	11/9
more than ten objects		✓	11/9
6. Can follow directions involving the following concepts			
first	✓		
middle		✓	11/16
last		✓	12/13
7. Demonstrates understanding of			
more than		✓	3/7
less than		✓	4/2

Advantages and Disadvantages of Checklists

Checklists are useful for classroom teachers and other service professionals because they are so easy to use. The teacher can identify instructional or behavioral objectives, translate them into behavioral statements, and then simply check off these behaviors as he or she sees them occur in the course of normal teaching duties.

The major advantage of the checklists is that it allows the observer to record the presence of a behavior very quickly and very efficiently. It takes a minimum amount of observer energy. This is due in part to the simplicity of the method, and in part to the planning that goes into the development of the checklist.

Another advantage of the checklist for observers who chose to record the date behaviors are first seen is that the observer can either note behaviors as soon as they occur or can sit down at the end of the day and review the checklist to see what new behaviors can be checked off. If the checklist is a simple one, an entire class can be listed on a single sheet. For example, Mrs. Fisher has been recording her day-care infants' "developmental firsts." Because infants can enter the day-care center as young as six weeks of age, she has a good opportunity to observe many "firsts." At the end of the first year of recording, her checklist looks like this:

CHILD / ACTIVITY	Hand Regard	Foot Regard	Crawling	Stands Alone	Walks Alone	Babbling	Single Word Sentence	Object Concept
BRIAN	77d	159 d	34 w	48 w		6 w	12M	10 M
DAVID	54d	136 d	31 w	45 w	11M	5 w	11 M	8 M
JASON	61 d	145 d	32 w	46 w	11 M	6 w	11 M	9 M
KATHY	59 d	140 d	32 w	45 w	10 M	6 w	10 M	9 M
LESLIE	45 d	133 d	29 w	40 w	9 M	4 w	9 M	7 M
MATTHEW	81 d	180 d	43 w	53 w		9 w		12M
MEGAN	66 d	141 d	34 w	47 w	12M	5 w	11 M	9 M
MELISSA	74d	162 d	36 w	57 w		7 w	12M	10M
GROUP AVRG	65d	149 d	34 w	47 w		6 w		9 M

Key: d = days; w = weeks; m = months

Notice that the teacher has recorded some of the developmental firsts by days, others by weeks, and some by months of age. She has used the time frame that is most meaningful for the behavior observed. A checklist makes it easy to incorporate this kind of recording flexibility. When the teacher notices a new behavior, she simply records the age of the infant at the time on her checklist. When all of the children have exhibited a particular behavior, the teacher can compute the average age for the emergence of that behavior in that group.

The senior author used a class checklist to record daily participation in indoor activities in her four-year-old group at a laboratory nursery school. The children's names and the grid itself were mimeographed as the basic recording sheet. Enough copies were run off to cover all class sessions for a quarter and she simply filled in the activities that were planned for each day and identified which teacher was supervising each activity.

The four teachers filled out the form together. This made it less likely that a child's participation in an activity would be missed and helped them to share information. The form provides a useful record of the daily activities plus a list of participants for each.

Notice that this list also contains another piece of information: We can circle any activity that a child spends a great deal of time doing. Thus we know that Kerry participated in seven different activities but spent most of her time at the easel. We could look at the lists for an entire week and notice patterns of participation for a child. We might find, for example, that Billy has not participated in any of the art activities during the week. The list would prompt us to watch him during the next week. If Billy continues to avoid art, we might decide to try to encourage him or to discover why he avoids art activities.

This type of checklist, called a participation checklist, serves three functions: (1) it is a record of daily activities; (2) it provides diagnostic information relating to participation in the various indoor activities; and (3) it is useful for curriculum planning. It is a very quick and efficient observational tool.

The major disadvantage of checklists is that they provide little or no information about the quality of behavior—*how* children babble or *how* they participate, for example.

Rating Scales

If you have been the first in your group to go to the new pizza parlor, your friends might say to you, "On a scale of 1 to 10, how does it rate?" If you thought the sauce was good but the crust was too thick, you might rate it 6 or 7. If the crust was soggy and the sauce was cold, you might rate it a 1 or 2. If it was the best pizza you ever had you might rate it a 9 or 10. In rating your reaction to the pizza, you would be using a kind of rating scale. Rating scales are simply measures designed to quantify impressions gained from observation. Because such procedures do not necessarily involve direct observation with on-the-spot recording, some researchers do not include them as direct observation techniques (see, for example, Medley and Mitzel, 1963, p. 252). Rating scales do not take the place of on-the-spot recordings of observations, but they do provide a quick and

DATE _____ ACTIVITY	Puzzles	Magnastix	Farm Lotto	String Painting	Easel/Collage	Floating Table	Felt Board Shapes	Dram.Play Shoe Store	Blocks: Unit Blocks	Group Time Punchinello	Piano	Animals	Book Corner	Comments
SUPERVISING TEACHER	M	M	M	C	C	D	D	B	B	C	B	B	D	
DEBBY	✓		✓	✓	✓			✓		✓				
KERRY		✓	✓		⊘		✓	✓		✓			✓	
PETER														Absent
RACHEL		✓	✓	✓		✓		⊘		✓	✓			
SANDY	✓			✓	✓				⊘	✓		✓		
MARK	✓	✓				✓			✓					Didn't want to join group — worked at Fl. Tbl.
TODD			✓				✓	⊘	✓	✓				
CARRIE	✓			⊘	✓	✓				✓	✓		✓	
JON	✓	✓	✓	✓	✓	✓	✓		✓		✓	✓		excited about trip to grandparents
TOMMY						✓		⊘	✓	✓		✓		
CHRIS				⊘	✓					✓			✓	
BILLY	✓	✓	✓				✓		✓	✓				
NOAH		✓	✓	✓			✓	✓	✓	✓				
TAMARA	✓	✓		✓		✓	✓	✓		✓			✓	Did 1 to 1 Corresp/felt shp.
ANN	✓				✓	⊘	✓			✓			✓	
JOHN PAUL			✓			✓		✓		✓			⊘	Didn't cry today!
KATHY		✓		✓	✓	✓		✓	✓	✓		✓	✓	
PAULA	⊘		✓		✓			✓		✓	✓		✓	

easy means of summarizing impressions gleaned from observations. Because rating scales are frequently used and are a product of observational perceptions, they are briefly described in this chapter.

Medley and Mitzel (1963) point out that checklists and rating scales are similar in that both call for observer judgment, but different in the kind of judgment required. Checklists call for *qualitative* judgments about the presence or absence of behaviors. Rating scales call for *quantitative* judgments about the degree to which a behavior is present or how it is exhibited (p. 252–253). Both can be recorded on-the-spot or after the fact. Both can be used with single observations or over longer periods of time.

It is difficult to track down the first research study that used rating scales. Wright's 1960 review cites Haggerty, Olson, and Wickman's behavior rating schedules published in 1930 as his earliest reference. The Twenty-Eighth Yearbook of the National Society for the Study of Education (1929) describes the emerging techniques for recording the behavior and development of children. It lists rating scales as one of the methods available and states that "the use of ratings is one of the common methods of getting information about the child's personality" (p. 778). The Yearbook cites four studies, published from 1925–1928, that used rating scales.

The Blanton chart (1925–26) is a graphic scale for use in rating preschool children in twelve groups of behavior traits. The Marston scale (1925) for rating extrovert and introvert behavior is also adapted to the preschool age. Bridges (1928) has developed a scale for preschool character rating. . . . Berne (1928) in measuring children's social attitudes has developed a rating scale for use with preschool children (1929, p. 778).

The Yearbook states that for rating scales to be of value, ratings must be precisely done:

For the person, place, object, or performance to be rated, definite items are noted and a numerical value or some graphic measure is assigned to each one. Such records are used for types of material which cannot easily be measured in any other way. As they are subjective judgments, depending upon the person making them, it is usually valuable to have them repeated by different persons (p. 771).

This early quote describes a primary advantage of rating scales (they can be used for behaviors not easily measured by other means), and a primary disadvantage (they are highly subjective). Fifty years later, that quote still captures the essence of rating scales.

One of the four early studies—Leslie R. Marston's 1925 study—was described by Goodenough in 1934. Marston's study took off from Carl Jung's belief that everyone could be classified as one of two general emotional types: extroverted or introverted. Marston wanted to see whether or not the behavior of individual young children would fall into this pattern. He selected 100 children two to six years of age who were enrolled at the University of Iowa's nursery school. First, teachers rated each child as introverted or extroverted using paired descriptions, one the characteristic of an introvert and the other the characteristic of the extrovert. Teachers were instructed to use two ++ marks next to descriptions that clearly fit the child, one + mark for moderate matches and a − mark if the child was midway between the two descriptions. A numerical value of 1 (two ++ marks in front of extreme introversion descriptions) to 5 (for two ++ marks in front of extreme extroversion descriptions) was assigned each rating and the child's score was simply the sum of the ratings for the 20 pairs of descriptions. Goodenough gives the following examples of Marston's descriptions:

Introversion	*Extroversion*
1. Is self-conscious; easily embarrassed; timid, or "bashful."	Is self-composed; seldom shows signs of embarrassment; perhaps is forward or "bold."
2. Deliberative; slow in making decisions; perhaps even on minor matters is overly cautious.	Impetuous and impulsive; may plunge into situations where forethought would have deterred him.
3. Reserved and distant except to intimate friends; does not form acquaintanceships readily.	Hearty and cordial even to strangers; forms acquaintanceships very easily.
4. Marked perseveration tendency; does not abandon an activity readily, regardless of success.	Turns from one activity to another in rapid succession; slight perseveration tendency (pp. 340–341).

Marston carried his study one step further by designing five experimental situations that would allow him to measure observable reactions in children. He found that girls were more introverted than boys and that this apparent sex difference increased with age. He also found that introversion and extroversion were not two separate types of behavior, as Jung had hypothesized, but were two poles of a single means of classifying behavior, with most children falling in the middle of the two extremes.

Rating scales became popular as soon as they were developed. This was partially due to the fact that they could be used to measure traits or behavioral characteristics that were not easily measured by any other means. It was also a reflection of the fact that they were quick and easy to complete: the rater did not have to be trained (parents or teachers could readily use rating scales) and they took relatively little time to complete.

Rating scales continue to be popular today and are used in many studies of child development. In his chapter on rating scales, J.P. Guilford (1954) notes: "of the psychological-measurement methods that depend upon human judgment, rating-scale procedures exceed them all for popularity and use" (p. 263).

Every observation technique introduced so far involves the observer in on-the-spot recording of events as they occur. Rating scales differ procedurally in that the bulk of the observer's recording task comes about after the observation. As a matter of fact, the observer may not even be aware at the time of observation that he or she will be asked to rate or evaluate later. This is true, for example, in some college classes where students are asked on the last day of class to evaluate how well their professor has taught the course.

In most cases, however, the researcher collects perceptions and information about a subject or situation over a period of time and then makes judgments about the behavior or events after the fact. In some cases, the observer makes no attempt to take notes, simply relying on memory to aid in doing the ratings. In other instances, the observer takes brief notes or records happenings that he or she feels might be helpful in later recall and evaluation. Thus, the technique supports *assessment* of behavior to a greater extent than it does *description* of behavior.

We might compare the difference between observational techniques like specimen descriptions and rating scales with the difference between the techniques of a photographer and an artist. The photographer makes an on-site record of a subject, much like the specimen recorder does, with all details intact. The artist, on the other hand, may make a number of quick sketches and then use these as raw material for a painting done later in his or her studio—or he or she may simply rely on memory—like a rater would do.

Types of Rating Scales

While all rating scales ask the rater to make a judgment about a behavior, not all rating scales are alike. J.P. Guilford (1954) identified five different types of rating scales: numerical, graphic, standard, cumulated points, and forced-choice. In all five, numbers can be used and given as ratings. According to Guilford, the five differ in the physical arrangements of the scale, the kinds and numbers of steps on the scale, and the level of discrimination required of the rater.

Numerical: A sequence of defined numbers is assigned to descriptive categories. The observer or rater selects the most appropriate number for the behavior being rated—either at the time of observation or later. For example, a study by Aletha Huston-Stein, Lynette Friedrich-Cofer, and Elizabeth J. Susman (1977) on the relation of classroom structure to social behavior, imaginative play, and self-regulation of economically disadvantaged children, used three different numerical scales. The first was a five-point scale intended to measure attentiveness and participation. Raters watched during circle time and clean-up time (two regularly occurring group activities) and observed each child just long enough to score him or her on this activity. The points on the scale were defined as:

1—overt disruptive activity or leaves group
2—inattention, no overt disruption
3—follows teacher visually
4—follows teacher, facial expression shows interest
5—follows teacher and adds to instruction through appropriate verbal or motor activities (p. 910).

The authors used a six-point numerical scale to assess the child's efforts to take responsibility during clean-up time. The points were defined as follows:

1—obstructs efforts to pick up
2—refuses to stop or give up toys until teacher insists
3—does not participate
4—assists in routine pick up by working with teacher's supervision

5—picks up cooperatively with other children without direct supervision from teacher

6—picks up without supervision from teacher and without help from other children (p. 911).

The researchers observed a number of different times during the course of 10 or 11 different days and then averaged each child's scores for a final score. They also used a 27-item scale designed to measure teacher warmth and support, use of harsh disciplinary practices, and amount of structure in the classroom. This scale provided five alternatives for the rater to check for each of the 27 items. The alternatives ranged from *strongly agree* to *strongly disagree*. This study illustrates the use of ratings both during the observation period (the two child rating scales) and after repeated observations (teacher scale). When the three rating scales were compared with time-sampling data on classroom structure and children's behavior, the researchers found that:

"Children in high structure classes engaged in less prosocial behavior to peers, less imaginative play, and less aggression than children in low structure classes but had slightly more friendly peer interactions. Children in high structure classes were more attentive in circle time and helped to clean up more after free play, but they did not show more independent task persistence. The latter finding suggested that high levels of adult direction produce conformity when adults are present but do not facilitate independent task-oriented behavior" (p. 908).

Graphic: A straight line display, either horizontal or vertical, is provided with cues along the line to help raters decide where to record their judgment. Graphic scales do not usually involve the rater in numbers, but allow a quick and easy recording along a visual scale from high to low. The graphic display is the most popular of the five forms of rating scales. In rating a child's social interactions with other children, for example, the graphic rating scale might look like this:

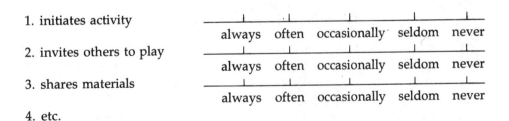

1. initiates activity

2. invites others to play

3. shares materials

4. etc.

The *semantic differential*, developed by Charles Osgood, is a popular form of graphic rating scales. The semantic differential is a seven-unit scale with opposing (bipolar) adjectives at either end. A teacher may rate a child's behavior on a semantic differential scale like the following:

	(1)	(2)	(3)	(4)	(5)	(6)	(7)	
a. cooperative								uncooperative
b. active								passive
c. initiating								responding
d. neat								messy
e. sharing								selfish
f. friendly								hostile

In 1941, H. Champney devised the vertical form of graphic rating scales. The advantage of a vertical display was that it allowed the researcher or observer to include a fuller description of cues. Champney used the vertical form in the famous Fels Parent Behavior Rating Scales at the Fels Research Institute in Yellow Springs, Ohio. The following (number 7.2) is an example taken from that scale.

Definitions: Acceptance of child (devotion-rejection). Rate the parent's acceptance of the child into his own inner circle of loyalty and devotion. Does the parent act in such a way as to indicate that the child is considered an intimate and inseparable partner? Or does the parent act as though he resents the child's intrusion and rejects the child's bid for a place in his primary area of devotion? Consider all evidence which in any way may impinge upon the child as acceptance-rejection, however subtle, vague, or indirect. It is not the parent's true feeling, but his *attitude,* as a functioning unit in the child's environment, which we are rating.

Parent's behavior toward child connotes utter devotion and acceptance into his innermost self, without stint or suggestion of holding back in any phase of his life.
Parent clearly accepts child. Includes child in family councils, trips, affection, even when it is difficult or represents considerable sacrifice.
A "charter member" of the family but "kept in his place." Parent accepts child in general, but excludes him from certain phases of parent's life.
Tacit acceptance. Excludes child so frequently that to the child the rejection attitude may seem to predominate even though parent takes acceptance for granted.
Parent's predominant tendency is to avoid, repulse, and exclude the child, but without open rejection.
Child openly resented and rejected by parent. Never admitted to inner circle. Made to feel unwanted, ostracized (From Fels Parent Behavior Rating Scale Number 7.2).

Standard: The rater is presented with a set of standards against which to judge others. Many university application forms ask people writing letters of recommendation to judge the applicant against other students they have taught:

	top 1%	top 5%	top 10%	top 25%	top 50%	lower 50%	lower 25%
intellectual ability							
creativity							
independence							
responsibility							
efficacy of written expression							
potential as a teacher							
potential as a researcher							

Cumulated points: This category of rating scale arranges items to be rated so that each one acts as a separate indicator of an overall trait. Cumulated points rating scales result in a total score which is the sum or average of the items rated. For example, a field supervisor may wish to evaluate how a student teacher handles discipline in the classroom and might construct a list of positive and negative behaviors related to classroom management. The following pairs of items might be on such a list:

Column A	*Column B*
_____ gives clear directions	_____ gives ambiguous directions
_____ is able to take the child's point of view into consideration	_____ views things from an adult's or teacher's perspective only
_____ gives clear and consistent expectations for behavior	_____ is inconsistent in messages

The rater would total the number of behaviors checked in Column A and the number checked in Column B. The student teacher's final score would be the total of Column A minus the total of Column B.

A second type of cumulated point rating scale identified by Guilford is the guess-who description where the rater is asked to identify a person that fits a given description. This method was originally developed by H. Hartshorne and Mark A. May in their 1928–30 study of character development in children, as a means of allowing children to function as raters. Children were given a series of short simple sentences and asked to identify classmates who fit the descriptions. This method has commonly been employed in sociometric studies where a member of the group is asked to give information about others in the group. A classroom teacher who wanted to elicit the children's perceptions about the on-task behavior of their classmates might ask the following questions:

Guess who–

1. Always gets their work done on time   _____

2. Likes to tease people when they are working on their lessons   _____

3. Never needs help with lessons   _____

4. Has a hard time sitting still when others are working _____

Forced Choice Ratings: This form of rating scale was created to meet needs to evaluate personnel in business and the military. The rater is given a set of descriptive phrases and is forced to choose which one is the most like the person being rated. A teacher may ask his or her aide to use a forced choice rating scale to judge children's classroom behavior. There may be one to five statements in a cluster. Some clusters may force the rater to select between several favorable (or unfavorable) items:

This child can best be described as:
_____ friendly
_____ cooperative
_____ a good leader
_____ hard working

Other clusters may include favorable and unfavorable items within the same cluster. *Only one* can be checked.

At group time, this child is most likely to:
_____ pay close attention and follow the teacher's directions
_____ tease other children
_____ sit quietly and watch but not participate
_____ ask to be first to do everything

Advantages and Disadvantages

The most obvious advantage of rating scales is the ease of both developing the scale and using it. The scale takes very little time to complete in comparison to on-the-spot recording of observations. A teacher might complete a rating scale in 10 or 15 minutes, whereas he or she could spend hours or days gathering observational records. Rating scales are often more interesting for the observer to use, perhaps because they do require observer judgment rather than straightforward objective recording of data. Unless the rater is concerned about the problems of scaling from a statistical measurement perspective, rating scales are also easy to score and quantify.

Because they can be used to record judgments about traits or behaviors that are otherwise difficult to measure, rating scales can be used to study a wide range of behaviors. It is difficult, for example, to develop an adequate measure of humility, yet we all know that some people are more humble than others. A rating scale allows us to generate a humility score for one individual that can then be compared to the score of other individuals or to other data gathered about the same individual.

Rating scales have another advantage in that they require a minimum of training and can be used with "psychologically naive raters" (Guilford, 1954, p. 297). A teacher, for example, can ask parents to complete a rating scale about how children spend their free time at home. The parent does not need to be trained in an observation procedure but simply completes the form and returns it to the teacher.

Another advantage of rating scales is that they can provide a good check on the match between reality and a person's perceptions. A researcher may ask the teacher to rate children on helpfulness and then compare the teacher's ratings with actual observations of helpfulness. Rating scales are frequently paired with time-sampling observations to provide two different sources of information. If the two measures agree, the teacher or researcher feels that the observations are more likely to be accurate. If they disagree, one of the measures may be inappropriate or there may be a significant difference between perceived reality and the actual situation. The observer would need to explore the situation further to determine the reason for the discrepancy.

There are drawbacks to the use of rating scales that make them less reliable than other observational measures. Because they demand a judgment from the rater, they are subject to rater errors and biases. Guilford (1954) identifies six potential rater errors and suggests that the best way to guard against them is to teach raters that they exist. To be forewarned is to be forearmed!

1. The first is the *error of leniency*. Raters tend to rate people they know higher than they deserve to be rated, or, to compensate for possible error, they rate them lower than they deserve to be rated.
2. The second is the *error of central tendency*. Raters tend to avoid extremes of high or low in their judgments and rate toward the middle.
3. The third error was originally identified by Edward L. Thorndike in 1920 as *"the halo effect."* This is the tendency to let other information influence the rating. Often raters have a tendency to contaminate their judgments with irrelevancies—a human failing with which all judges and juries are familiar. A child may be rated as aggressive because the rater knows his older brothers who are aggressive.
4. The fourth problem is the *error of logic*. Raters are apt to give similar ratings for

two items that seem logically related. A child who is rated high on "shows initiative" may be rated high on "works well independently" because the rater assumes that the two are logically related and should be treated in the same manner.

5. The fifth error identified by Guilford is the *error of contrast*. This error is two-pronged in that we either tend to rate people in the opposite direction from ourselves or rate them as similar to ourselves, depending on how we perceive them and how we view or value the trait being rated.

6. The last type of error is called the *proximity error*. This was discovered when researchers did intercorrelations of items on a rating scale and found that items that were next to each other or close together in time or space were rated more similarly than items further apart.

No matter what form the rating scale might take, Guilford suggests that a rater should rate all members of a group on one trait before going on to another trait. This helps in the recognition of differences among individuals through the rater's making immediate and frequent comparisons while concentrating on a single measure.

Another disadvantage of rating scales relates to the ambiguity of the terms used in rating scales. Unlike time or event sampling, where operational definitions are a part of the directions to the rater, terms used in rating scales are seldom defined and different raters may attach different meanings to words like *cooperative, curious, sarcastic,* etc. They may also attach different meanings to words used in the scale like *extremely* or *frequently* or *sometimes.*

A related problem is the fact that some behaviors or attitudes are more socially acceptable than others and unconscious attitudes can influence ratings in ways that make them less a reflection of objective than of subjective reality.

A final disadvantage of rating scales (and checklists, too) is that they tell us little about the causes of behavior. We must keep in mind that a rating provides us with someone else's judgment—not straightforward objective reporting of actual behavior.

One needs to weigh the ease of construction and ease of use of rating scales with the fact that they are also the least objective of all the measures discussed and by the very fact that they call for judgments or opinions rather than descriptions of behavior, they allow room for more biases, conscious or unconscious, to enter the picture.

Guidelines for Observation

The developers of rating scales have offered a variety of guidelines for those who would like to construct their own scales. Guilford (1954) and Brandt (1972) summarize the major guidelines as follows:

1. *Be as clear and concise as possible.* Use short, simple, unambiguous terms.
2. *Be sure that the words or cues are consistent with the trait being rated.*
3. *Use words that imply a specific point on a scale.* Do not overlap the meanings of scale descriptors.

4. *Avoid the use of terms that are general in nature,* such as *average, excellent,* or *very.*
5. *Avoid terms that imply value judgments*—words that imply good or bad behavior or attitudes that may influence the rater.
6. *Do not use scales for traits that can be measured with more reliable means* like time sampling or specimen descriptions.
7. *When using examples of traits to be rated, be sure that the examples distinguish behavior included from behavior not included by the definition.*
8. *Rate all individuals on one trait before going on to the next trait.*
9. *Rate blindly whenever possible.* You are more likely to be objective if you don't know the individuals you are rating. This guideline is appropriate for situations in which the observer is asked to watch a situation or setting for a specified length of time (e.g., 30 minutes) and then rate the children in the setting on a predetermined list of traits.
10. *Select the observation and rating situations carefully.* Brandt says that "if the quality of pupil study habits is to be rated, teachers are well-advised to pay close attention to how their pupils behave during particular study periods and rate them immediately afterward, rather than the night before report cards are due when they are assigning marks and rating other traits" (1972, p. 124). The validity of ratings will depend upon the amount of time the rater has observed and the number of settings and situations that have been observed. Both the observations and the time of the ratings need to be carefully selected.

Summary

Rating scales, used primarily for the study of behavior or personality, first appeared in the 1920s and have been popular ever since. Unlike other techniques which require on-the-spot recording, most rating scales ask the observer to reflect on past impressions to generate ratings.

Five types of rating scales are identified and defined: numerical, graphic, standard, cumulated points, and forced choice ratings. Potential errors raters tend to make are described and include the error of leniency, the error of central tendency, the "halo" effect, the error of logic, the error of contrast, and the proximity error.

The advantages of rating scales revolve around the ease with which they can be constructed and used. The disadvantages tend to cluster around the subjective nature of a rater's assessments.

Suggestions for Further Reading

Brandt, R.M. *Studying Behavior in Natural Settings.* New York: Holt, Rinehart and Winston, 1972. Chapter 4, Measurement through Observational Procedures (pp. 94–127), draws heavily on the work of Guilford, Kerlinger, and Remmers. It provides a very readable overview of rating methods, the problems associated with them, and guidelines for raters.

Guilford, J.P. *Psychometric Methods, 2d ed.* New York: McGraw-Hill, 1954. Chapter 11, Rating Scales (pp. 263–301), is a sophisticated presentation of the psychometry of rating scales. A good statistical background is needed for thorough understanding of Guilford's advice on scale construction and the special conditions that bear upon the use of ratings. A must for researchers—a bit heavy for classroom teachers.

Remmers, H.H. Rating methods in research on teaching. In N.L. Gage, ed., *Handbook of Research on Teaching.* Skokie, Ill.: Rand McNally, 1963, pp. 329–378. This analysis of rating methods includes a description of the five types of rating scales outlined by Guilford, plus a discussion of sociometric methods, the semantic differential, and the Q-technique. All of the methods are illustrated with examples from research on teaching. The review will be most helpful to students with a solid background in statistics.

Checklist Inventories

Checklists serve many purposes. They can tell us about the presence or absence of behavior, they can be used to help us analyze data gathered through narrative observations, and they can help us survey or inventory a situation. The following assignment is designed to give you an experience with checklists as a means of surveying or taking inventory of a situation. In this case, the setting is a preschool classroom and playground. The focus of the observation is the physical environment itself.

It is common for both agency consultants concerned with licensing group care facilities and for researchers concerned with program evaluation to use a checklist to help them evaluate the physical setting. Jane Stallings and her associates at the Stanford Research Institute (SRI) developed the following Physical Environment Inventory as part of their *Preschool Observation Instrument*. It is a simple checklist that provides a means of comparing the physical environments of different preschools.

Procedure: Observe a preschool classroom and its adjoining playground for 15 minutes during indoor free-play and 15 minutes during outdoor free-play. At the end of the observation period, complete the Physical Environment Inventory on the next page. After you have completed the inventory, answer the questions below.

1. If we had asked you to do a narrative description of the physical environment, what information would you have included that is not accounted for on the checklist.

2. How would you revise the checklist to include this information?

3. Stallings' checklist is a rather simple one. Some physical environment checklists go on for pages in an attempt to cover every aspect of the physical setting in detail. If you wanted to know more information about the classroom environment, you would use a more detailed checklist. How would you extend the dramatic play portion of the checklist to provide more detailed information about the kinds of dramatic play activities that can and do occur in the classroom? Indicate the items that you would add below.

PHYSICAL ENVIRONMENT INVENTORY
(Mark All That Apply)

Code those that apply:

SOFTNESS OF ENVIRONMENT
- ○ Child/adult cozy furniture
- ○ Carpet/rug
- ○ Grass to be on
- ○ Sand to be in (box or area)
- ○ Dirt to dig in
- ○ Animals to hold (rabbits, etc.)
- ○ Sling swings
- ○ Dough
- ○ Messy materials: fingerpaint, clay, mud, etc.
- ○ Water as an activity
- ○ Stuffed toys

SPACE AVAILABLE
Number of rooms available	①	②	③	④	⑤
Number of play yards	①	②	③	④	⑤
Secure safety fences/gates	Ⓨ	Ⓝ			

Present and/or Used

PLAY EQUIPMENT
- Ⓟ Ⓤ Dramatic play props
- Ⓟ Ⓤ Structured games and puzzles
- Ⓟ Ⓤ Books, magazines, comic books, etc.
- Ⓟ Ⓤ Water play equipment
- Ⓟ Ⓤ Large vehicles to ride
- Ⓟ Ⓤ Dolls
- Ⓟ Ⓤ Outdoor physical: slides, swings, climbers
- Ⓟ Ⓤ Construction, table-type toys: leggo blocks, tinker toys, etc.
- Ⓟ Ⓤ Work tools
- Ⓟ Ⓤ Floor blocks
- Ⓟ Ⓤ Small wheel toys, cars, trucks, etc.
- Ⓟ Ⓤ Skill equipment: carpentry/sewing, cooking equipment, etc.
- Ⓟ Ⓤ Art materials: pencils, crayons, paper, scissors
- Ⓟ Ⓤ Swimming pool
- Ⓟ Ⓤ Child sized furniture, tables and chairs

SPACE OR PLAY EQUIPMENT PROBLEMS
- ○ None
- ○ Lack of shade
- ○ Broken or shabby equipment
- ○ Space is used as a pathway for other people
- ○ Two groups in one space which are interfering with one another
- ○ Little privacy for children
- ○ All asphalt or rough ground

SPACE SELECTION
How much choice do children have about the space they use?
- ○ No Choice
- ○ Some Choice
- ○ High Choice

Adapted from the "Day Care Environmental Inventory" by Prescott, et al.

Rating the Physical Environment

Rating scales require more judgment than checklists. In addition to classifying specific features of the environment or to indicating presence or absence of certain behaviors, activities, or materials in the environment, rating scales require the observer to estimate how much or what quality is present. This assignment gives the student a chance to compare the information generated by checklists and rating scales.

Part I: Using a Rating Scale

Procedure: We have seen an increased interest in children's play and play facilities during the past two decades. One of the most recent books on the subject is *Children's Play and Playgrounds* by Joe Frost and Barry Klein (Boston: Allyn and Bacon, 1979). Their book includes a playground rating system developed by the senior author. Use this scale to rate the same playground that you observed as part of Lab Assignment 25.

Playground _____ Date_____Time _____

PLAYGROUND RATING SYSTEM*

Instructions: Rate each item on a scale from 0-5. High score possible on Section I is 100 points; Section II is 50 points; and Section III is 50 points, for a possible grand total of 200 points. Divide the grand total score by 2 to obtain a final rating.

Section I. What does the playground contain?

Rate each item for degree of existence and function on a scale of 0-5 (0 = not existent; 1 = some element(s) exists but not functional; 2 = poor; 3 = average; 4 = good; 5 = all elements exist, excellent function).

_____ 1. A hard-surfaced area with space for games and a network of paths for wheeled toys.
_____ 2. Sand and sand equipment.
_____ 3. Dramatic play structures (play house(s), old car or boat with complementary equipment, such as adjacent sand and water and housekeeping equipment).
_____ 4. climbing structure(s) (with room for more than one child at a time and with a variety of entries, exits and levels).
_____ 5. Mound(s) of earth for climbing and digging.
_____ 6. Trees and natural areas (including weed areas).

*Joe L. Frost © 1977

_____ 7. Zoning to provide continuous challenge; linkage of areas, functional physical boundaries, vertical and horizontal treatment.

_____ 8. Water play areas, with fountains, pools and sprinklers.

_____ 9. Construction area with junk materials such as tires, crates, planks, boards, bricks and nails. Tools should be provided and demolition allowed.

_____ 10. An old vehicle, train, boat, car that has been made safe, but not stripped of its play value. (This item should be changed or relocated after a period of time to renew interest.)

_____ 11. Equipment for active play: A _slide_ with a large platform at the top (best if slide is built into side of a hill); _swings_ that can be used safely in a variety of ways (use of old tires as seats); _climbing trees_ (mature dead trees that are horizontally positioned); _climbing nets._

_____ 12. A large grassy area for organized games.

_____ 13. Small private spaces at the child's own scale: tunnels, niches, playhouses, hiding places.

_____ 14. Fences, gates, walls and windows that provide security for young children and are adaptable as opportunities for learning/play.

_____ 15. Natural areas that attract birds and bugs. A garden and flowers located so that they are protected from play, but with easy access for the child to tend them.

_____ 16. Provisions for the housing of pets. Pets available.

_____ 17. A transitional space from outdoors to indoors. This could be a covered play area immediately adjoining the playroom areas which will protect the children from the sun and rain and extend indoor activities to the outside.

_____ 18. Adequate protected storage for outdoor play equipment, tools for construction area, and maintenance tools. Storage can be separate, wheel toys stored next to the roadway; sand equipment near or next to the sand enclosure; tools in the workshop area. Or storage can be the lower level of the climbing structure, or separate structures attached to the building or fence. _But storage should aid in pick-up_ (that is, make it easy for children to put equipment away at the end of each play period).

_____ 19. Easy access from outdoor play areas to coats and toilets.

_____ 20. Places for adults, parents and teachers, to sit within the outdoor play areas. Shade structures with benches can provide for this as well as for seating for children.

Section II. Is the playground in good repair and relatively safe?

Rate each item for condition and safety on a scale of 0-5 (0 = not existent; 1 = exists but extremely hazardous; 2 = poor; 3 = fair; 4 = good; 5 = excellent condition and relatively safe yet presents _challenge_).

_____ 1. A protective fence next to hazardous areas (streets, etc.).

_____ 2. Eight to ten inches of noncompacted sand (or equivalent) under all climbing and moving equipment, extending through fall zones and secured by retaining wall.

_____ 3. Size of equipment appropriate to age group served.

_____ 4. Area free of litter (e.g., broken glass, rocks).

_____ 5. Moving parts free of defects (e.g., no pinch and crush points, bearings not excessively worn).

_____ 6. Equipment free of sharp edges, protruding elements, broken parts, toxic substances.

_____ 7. Swing seats constructed of soft material (e.g., rubber, canvas).

_____ 8. All safety equipment in good repair (e.g., railings, padded areas, protective covers).

_____ 9. Fixed equipment secure in ground and concrete footings recessed in ground.

_____ 10. Equipment structurally sound. No bending, warping, breaking, sinking, etc.

Section III. What should the playground do?

Rate each item for degree and quality on a scale of 0-5 (0 = not existent; 1 = some evidence but virtually nonexistent; 2 = poor; 3 = fair; 4 = good; 5 = excellent). Use the space provided for comments.

_____ 1. Encourages Play:
Inviting, easy access
Open, flowing and relaxed spaces
Clear movement from inside to outside
Appropriate equipment for the age group

_____ 2. Stimulates the Child's Senses:
Change and contrasts in scale, light, texture and color
Flexible equipment
Diverse experiences

_____ 3. Nurtures the Child's Curiosity:
Equipment that the child can change
Materials for experiments and construction

_____ 4. Allows Interaction Between the Child and the Resources:
Systematic storage which defines routines
Semi-enclosed spaces to read, work a puzzle, or be alone

_____ 5. Allows Interaction Between the Child and Other Children:
Variety of spaces
Adequate space to avoid conflicts
Equipment that invites socialization

_____ 6. Allows Interaction Between the Child and Adults:
Easy maintenance
Adequate and convenient storage
Organization of space to allow general supervision
Rest areas for adults

_____ 7. Supports the Child's Basic Social and Physical Needs:
Comfortable to the child
Scaled to the child
Free of hazards

_____ 8. Complements the Cognitive Forms of
Play Engaged in by the Child:
Functional, exercise, gross-motor, active
Constructive, building, creating
Dramatic, pretending, make believe
Organized games, games with rules

_____ 9. Complements the Social Forms of
Play Engaged in by the Child:
Solitary, private, meditative
Parallel, side-by-side
Cooperative interrelationships

_____ 10. Promotes Social and Intellectual Development:
Provides graduated challenge
Integrates indoor/outdoor activities
Involves adults in child's play
Adult-child planning
The play environment is dynamic,
continuously changing

_Part II: Comparison and Analysis of Checklists and
Rating Scales_

1. One of the problems with most rating scales is that they lack definitions of terms. Were there any terms in the scale or on the items to be rated that you either found ambiguous or did not understand fully? If so, identify which ones.

2. The SRI inventory and Joe Frost's rating scale are not comparable in that they contain different items. The SRI inventory surveys both the classroom and the playground in snapshot fashion. Frost's rating scale goes into more detail about the playground and asks the observer to make a judgment about the quality of the playground facilities. Both instruments, however, provide a means of summarizing information about the physical environment. Discuss the differences in information gathered by each _method_ (i.e., focus on the strategy itself, not the specific items on the checklist or scale).

3. Which method allows the most room for observer bias or error? What safeguards could you use to minimize this?

Comparing Different Types of Rating Scales

J. P. Guilford (1954) identified five different types of rating scales: numerical, graphic, standard, cumulated points, and forced-choice. Each kind of rating scale yields information that can be treated numerically. Scores can be tallied and data can be quantified. They make different demands on the developer and user, however. This assignment is designed to help you better understand the various kinds of rating scales and the information that they generate.

Procedure: Spend a half hour observing a teacher of young children (preschool or early elementary grades) during a group-time activity. Pay particular attention to the kinds of attention bids children make and to how the teacher responds to the children's bids for attention. At the end of your observation period, fill out the rating scales that follow. These rating scales contain items that are based on a numerical scale, graphic scale, standard scale, cumulated points scale, and a forced-choice scale.

Setting _____ Teacher_____Date _____

Part I: Numerical Scale

Rate the teacher on how he or she gets and holds the children's attention:

_____1. Waits for all children to be clearly paying attention before beginning activity.

_____2. Starts activity as soon as most of the children have gathered and are quiet.

_____3. Starts activity as soon as half of the children have gathered and are quiet.

_____4. Waits until most of the children have gathered and then signals for attention, waits a few seconds, and begins (whether all of the children are attending or not).

_____5. Starts activity by shouting over the din and waiting for it to die down.

Rate the teacher on how he or she monitors attention during activities:

_____1. Scans group regularly throughout activity to see if children are paying attention and to observe for signs of confusion or difficulty.

_____2. Scans group once or twice during the activity to see if children are paying attention and to observe for signs of confusion or difficulty.

_____3. Focuses on one particular child (or small group) throughout most of the activity.

_____4. Focuses on material (book, chalkboard, etc.) rather than on the children throughout most of the activity.

_____5. Focuses on other adults (teachers, aides, parents) throughout most of the activity.

Part II: Graphic Scale.

Rate the teacher on the variety of questions and response demands he or she makes in leading a group activity.

1. Asks a variety of questions.

                              always often occasionally seldom never

2. Goes around the group asking each child to respond in turn

                              always often occasionally seldom never

3. Comments on the children's responses.

                              always often occasionally seldom never

4. Asks children to comment on other children's responses.

                              always often occasionally seldom never

5. Asks questions before naming a child to respond.

                              always often occasionally seldom never

6. Insures that every child is invited to respond during the activity.

                              always often occasionally seldom never

Rate the teacher's methods of dealing with inattention and misbehavior on the following semantic differential graphic rating scale:

	1	2	3	4	5	6	7	
a. attends to each misbehavior								ignores misbehavior
b. eliminates disruptive behavior quickly								waits to deal with misbehavior until just short of chaos
c. redirects attention by distracting child								focuses directly on misbehavior
d. praises desirable behavior								does not use praise
e. goes on with activity								stops activity to deal with misbehavior

Part III: Standard Rating Scale.

Rate the teacher on the following scale, comparing the teacher with other teachers you have observed in the past.

	Top 5%	Top 10%	Top 25%	Top 50%	Lower 50%	Lower 25%
1. alert to children's needs						
2. spots potential problem situations						
3. attends to demands for attention						
4. attends to the quiet as well as to the demanding children						
5. models good professional behavior for staff						

Part IV: Cumulated Points

Rate the teacher on the following scale, which focuses on teacher response to disruptive children. Remember that each item acts as a separate indicator of an overall trait. Cumulated points rating scales result in a total score which is the sum or average of the items rated.

Column A	*Column B*
_____ notices problem situations early	_____ notices problem situations only after they are well underway
_____ responds quietly and firmly to child's anger	_____ raises his or her voice in response to child's anger
_____ attends almost immediately to child's bid for attention	_____ doesn't respond to child's attention bid until child has made several attempts
_____ responds promptly to noisy and persistent child	_____ tends to put off or ignore quiet child
_____ listens thoughtfully to child's message	_____ attends poorly to child's message

Part V: Forced Choice Ratings

Check *one* statement in each cluster that best describes the teacher's response to disruptive children.

When a child tugs at the teacher for attention, the teacher

_____ responds immediately, even if it means turning attention away from another child.
_____ recognizes the child's presence but lets the child wait his or her turn.
_____ asks the child to wait a moment.
_____ ignores the child until the child has repeatedly tried to get the teacher's attention.
_____ shows irritation at the child's persistence.

When the child finally gets the teacher's attention, the teacher

_____ listens attentively and focuses attention on that child.
_____ listens, but focuses visually on other children in the room.
_____ is obviously in a hurry to close the conversation with the child.
_____ allows other children to interrupt and divert attention away from the child.

Part VI: Analysis and Comparison

1. Which of the five types of rating scales did you find easiest to use in rating teacher behavior? Why was this so?

2. Which of the five types of rating scales did you find most difficult to use? Why?

3. This assignment only required a brief observation period—30 minutes. If you were going to judge teacher behavior, how long do you feel you would need to observe to have an adequate basis for making judgments? Why?

4. Are there any teacher behaviors that could easily be rated after a short period of observation? Identify those behaviors.

Chapter 10

Observation
Systems

Observation strategies began with the simple diary notations of scientifically minded parents. When groups of young children became available in lab schools for child study in the 1920s other strategies emerged. Anecdotal and running records and specimen descriptions preserved the richness of detail characteristic of narrative observations. The popularity of experimental research in child study, however, led many researchers to abandon the narrative observational strategies and develop new strategies that made quantification and analysis of data collected an easier process. The challenge for the researcher was how to collect the rich supply of detail contained in narrative descriptions in such a way that it could be managed. How could the detail be reduced to a form that made it relatively easy to analyze and use?

The answer was two-fold. One way was to sample behavior rather than describe it. This led to time and event sampling. The other was to develop observation systems that allowed the observer to use a coding system to divide behavior and events into meaningful and manageable categories. The observer recorded the ongoing behavior and then analyzed the resulting data according to some predetermined method of data analysis.

Observation systems can be built upon any type of observation strategy—narrative, sampling, or rating. Most observation systems involve time sampling, but they can use any single strategy or a combination of strategies.

The advantage of using an observation system is that the coding categories are already worked out. Reliability and validity (whether the system measures what it is supposed to measure) have already been determined, and the means of data analysis defined and refined. The observer has only to concentrate on learning the system.

Devising a Coding System

A technological development that has changed the face of observational research is the development of the computer with its vast capabilities for information storage and retrieval. But decades before the computer was available, researchers were coding responses. Ernest Horn in his study of pupils' opportunities for participation in classroom recitation (published in 1914 and copyrighted by Horn in 1915) used a circle on the seating chart or class list to identify the fact that a pupil responded by doing something. He used interlinking circles to indicate that a pupil recited more than once without the recitation of any other pupil intervening; when a pupil failed "utterly" an F was placed inside the circle or square.

Horn's research was fairly ambitious for its time. He reported that "Records were made in the classes of 229 teachers in twenty-two different schools, in nineteen different systems, in eleven different states. . . . Records were taken from the kindergarten, from each of the elementary grades, from the high school and from the college" (1915, p. 10).

Roswell C. Puckett (1928) added to and refined Horn's circle and square code by creating additional symbols using the circle and square as the basic elements. A dot inside the circle signified that the pupil raised a hand and was called on by the teacher; a dot in the circle plus a short vertical line at the bottom of the circle signified that the pupil raised a hand, was called on by the teacher, and made a single word response—and so on through 14 variations.

CATEGORIES FOR

PUCKETT SYSTEM

Roswell C. Puckett

- •   Pupil raised hand.
- ⊙   Pupil raised hand and was called on by teacher.
- ⊙   Pupil raised hand, was called on by teacher, and made a single-word response.
- ⊙-   Pupil raised hand, was called on by teacher, and made a fair response.
- ⊙   Pupil raised hand, was called on by teacher, and made a good response.
- -⊙   Pupil raised hand, was called on by teacher, and made a very good response.
- ☐   Pupil called on when he did not have hand raised.
- ☐   Pupil called on when he did not have hand raised; made a single-word response.
- ☐-   Pupil called on when he did not have hand raised; made a fair response.
- ☐   Pupil called on when he did not have hand raised; made a good response.
- -☐   Pupil called on when he did not have hand raised; made a very good response.
- ☒   Pupil called on when he did not have hand raised; made no response.
- >   Pupil asked a question.
- | Pupil spoke without being addressed by teacher.

Puckett's system was designed for use by a supervisor evaluating a secondary school teacher. His aim was "to get away from the old method of stating general impressions and to make supervision objective so that it will be of real service to the teachers in increasing their efficiency" (*Mirrors for Behavior*, 1970, Vol. B, p. 89.1–1). He then combined the coding system with a seating chart so that his tabulation "will show not only the actual distribution of questions but the nature of the responses by the pupils and the extent to which the pupils entered into the work" (89.1–2). A sample of his codes on a seating chart taken from *Mirrors for Behavior*, 1970, p. 89.4) follows:

SAMPLES OF CODES

ON A SEATING CHART

From this we can decipher a great deal of information. For example, we can tell that the class normally contained 28 children but that two were absent on the day of the observation (students #18 and #19). Four students never raised their hands (#10, 14, 26, and 28); five students asked questions (#1, 7, 15, 17, and 27) and four students spoke without being addressed by the teacher (#11, 12, 13, and 15). Student #7 made the best responses. Students #11, 15, 21, and 25 made a lot of responses but most of them were single-word responses. As we can see, a great deal of information is recorded in a very small space.

When a code is used, the observer needs to memorize it beforehand so that its use is almost automatic. The simpler the code, the less time it takes to master it. Puckett's system can be mastered in a matter of minutes. The coding system outlined by Ray Birdwhistell for recording precise nonverbal behavior or movements (see page 105) is a very complicated code and takes weeks to master.

Developing a shorthand representation for behavioral events and circumstances—creating a proper code —is a great deal easier today than it was when Horn and Puckett made their pioneer attempts to control their recording task. Perhaps part of the reason is that we are familiar with a variety of codes used in everyday life. Codes we use daily take at least two forms:

1. abbreviations: for example, F-female: M-male: Mn-Minnesota: Vt-Vermont
2. encoding narrative information in numerical form: zip codes are examples of this form of coding as are the Dewey Decimal System for the storage and retrieval of library books and the HEGIS Code (Higher Education General Information Survey) for coding academic disciplines and concentrations.

Another reason is that we now have the technology to develop computer systems designed for rapid hierarchical coding of behaviors. We can enter and store coded data that represent various dimensions of behavior as quickly as we can push the buttons. The advances in methodology and data analysis made possible by computer technology help explain the recent increase in popularity of naturalistic research and direct observation.

Observation Systems: Some Examples

Developing a coding system is just one part of developing an observational system. A spate of observational systems have been constructed in the past two to three decades. These systems are divided into two types:

1. *specific observation system*—in which only one dimension is being observed and others ignored
2. *general observation system*—in which a number of important dimensions are attended to at the same time

We will review three observation systems in this chapter. The first is a frequently used system that illustrates a *specific observation system*. The other two illustrate research and classroom applications of *general observation systems*.

1. *Flanders' Interaction Analysis System.* Interaction analysis is "a label that refers to any technique for studying the chain of classroom events in such a fashion that each event is taken into consideration" (Flanders, 1970, p. 5). Such procedures allow the researcher to measure, not simply describe, classroom behavior. The most popular such system is that developed by Ned Flanders and his associates at the University of Minnesota in the late 1950s.

Flanders was particularly interested in studying the relationship between teacher behavior and the nature of classroom interaction. In 1975, Flanders summarized the result of 20 years of research dealing with the influence of teachers on pupil attitudes. While his research covers pupils from second grade to teachers in in-service training, most of it was conducted on pupils in junior high. The specific aspect of teacher behavior that Flanders studied was teacher statements—how teachers talk to children. He chose to study teacher talk during those times of day when pupils have a chance to respond—i.e., when there is interaction between teachers and pupils. He developed a category system that accounted for every possible type of classroom interaction. His system includes seven teacher-talk categories, two pupil-talk categories, and one category to indicate silence or confusion:

Teacher Talk
1. *Accepts feeling.* Accepts and clarifies an attitude or the feeling tone of a pupil in a nonthreatening manner. Feelings may be positive or negative. Predicting and recalling feelings are included.
2. *Praises or encourages.* Praises or encourages pupil action or behavior. Jokes that release tension, but not at the expense of another individual; nodding head, or saying "Um hm?" or "go on" are included.

3. *Accepts or uses ideas of pupils.* Clarifying, building, or developing ideas suggested by a pupil. Teacher extensions of pupil ideas are included but as the teacher brings more of his own ideas into play, shift to category five.
4. *Asks questions.* Asking a question about content or procedure, based on teacher ideas, with the intent that a pupil will answer.
5. *Lecturing.* Giving facts or opinions about content or procedures; expressing *his own* ideas, giving *his own* explanation, or citing an authority other than a pupil.
6. *Giving directions.* Directions, commands, or orders with which a pupil is expected to comply.
7. *Criticizing or justifying authority.* Statements intended to change pupil behavior from nonacceptable to acceptable pattern; bawling someone out; stating why the teacher is doing what he is doing; extreme self-reference.
8. *Pupil-talk—response.* Talk by pupils in response to teacher. Teacher initiates the contact or solicits pupil statements or structures the situation. Freedom to express own ideas is limited.
9. *Pupil-talk—initiation.* Talk by pupils which they initiate. Expressing own ideas; initiating a new topic; freedom to develop opinions and a line of thought, like asking thoughtful questions; going beyond the existing structure.
10. *Silence or confusion.* Pauses, short periods of silence and periods of confusion in which communication cannot be understood by the observer (Flanders, 1970, p. 34).

Flanders classifies items #1,2,3, and 8 as *response* and items #5,6,7, and 9 as *initiation.*

Observers using the Flanders Interaction Analysis System (FIAS) must first memorize the code and then practice from 3 to 12 hours until they reach a criterion of coding at a constant rate during the observation period—about 20 to 25 tallies per minute or one tally every three seconds.

Through his research, Flanders has demonstrated that interaction patterns affect educational outcomes (in terms of both pupil attitudes and subject matter achievement). Basically, "when teachers encourage the expression of pupil ideas by supporting and accepting what the pupils say, and when they are able to combine such support with a minimum of directions and criticism, then pupils tend to like the teacher and learning activities and to have more positive perceptions of their own participation" (Flanders, 1975, p. 67). Flanders has further demonstrated that "when teachers analyze their interactions, in either preservice or inservice programs, and have a chance to plan and practice modifications, they tend to increase the ratio of supportive and acceptant statements to directive and critical statements" (p.71).

2. *SRI Classroom Observation System.* Jane Stallings and staff members at the Stanford Research Institute (no connection to Stanford University) used Flanders's system as a starting point in developing an observation system to use in evaluating Project Follow Through classrooms. Project Follow Through was established by Congress in 1967 as a means of extending Head Start interven-

tion programs into the primary grades. Twenty-two different intervention models were originally developed (many of them based on Head Start models). Stallings and her associates selected seven models to evaluate and then developed a classroom observation system to use in gathering information about how closely the classroom implementation of the model matched the sponsor's description of the model. This allowed the researchers to focus both on real and intended differences among the various models.

The SRI system was built from the Flanders system but expanded to include teacher verbalization outside of discussion groups and also to include nonverbal teacher clues. The system contains three separate instruments:

1. *Physical Environment Information,* filled out once a day to provide information on seating patterns and use of equipment and materials.
2. *Classroom Checklist,* filled out four times an hour, five hours a day for three days, yielding 60 grids per classroom. This provides a "snapshot" of the classroom at different times during the day and gives information on the type of activities occurring in the classroom and on the grouping of children and the teaching staff.
3. *Five-Minute Interaction,* filled out four times an hour, five hours a day for three days following the completion of each Classroom Checklist. It provides information about the type of interactions that occur in the classroom: who the speaker was, to whom the speaker was speaking, what the message was, and what the intention of the message was.

The combination of measures tells the observer what materials are used in the classroom, what activities occur, and what happens between teachers and children in a classroom.

The Flanders system involves a straightforward recording of 10 code numbers and takes less than a day to master. The SRI system involves many more codes to memorize plus three instrument formats to learn to use. It takes about seven days to master. The following example of the SRI format and coding system is taken from the five-minute interaction instrument. The record sheet for this instrument includes a series of 76 grids like the one below:

List of Codes

The list of codes for this instrument is as follows:

Who/To Whom	What	How
T - Teacher	1 - Command or Request	H - Happy
A - Aide	2 - Open-ended Question	U - Unhappy
V - Volunteer	3 - Response	N - Negative
C - Child	4 - Instruction,	T - Touch
D - Different Child	Explanation	Q - Question
2 - Two Children	5 - Comments, Greetings;	G - Guide/Reason
S - Small Group (3-8)	General Action	P - Punish
L - Large Group (9 up)	6 - Task-related Statement	O - Object
An - Animal	7 - Acknowledge	W - Worth
M - Machine	8 - Praise	DP - Dramatic Play/Pretend
	9 - Corrective Feedback	A - Academic
	10 - No Response	B - Behavior
	11 - Waiting	
	12 - Observing, Listening	
	NV - Nonverbal	
	X - Movement	

R - Repeat the frame
S - Simultaneous action
C - Cancel the frame

Each code word or phrase is operationally defined and examples are given to help the observer learn how to code correctly classroom behavior. According to Stallings, the five-minute interaction schedule allows the researcher to study such things as "teachers' questioning patterns, reinforcement methods, control systems, and positive and negative displays of emotions. Also, the independence, task persistence, cooperativeness, and inquiry of children . . . could be assessed" (1977, p. 34).

Stallings summarized the findings from her Follow Through study observations as follows:

Highly controlled classroom environments in which teachers used systematic instruction and a high rate of positive reinforcement contributed to higher scores in mathematics and reading. Flexible classroom environments which provided more exploratory materials and allowed for more choice on the part of the child contributed to higher scores on a test of nonverbal reasoning, lower absence rates, and a willingness on the part of children to work independently (Stallings, 1975, Abstract).

3. *APPROACH.* One of the biggest problems for ecological researchers is what to do with the masses of observational data once they are collected. Computers have greatly assisted ecological researchers. The early pioneers like Roger Barker and Herbert Wright, who worked with masses of data despite the inconvenience, are no longer alone in their research efforts in human ecology. They have been joined by a growing cadre of researchers. Two of the additions to the ecological ranks are Bettye Caldwell and Alice Honig.

Caldwell and Honig created APPROACH, an acronym for *A Procedure for Patterning Responses of Adults and Children*. APPROACH was specifically developed "for translating data from records of behavior in situ into a numerical code which is eminently suitable for computer summarization and analysis" (1969, p. 76). It is a numerical language into which ongoing behavior can be coded, summarized, and analyzed.

It follows the ecological tradition of seeking to help the researcher better understand the relationship between setting and behavior through the careful study of social behavior in natural settings. Caldwell and Honig use the specimen description observation strategy for recording data. The behavioral record is obtained by having the observer stationed near the target individual or central figure. The observer uses a tape recorder and whispers all actions, interactions, and relevant statements or stimuli within the selected setting into the microphone. Observations are scheduled for 20-30 minute chunks during times of the day most likely to provide the behavioral interactions under study. The taped information is then coded directly from the tape or a typescript is prepared as a basis for coding.

APPROACH has two major coding divisions: one for emitted behaviors, the other for settings in which the behavior occurs. The behavior code involves a five-digit numerical code that describes four components for each action:

1. the *subject*—who or what does something
2. the *predicate*—what is done
3. the *object*—toward whom or what the action is directed
4. *qualifiers* (adverbs)—that tell how or provide other supplementary information

The behavior categories are on page 238. The setting categories are on page 239. The five-digit code summarizes information about the setting, including a *setting alert* to indicate a setting change and to define characteristics of the new setting, an *activity identification* to identify the kind of activity occurring, the *geographic region* to indicate where the action is taking place, and the *supporting cast* to identify people other than the central figure present during the observation. The setting categories used by Caldwell and Honig in their studies at the Children's Center at Syracuse University are as follows:

Table 10.1 Summary of the major APPROACH Behavior Categories and the numbers assigned each in the code

BEHAVIORS

I. *Subject of Behavioral Clause* (1st digit)
0 Central Figure (CF)
1 The environment
2 Female adult
3 Female child
4 Item
5 Male child
6 Group, including CF
7 Group, excluding CF
8 Male adult
9 Setting alert

II. *Behavioral Predicates* (2d and 3d digits)

Environmental Contact (00-09)
00 Ignores
01 Attends
02 Establishes or maintains contact
03 Terminates contact
04 Scans

Information Processing (10-19)
10 Confirms
11 Shows (to) or demonstrates (for)
12 Communicates or converses
13 Writes or draws (for)
14 Reads (to)
15 Corrects or disconfirms
16 Inquires
17 Informs or teaches
18 Informs about culture
19 Role plays (with)

Food Behavior (20-24)
20 Gives food (to)
21 Takes or handles food
22 Prepares food (for)
23 Transports food (to)
24 Disorganizes with food

Manual Activities (25-29)
25 Transfers item (to or toward)
26 Takes (from) or handles item
27 Manipulates item
28 Transports item (to)
29 Throws or rolls item (to)

Negative Reinforcement (30-39)
30 Withholds sanction (from)
31 Shows discomfort
32 Expresses displeasure (to)
33 Criticizes or derogates
34 Expresses hostility
35 Interferes or restricts
36 Resists or rejects
37 Threatens or frightens
38 Assaults

Positive Reinforcement (40-49)
40 Permits or sanctions
41 Expresses solicitude
42 Shows pleasure
43 Approves, encourages
44 Expresses affection
45 Facilitates
46 Excuses
47 Bargains, promises
48 Protects, defends

Body Activities (50-59)
50 Increases or accelerates activity
51 Decreases or retards activity
52 Perioralizes
53 Acts in situ
54 Adjusts or accommodates
55 Provides kinesethetic stimulation
56 Locomotes (toward)
57 LMA's
58 Marches, dances or rhythmicizes
59 Voids or excretes

Miscellaneous (60-69)
60 Acts or occurs (in)
61 Caretakes
62 Consummates activity
63 Consummates activity, with failure
64 Disorganizes
65 Disintegrates emotionally
66 Makes music or sound patterns (by means of or to)
69 Garbled record

Control Techniques (70-79)
70 Suggests
71 Requests
72 Inhibits
73 Forbids
74 Offers

III. *Object of Behavioral Clause* (4th digit)
0-8 Same as for 1st digit
9 No information or self

IV. *Supplementary Information* (5th digit)
0 Ineptly
1 Accompanied by verbalization (or with sound if subject is 1 or 4)
2 Involving interpersonal physical contact
3 With intensity
4 In a specified manner, place, or time
5 In a manner, place, or time other than that specified
6 Imitatively
7 In continuation
8 Complexly
9 No information

Table 10.2 Summary of the major APPROACH Setting Categories and the numbers assigned each in the code

SETTINGS

I. *Setting alert* (1st digit)
9 Setting code

II. *Activity Identification* (2d and 3d digits)
00 Lunch or snack
01 Pre-nap or nap
02 Diapering or toileting or associated dressing or undressing
03 Free or unstructured activity
04 Structured learning time
05 Book or story
06 Record, singing, instrumental music or rhythm activities
07 Art, cutting, pasting
08 Gym or outdoor play
09 Transition times
10 Medical or psychological experience
11 Assembly or program
12 Open
13 Open
14 Open
15 Perceptual-motor exercises
16 Field trip
17 TV time
20 Other

III. *Geographic Region* (4th digit)
1 School
2 Home
3 Laboratory or examining room
4 Special teaching area (e.g. science corner, principal's office, etc.)
5-9 Other

IV. *Supporting Cast* (5th Digit)
0 Central figure alone
1 Mother (or mother figure) also present
2 Father (or father figure) also present
3 Mother and father (or father figure) also present
4 One other child present
5 More than one other child present
6 Non-family adult also present
7 Non-family adult or adults and child or children also present
8 One or both parents plus other adult, with or without other children
9 Other

The APPROACH system is not limited to the categories presented in Tables 10.1 and 10.2. A researcher could substitute other items or add more items to the existing categories. A major feature of the system is its adaptability for computerization.

Neither APPROACH nor the SRI system have been used as broadly as the Flanders Interaction Analysis System (FIAS). The relative recency of AP-PROACH and the SRI system is certainly a factor in their more limited use. The relative simplicity of FIAS compared to the complexity of APPROACH and the SRI system is another factor. As Caldwell states:

> . . . the technique is complicated and time-consuming and "hard to sell," and in spite of the investment of time and effort that went into developing the technique, we have used it minimally. Research technicians using the procedure must undergo something tantamount to a religious conversion as to its merits to be willing to endure the tedious coding that it requires. I personally cannot stand to do so for more than an hour at a time. Yet every time we carry out an analysis of behavior in the affective domain using an "available" rating scale, I feel suffused with guilt (Caldwell, 1977, p. 79).

The systems take time and effort to learn, but the data payoff is well worth the effort.

Adapting Observation Systems

Observation systems offer the researcher a convenient, well-developed, validated tool for observation. They do not, however, always meet the specific needs of the researcher. Sometimes they have to be extended or adapted for a specific purpose.

One method of altering an existing system is to subscribe it. In subscripting, a single category is subdivided into additional categories. This is in effect what Puckett did with Horn's system in the 1920s.

Another method of altering an existing system is to extend or expand it. We will use several expansions of the Flanders Interaction Analysis System to illustrate this form of alteration.

John B. Hough expanded on Flanders' 10 categories and developed 16:

Indirect Teacher Verbal Influence
1. Affective clarification and acceptance
2. Praise and reward
3. Cognitive and skill clarification and acceptance
4. Teacher questions
5. Response to questions

Teacher Direct Influence
6. Initiates information or opinion
7. Corrective feedback
8. Requests and commands
9. Criticism and rejection

Student Verbal Behavior
10. Elicited responses
11. Emitted responses
12. Student questions

Silence
13. Directed practice or activity
14. Silence and contemplation
15. Demonstration

Nonfunctional Behavior
16. Confusion and irrelevant behavior *(Mirrors for Behavior*, Summary Volume, 1970, pp. 9.1-9.4)

Other researchers have used the Flanders Interaction Analysis System as a starting point for creating an adaptation that extends the original purpose of the Flanders system. One such adaptation is COMIC (Cognitive Operations Monitored in the Classroom) developed by John R. Anderson and Richard M. Bingham (1970, 80). COMIC

was used to investigate inquiry behaviors of students interacting within small groups and with their teacher. The basic instrument contains nine cognitive categories which were designed to be used simultaneously with an adaptation of the Flanders Interaction Analysis Categories by using a three-digit code. The first two digits represent Flanders's categories and the third digit is used for the COMIC categories. Coding is usually done from tapescripts of verbal exchanges in the classroom, although the system has been used for on-the-spot coding.

Column One: Modification of Flanders

1. Teacher accepts feeling
2. Teacher praises
3. Teacher accepts ideas
4. Teacher asks questions
5. Teacher gives opinion
6. Teacher gives direction
7. Teacher criticizes
8. Pupil response
9. Pupil initiated talk

Column Two: Modification of Flanders
1. Student expresses or accepts feeling
2. Student gives praise
3. Student accepts ideas
4. Student asks
5. Student gives opinion
6. Student gives direction
7. Student criticizes

8. Decision by class groups
9. Noninquiry talk by class members (pupil or teacher)

Column Three: COMIC Categories
—Unclassified Inquiry Statements
1. Factual information or single idea
2. Comparisons and generalizations
3. Predicting and planning
4. Inquiry into inquiry operations
5. Inquiry into inquiry attitudes
6. Present procedures to obtain knowledge
7. Sensory observations
8. Formulating or identifying question or discrepant event
9. Assessing content, goal, or procedure

Special
001 Pupil exchange
010 Silence or confused state
020 Disruption

The Flanders Interaction Analysis instrument has been extended and adapted for use with teacher-group communication research in an attempt to develop information on a teacher's style. Thomas Good and Jere Brophy (1971) suggest that the individual student could become the unit of analysis rather than the class. The authors cite Horn's focus on individual pupil's patterns in classroom recitation patterns and indicate that several early researchers in the area of classroom interaction also focused on the child rather than on the teacher. Horn wrote:

The final test for any educational procedure whether it be making, administering, or teaching the course of study, is its effect on individual pupils in the school . . . the author has felt many times the need of definite knowledge, with regard to the exact nature of the practice in meeting this difficulty of reaching the individual child (1915, p. 1).

Years of work in the area of defining and describing and testing for individual differences also created questions about what a teacher could do to meet individual needs within a class group. When researchers began to look at teacher behaviors, the tendency was to treat the class as a pupil unit. Good and Brophy argue that to treat the class as a unit overlooks the fact that teachers interact differently with different pupils within a group and that these interactions often affect group—as well as individual—behavior. They also feel that information of value can and should be developed on individual pupil's interactions as well as on teacher interactions. For example, they point out that with the emergence of behavior modification techniques, attention must be focused on the individual pupil in order to develop those perceptions required for planning an appropriate behavior modification prescription. Some educators feel that the kind of information now being developed for children with special problems should be developed for all children so that all teacher-pupil interactions can be made more productive.

Jane Stallings extended the Flanders system to look at the entire interaction system operating within the classroom. She added categories to include nonverbal communication and developed two companion instruments to provide a total classroom picture. Since she also wanted the protocols or record sheets to be easy to score, she changed the coding procedure.

All four observation systems just cited started with Flanders as a base, as have literally dozens of other systems. Some, like John Hough's system are easily recognizable as a Flanders expansion. Others, like Jane Stallings' SRI system, look totally different. The purpose and needs of the researcher determine the amount of alteration needed. The system should be as simple as possible and still meet the needs of the researcher. Richard Holm offers good advice regarding the coding format for observation systems:

As the recording technique becomes more complex, it increases initial development time, probability of data loss, and number of areas of expertise required to maintain the system, so increases in complexity should not be considered lightly. Initial setup time for a digital keyboard system, including the development of computer programs to summarize and combine trials, is several months, whereas setup time for a checklist system can be only a few days. Two advantages of the more complex recording methods are relative ease of handling large volumes of data once the system is operational, and added flexibility in both the type and level of data analysis possible. In general, the adopted recording technique should be the simplest one that will meet the research needs and *proven* resources available for electronic and computer assistance (Holm, 1978, p. 99).

Guidelines for Developing Observation Systems

For researchers interested in using or creating a system of their own, there are criteria that have been developed to serve as guidelines. John Herbert and Carol Attridge (1975) have identified 33 criteria which observation systems should meet. They have sorted these into three types:

1. Identifying Criteria: information which enables the user to select the correct instrument for his purpose (6 items).
2. Validity Criteria: information which enables the user to decide whether the instrument represents accurately and consistently the events it claims it describes (15 items). This category includes such subcategories as item characteristics, inference, context, observer effect, reliability, and validity procedures.
3. Practicality Criteria: Pertains to the administration of the instrument, to the ease with which it is used and the results disseminated (12 items). The category includes as subcategories instrument items, observers, and collection and recording of data.

Bettye Caldwell provides some additional considerations relating to practicality criteria. Based on her experience in developing APPROACH, she offers the following suggestions for specific requirements of the coding procedure:

1. The system should not only describe the behavior of the central figure of the observation but also report all the significant behaviors directed to the central figure, or even salient behaviors that occur in his vicinity and to which he could be expected to react.
2. The system should adequately handle the behavior of a person in any type of social grouping (monads, diads, polyads) and any type of social setting (informal play, formal learning situations, mealtimes, etc.).
3. The same behavior categories should apply to all members of the social grouping (avoid separate categories for children/adults).
4. The system should permit detailed analyses of sequences of behavior, both between and within individuals.
5. The system should be able to describe the contribution to the stimulus field made by nonhuman objects as well as by people.
6. The system should be convertible to a simple numerical code for rapid reading, summarization, and data analysis by computers . . . the direct number designation has proven no more difficult to memorize than an alphabetical code and has saved one step in the transmission of information to the computer.
7. The system should not be too complicated to be learned fairly quickly and to be used and coded reliably (1969, p. 77-79).

Summary

The growing popularity of experimental child psychology in the 1920s and 1930s led many researchers to abandon narrative observational strategies and develop observational methods of sampling behavior. The major drawback to the narrative methods was the problem of reducing the masses of data collected to some manageable form.

The combination of coding data during the recording of observations and computer technology for data storage and analysis made direct observation feasible once again. As researchers sought to improve the old observation strategies, observation systems developed.

Two kinds of systems are identified and described:

1. *specific observation systems*, exemplified by the Flanders Interaction Analysis System (FIAS), in which a single dimension is focused on
2. *general observation systems*, exemplified by Caldwell and Honig's APPROACH and Stallings's SRI observation systems, in which a number of important dimensions are attended to at the same time

Observation systems have the advantage of having the coding and scoring systems already worked out, reliability and validity established, and usually the benefit of others' experience with the system. They can be used as they are or subscribed or expanded to suit specific purposes.

Some guidelines for using or creating an observational system are given as well as suggestions specific to the coding procedure itself.

Suggestions for Further Readings

Caldwell, Bettye M. A new "approach" to behavioral ecology. In John P. Hill, ed., *Minnesota Symposia on Child Psychology*, vol. 2. Minneapolis: The University of Minnesota Press, 1969. Provides a description of the development of the APPROACH system, its relation to ecological psychology, and how it can be adapted for other needs.

Flanders, Ned A. *Analyzing Teacher Behavior*. Reading, Mass: Addison-Wesley, 1970. This book is devoted to interaction analysis as a means of studying teaching behavior. It details the Flanders Interaction Analysis System and how to use or adapt it. It contains a good section on computer assisted encoding and decoding and the last half of the book is devoted to questions, strategies, and research on teacher behaviors.

Herbert, John, and Carol Attridge. A guide for developers and users of observation systems and manuals. *American Educational Research Journal*. (Winter 1975), 12 (1), 1-20. A detailed outline of guidelines for observation system developers. The guide is a useful list of considerations for preplanning and of points to check for inclusions and clarity in the final stages of planning.

Medley, D.M., and H.E. Mitzel, Measuring classroom behavior by systematic observation. In N.L. Gage, ed., *Handbook of Research in Teaching*. Skokie, Ill.: Rand-McNally, 1963. An excellent review chapter on the observation methods and systems that have been developed for measuring classroom behavior. The statistical discussions included make the reading tough going for the nonstatistically minded, but the chapter is a must for those who intend to develop their own methods or systems.

Sackett, Gene P. ed. *Observing Behavior: Theory and Applications in Mental Retardation*, vol. I; *Data Collection and Analysis Methods*, vol. II. Baltimore: University Park Press, 1978. While Volume I focuses specifically on theory and applications in mental retardation, the discussion of ethological and ecological approaches to understanding behavior will be helpful to all researchers and observers. Volume II concerns identification and solution of problems encountered in performing observation research under either laboratory of field conditions. It contains the most recent information about system development (many advances have been made since 1975) and is a must for the serious researcher.

Simon, Anita, and E. Gil Boyer, *Mirrors for Behavior*. Philadelphia: Research for Better Schools, 1967-1974. A summary of existing observation systems. The first six volumes came out in 1967 and reviewed 26 instruments; the next eight volumes, published in 1970, reviewed 53 instruments, and an additional volume provided a summary. In 1970, two supplemental volumes were published covering 13 instruments and in 1974 additional publication brought the total number of systems covered to 99. *Measures of Maturation* by E. Gil Boyer, Anita Boyer, and Gail Karafin, focused on observation systems available for use with young children. It was published in three volumes in 1973 and reviews 73 systems.

Stallings, Jane A. *Learning To Look*. Belmont, Ca.: Wadsworth, 1977. A how-to observation manual based on the SRI system developed for Follow Through. Stallings takes readers through a series of exercises designed to help them gain competence with the system and also to alert them to the benefits of analyzing classroom interactions. A very readable and useful manual.

Weinberg, Richard A., and Frank H. Wood, eds. *Observation of Pupils and Teachers in Mainstream and Special Education Settings: Alternative Strategies*. Reston, Va.: Council for Exceptional Children, 1975. An excellent overview of four approaches to observation: interaction analysis, behaviorist, ecological, and ethological. While the book does not focus specifically on observation systems, it describes the theoretical and applicative approaches of each of the perspectives and includes good discussions of the use of systems.

Developing and Using Coding Symbols

A number of recording aids can be developed by an observer to make the task of detailing events and behavior easier. One thing is to streamline the recording sheet and premark as many recording aids (like time frames) as possible. Another is to develop a set of symbols or a code to be used as a shorthand system of making notes. Your task in this assignment is to work out a coding system for recording parental discipline techniques.

Procedure: We know that many parents discipline their children differently in public than they do at home. Children know that too, and sometimes take advantage of the opportunity to "get their own way." Your task is to develop a coding system for recording parental discipline techniques used in public places. Select a local fast food service or family restaurant for the setting for this observation.

1. Identify and operationally define the various parental discipline techniques you would expect to find in a public eatery.

2. Outline the coding system you would use to record your observations.

3. Use your coding system in a 30-minute observation. You will need to decide what observational strategy you want to use—specimen description, time sampling, event sampling, etc. Identify the strategy you will use and briefly state your reason for selecting it. Then compose a recording sheet and attach your completed observation with this assignment.

4. Identify any changes or modifications that you would make in your operational definitions or your coding system as a result of your observation.

Chapter 11

Selecting a
Strategy

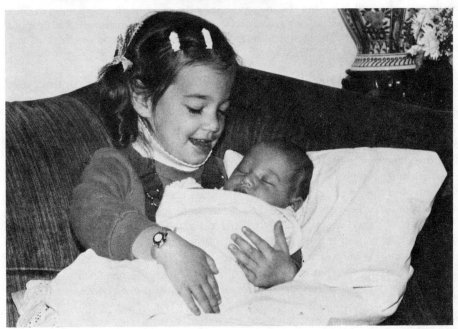

Any behavior or event can be studied through observation, but not all behaviors can be studied by all of the observational strategies we have discussed. Now that you have learned about each of the strategies and have had some practice in developing and using them, how do you decide which strategy to use? There are some obvious guidelines, like the fact that time sampling is appropriate only for behaviors that are easily observable and that are regularly or frequently occurring. Other guidelines are less obvious, like the fact that in research, specimen descriptions are probably best for hypothesis generating while time and event sampling are probably best for hypothesis testing. The table on pages 252–253 is designed to summarize some of the important information about each strategy. The observation interval, material covered, recording technique and analysis procedure columns are adapted from a table presented by Wright in his 1960 review of observation methods. Wright's original list of strategies has been expanded to include anecdotal records, running records, and checklists.

The various observational strategies can be divided into three major groups according to their basic purpose or function. The *narrative methods* are all designed to reproduce behavioral events as they naturally occur. The observer records the observations and then classifies, sorts, and analyzes them after the fact. The *sampling methods* do not preserve the original sequence of behavior in detail the way the narrative methods do. Instead they sample selected aspects of behavior according to predetermined criteria. The observer does a good deal of preparation prior to the observation. This usually includes selecting and defining the behaviors to be observed and deciding on what structure or format to use during the observation. The *rating methods* require that the observer not only observe but also judge behavior.

The *observation interval* refers to how the behavior stream is divided during observation. As Wright says:

The behavior of a person is a lifelong continuum. It is in the nature of a stream that can never be seen in its entirety. To observe it, therefore, one has to divide it into observable lengths. One can look in on the stream, say, once a day for an hour, once an hour for a minute, for as long as a quarrel or a greeting lasts, or from awakening time to bedtime of a day through as many hours, minutes, quarrels, greetings, or days as one may choose (1960, p. 73).

Some methods require the observer to record the behavior stream continuously or for the duration of a specific event; others allow the observer to impose a predetermined control on the observation interval—like a time frame.

Material covered refers to what behavior or events the observer focuses on and how much of the behavior or event the observer tries to record. Some methods allow the observer to impose some sort of structure on the observation through preselection of categories, definition of behaviors, precoded recording formats and control of observation time. Other methods are controlled by the behavior; the observer records everything he or she can for as long as the behavior lasts or, in the case of diary descriptions and anecdotal records, makes complete recordings when something noteworthy happens.

The *recording techniques* are designed to fit the different sampling plans or methods of coding the material. Time sampling allows the observer to focus on preselected aspects of behavior; the recording technique provides for on-the-spot coding of those selected dimensions of behavior. Diary descriptions, on the other hand, focus on developmental changes. The recording technique provides for regular biographical notations. The observer is free to record as the event or behavior is occurring, when he or she has a free minute, or at the end of the day.

The *major advantages and major disadvantages* columns highlight the chapter discussions of these topics. They do not provide an exhaustive list, but rather identify major points to keep in mind when trying to decide which method is best suited to your needs and purpose.

The *analysis procedure* column will mainly be of concern to researchers. The procedures are designed to fit the different sampling plans and basically either call for classification and interpretation or scoring and statistical analysis.

The *classroom uses* column identifies some of the more common ways that the various strategies can be used in the classroom. Some methods readily lend themselves to classroom use either because of their recording flexibility or because they do not require extensive training before use. This does not mean that other methods cannot be used in the classroom. It does mean, however, that the classroom teacher first needs to be comfortable with the method so that it can easily and readily be used and, second, that the teacher needs to know when to fit this kind of observation strategy into the busy teaching day. Diary descriptions, anecdotal records, checklists, and rating scales can all be recorded at the end of the day when the children have gone home and the teacher has time that is not likely to be interrupted. The wise teacher will not eliminate the other methods from his or her observational repertoire just because they require on-the-spot recording, however. Ten to fifteen minutes a day spent in time-sampling observations can yield rich results in assessing easily observable behaviors such as group activity level. Time sampling is also the easiest and quickest way to gather information about presence or absence of behavior—like cooperation or frequency of occurrence of behaviors—like inattention. One of the major benefits of gathering this kind of information is that it provides a check for your own perceptions. You may feel that a certain child is twice as active as anyone else in class when in fact he is not. Knowing that he is not is important in viewing and thus treating that child properly, and in identifying what you are reacting to.

Two of the strategies that we presented are very closely releated to each other. Running records and specimen descriptions both require on-the-spot continuous recording of behavior. The major difference is that specimen descriptions require predetermined criteria while running records do not, and specimen descriptions require an uninvolved observer—someone who does not have any responsibility for the individuals being observed. Running records allow the classroom teacher to snatch a few minutes and record what is happening. If a child interrupts in the process, the teacher notes it and continues recording when the interruption has been handled.

The narrative methods are often used to gather information on single individuals while the sampling methods are more frequently used to gather group data. This is in part a function of the history of their development. Diary descriptions were heavily used before groups of children became available. Time and event sampling were designed specifically to allow researchers to study groups of children. However, all of the methods can be used for both individual and

Table 11.1 Summary of Observation Strategies

Taxonomy	Strategy	Observation Interval	Material Covered	Recording Technique
Narrative Methods	Diary Descriptions	More or less regular day-to-day intervals	Developmental changes as they occur	Itemization of growth changes (can be recorded after the event), narrative summary
	Anecdotal Records	Sporadic intervals	Whatever seems noteworthy	Brief description of event (can be recorded after the event)
	Running Records	Continuous behavior sequences	On-the-spot records of behavior as it is occurring	On-the-spot sequential narration
	Specimen Descriptions	Continuous behavior sequences	"Everything" of ongoing behavior and the situation or setting	On-the-spot detailed sequential narration
Sampling Methods	Time Sampling	Intermittent short and uniform time intervals	Selected aspects of behavior or situation or both	On-the-spot coding
	Event Sampling	Event duration	Specified class of behavioral events	On-the-spot coding or narration or both
	Checklists	Can be intermittent or regular depending on purpose	Selected aspects of behavior or situation or both	Checks occurrence of behaviors (can be recorded after the fact)
Rating Methods	Rating Scales	Continuous behavior sequences	Selected aspects of behavior or situation or both	Ratings based on cumulative direct observation

Major Advantages	Major Disadvantages	Analysis Procedure	Major Classroom Uses
Record of developmental changes	Limited cases; costly in time and money	Classification and interpretive study	Document development or changes of individual or group
Can select topical focus or note things of interest; flexibility and informality of recording	Lack of continuity	Classification and interpretive study or coding, scoring and statistical analysis	Teacher training, case studies, study of selected behaviors
Maintains original sequence of events; record can be reviewed again and again	Costly in time and money; data reduction	Interpretive study or coding, scoring and statistical analysis	Teacher training, case studies
Describes behavior as it occurs and its environment; richness of detail; record can be reviewed again and again	Costly in time and money; data reduction; requires more training than running record	Same as Running Record	Case studies; classroom interaction; field studies
Easy to record, code, and analyze; can sample a larger number of individuals; greater control over what is observed; useful in determining frequency of occurrence	Limited to frequently occurring behaviors; loss of detail; loss of permanent record of events and actions; categories can bias observation; requires training to use	Scoring and statistical analysis	Recording presence/absence; frequency and/or duration of behavior
Reduces observation time; easy to record, code and analyze; structures data into natural units of behavior and situation	Have to wait for the event to occur	Scoring and statistical analysis	Study of selected behaviors; case studies, field studies
Ease of developing and using	Lack of detail; tells little about causes of behavior	Scoring and statistical analysis	Evaluation; recording presence/absence of behavior
Ease of developing and using; can use with wide range of behaviors; requires a minimum of training	Rater errors and rater bias; ambiguity of terms; tells little about causes of behavior	Scoring and statistical analysis	Evaluation

group observations. Your own needs and purposes will determine which strategy is most appropriate.

Anecdotal and running records have another important classroom use. Originally designed as teacher training techniques, these observation strategies provide an idea vehicle for helping student teachers, assistants, aides, and parents to learn more about how children think, learn, and behave and how the classroom itself functions as a learning environment.

Naturalistic and Experimental Research

Observation has long been the cornerstone of scientific inquiry. The natural sciences have traditionally used direct observation as a starting point in their search for meaning. Anthropologists, biologists, geologists, physicists, and astronomers have observed phenomena through microscopes, telescopes, and with the naked eye, and in observing they have learned about the properties, characteristics, and behaviors of what they watched.

Until computer simulations made it possible to "test" out the effect of different movements in the heavens, astronomy was totally dependent on direct observation as the source for gathering information. Even with the assistance of sophisticated computers, astronomy remains essentially an observational science.

Cultural anthropology also benefits from technology; recording by long-hand can now be supplemented with recording on film to supply detailed descriptions of events and behaviors. But like astronomy, anthropology also remains an observational science.

Psychology has been less tied to direct observation, preferring instead the experimental method as its chief means of collecting information. From the beginning, psychologists have devoted more of their energies to controlling, manipulating, and doing things to their subjects than to directly observing natural behavior in the natural environment. In 1967, Herbert Wright wrote:

The first psychological scientists worked in laboratories where, as new practitioners of the experimental method, they created special environments for their subjects. The experimenter supplied and arranged exterior conditions to suit his problem and then recorded the behavioral effects of these conditions. Until today, moreover, this model of manipulative control over the environmental determinants of behavior has largely ruled the scope as well as the procedures of psychological research. Psychologists have not often ventured as scientists into naturally occurring environments. They have not often sought to record and examine the characteristics and the behavioral effects of exterior conditions that nature and society create. In short, for whatever reasons, . . . psychology lacks a developed ecology of human behavior . . . Psychology appears to stand alone as a science without a substantial descriptive, naturalistic, ecological side (1967, pp. 1-3).

The push for experimental research started early. In 1898, in *Animal Learning*, Edward L. Thorndike wrote:

In abandoning the old method one ought to seek above all to replace it by one which will not only tell more accurately *what they do,* and give the much-needed information *how they do it,* but also inform us *what they feel* while they act. To remedy these defects experiment must be substituted for observation and the collection of anecdotes (Herrnstein and Boring, 1965, p. 538).

The "old method" to which Thorndike referred was the recording of direct observations, which was THE technique used by the early researchers of human and animal behavior and perhaps best illustrated by the baby biographies or diary descriptions written at the turn of the century. Thorndike and others complained of several defects in this procedure: too few cases to warrant generalizations, no repetition of observations, uncontrolled conditions, and no previous history of the subject.

They felt that a researcher should control as many variables as possible. To explain why a child behaved or learned in a particular way, they felt that causes or influences on that behavior or learning should be regulated by the researcher. It was reasoned that if only one factor or variable at a time were changed or manipulated, then resulting behavioral changes or reactions could be attributed to that variable. This *experimental method* requires the researcher to experiment with, rather than simply observe, the subject in natural surroundings.

Many early child-study researchers were interested in cataloging physical, sensory, and language development, which could easily be studied through direct observation. But as overt behavior claimed more and more attention, the difficulties of a study limited to naturalistic observation alone became obvious. B.F. Skinner in his *Science and Human Behavior* (1953) expressed strong reservations about the use of traditional observational techniques in the study of overt behavior, and by the time he wrote these comments, experimental studies were overwhelmingly more often done than simple observation alone:

Behavior is a difficult subject matter, not because it is inaccessible, but because it is extremely complex. Since it is a process, rather than a thing, it cannot easily be held still for observation. It is changing, fluid and evanescent, and for this reason it makes great technical demands upon the ingenuity and energy of the scientist (1953, p. 15).

By the time Harold Stevenson wrote his Introduction to the *Sixty-second Yearbook of the National Society for the Study of Education: Child Psychology* in 1963, experimental child psychology was firmly established as the major approach to child study:

Child psychology of the past decade differs greatly from that of earlier years. Longitudinal studies, observational methods, and a developmental orientation have largely been replaced or supplemented by short-term experimental studies of the effects of particular variables on child behavior (1963, p.2).

Although experimentalists from Thorndike to Stevenson were advocating experimental methods, researchers in the field of child study did not totally abandon the "old method" of direct observation in naturalistic settings. Some researchers simply found that experimental methods were less suitable for their subjects. Clinical psychologists and child psychologists studying preschool children found these "uncooperative subjects" (Hutt and Hutt, 1970) could best be studied in naturalistic rather than experimental settings. These young children and individuals with special problems had limited abilities to interact with researchers; they often had difficulty understanding the experimenter's instructions and their responses were unreliable.

An ethical issue also emerged with experimental laboratory studies. One could not intentionally abuse or abandon children to study the effects of child abuse or abandonment on behavior and development. In studying the effects of maternal deprivation, Ainsworth stated the problem as follows:

The experimental method, the backbone of laboratory research, has limited applicability to the study of maternal deprivation. Once the hypothesis had been put forward that prolonged deprivation experiences in early childhood may have lasting adverse effects upon subsequent development, it was out of the question to expose young children experimentally to deprivation in order to test the hypothesis (1966, p. 297).

Other psychologists felt that experimental methods were artificial and gave the researcher little insight into real-life interactions and reactions. They felt that the laboratory findings did not necessarily relate to similar situations in the natural environment. Nikolaas Tinbergen wrote:

It has been said that, in its haste to step into the twentieth century and to become a respectable science, Psychology skipped the preliminary descriptive stage that other natural sciences had gone through, and so was soon losing touch with the natural phenomena (in Hutt and Hutt, 1970, p. 4).

In 1970, S.J. Hutt and Corinne Hutt pointed out the fact that in carefully controlling everything in our experimental studies we could have reached the point where we would be able to generalize our findings to nothing but laboratory situations, leaving us with little to say or predict about behavior in the real world. Richard Brandt says, "For the most part, only the anthropologist and sociologist know something about life in ghettos and suburbs, factories and offices, stores and homes, churches and schools" (1972, p. 3). Hutt and Hutt estimated that over 95 percent of our total information about how human beings behave is based on experimental studies in which one or two responses to carefully controlled stimuli are taken to be representative of a whole constellation of behaviors. This does not mean that the data from experimental studies are erroneous; it does imply that verification of many of the theories developed from those experimental studies must await observational studies of those behaviors in natural as well as in laboratory situations.

More recently, Robert B. McCall has challenged the experimental method directly:

The axioms of the experimental method have served general psychology well, and they have provided developmentalists with much useful information. Certainly no one would want to exclude this approach from our discipline. But developmental psychology has embraced this attitude so completely that the experimental method now dictates rather than serves the research questions we value, fund, and pursue; as a result the process of development as it naturally transpires in children growing up in actual life circumstances has been largely ignored. . . . Bronfenbrenner (1974), for example, has charged that our discipline is the science of the influence of one strange environmental factor or one strange person on one isolated behavior of a single child placed in a largely artificial context.

. . . We rarely take the time to keep our experimental hands off a behavior long enough to make systematic descriptive observations in naturalistic settings of the several dimensions and circumstances of the behavior we wish to study. . . . Developmental psychologists should accord description the esteem other disciplines do because much has been learned at its hand: consider the theory of evolution, the plate theory of continental drift, and our knowledge of the early evolution of Homo sapiens. Paleontology, geology, and astronomy seem to be alive and well without manipulating fossils, continents, or heavenly bodies, and we might look into our own backyard at Jean Piaget to observe the impact detailed naturalistic description can have on a discipline even when the maximum number of subjects is only three (1977, pp. 334–337).

For fifty years naturalistic research has been "out of favor," taking second place to experimental research and then third place as tests and measurements became increasingly popular. The last decade, however, has seen a resurgence of interest in naturalistic research.

There are probably several reasons for this shift toward observation in a naturalistic setting and away from the laboratory situation or the manipulated environment—physical or psychological. One is the influence of ethologists whose productive speculations about animal and human behavior based on observations in naturalistic settings have begun to intrigue us. Nikolaas Tinbergen summarizes the current work in human ethology as follows:

I felt what is now just beginning to happen in human ethology is reminiscent of what occurred in the later 'twenties and early 'thirties to the science of animal behaviour; a new type of research worker is busy building the foundations of a science, by returning, with renewed attention and interest in detail, to the basic task of observation and description of the natural phenomena that have to be understood. . . . Rather than extrapolating interpretations from animals to man, a growing number of young ethologists have themselves begun to collect factual information about Man's behaviour, using ethological methods. . . . Working 30 years later than the early animal ethologists, they are naturally doing so with more sophistication (Preface to Blurton-Jones, 1972, pp. viii–ix).

A second reason for the rise in naturalistic research is the growing popularity of ecological psychology. For years Roger Barker and Herbert Wright and their students were lonely voices advocating ecological methods of research. Gradually the ranks have increased as researchers like Bettye Caldwell and Urie Bronfenbrenner have championed the ecological cause. Educators have found the ecological approach particularly well suited for the study of classroom interactions. As the anthropology of education and the ecology of education have gained popularity, so have observational studies of classroom behavior and classroom interactions.

A third factor influencing the renewal of interest in naturalistic settings is the extension of preschool care and education downward to infancy, where many of our laboratory techniques for the study of older preschoolers won't work. A fourth reason is that we have developed an impressive array of technological tools to help us with the arduous recording task: video and sound tape, for example. And the computer helps us deal with masses of data generated in this kind of observational research. A fifth reason may be that there are more safeguards for children who are used as research subjects in recent years, which have turned more researchers' attention toward natural rather than engineered situations requiring approval and permission from parents. And sixth, it just might be that naturalistic observation is an idea whose time has come—again.

Richard M. Brandt makes a strong statement for this viewpoint in his book, *Studying Behavior in Natural Settings:*

> Behavioral science research methodology has reached a point in its development where, despite the greater number of uncontrolled variables, naturalistic investigation should match, if not surpass, laboratory research in both quality and quantity (1972, p. v).

One effect of the move back to direct observation and away from experimental manipulation is a parallel move away from quantification to the more qualitative descriptions of behavior. In analyzing the problem of research in the human sciences, ethologist Konrad Lorenz differentiated between the study of inorganic and living systems and deplored the all too prevalent reliance on quantification to the virtual exclusion of descriptive analysis. He wrote: "I am convinced that approaching the urgent problems of humanity by quantifying methods *alone* is just plain stupid" (1975, p. 177). He continued:

> One of the most disastrous consequences of regarding the whole universe, nonliving and living, as nothing but homogeneous, quantifiable material lies in the fact that this kind of philosophy leads to the ultimate outrage of attempting to quantify the unquantifiable: human emotions. As a very witty reduction to the absurd, my wife used to answer my very silly question, how much she loved me, by saying: "eight" (1975, p. 179).

Today, many researchers are attempting to combine the best aspects of naturalistic and experimental methods by creating a "natural environment" in which certain facts can be controlled in a manner that appears natural rather than artificial to the subject. For example, Nancy Smothergill, Fran Olson, and Shirley Moore (1967) wanted to determine the effects of teacher verbalization style on children's learning. They divided day-care children into two similar groups, each of which met for an hour of special activities each day. The children perceived the group as a normal part of their school day. The researchers, however, were able to control the situation by having the same teachers teach exactly the same curriculum to both groups. The only difference was that the teachers used an elaborated verbalization style with one group of children and a directive style with the other group. Pre- and post-tests of different dimensions of learning allowed them to assess the effect of the teacher's verbal style on those learning behaviors.

This kind of creative engineering of a "natural" environment in which factors which are thought to be important influences on the way behavior under investigation can be controlled may prove to be the most productive method of testing our theories and hypotheses. It avoids some of the major criticisms of direct observation and allows for safer generalization of the findings beyond the artificial laboratory situation.

Epilogue

In the Introduction to this book we quoted Katherine Read who said that "the first and the continuing task of every student of child development is to learn to observe and record observations of child behavior." In the past ten chapters you have read about the different observational strategies used in child study and you have completed assignments designed to help you sharpen your observational skills. The fact that you are now at the end of the book does not mean that you have learned all that there is to know about observational child study. If you have been conscientious about your work, you will have a good beginning, but only a beginning. As Read said, "It is not easy to learn to see objectively and in depth, to record one's observations, and finally to organize and interpret them. . . ."

When you have finished the book, you should understand that observing and recording human behavior is indeed a challenging task. Much of what we see cannot be measured and quantified, despite our desire to do so. This does not mean that these qualities or factors are not important or do not exist. It simply means that in our study of a human being, we will be using every available strategy—plus our own good judgment. More than an accurate eye is required from a teacher and the researcher. It is hoped that the observer will also have a perceptive eye as well. In 1972, Ned O'Gorman wrote in *The Wilderness and the Laurel Tree:*

Sit down now and then and watch the children, write down what you see, bring it home and think about what you have seen. A teacher will learn about children by watching them first of all; not by reading about them or talking to experts about them (pp. 6–7).

What you do with children is of great importance. We are firmly convinced that the more you observe children, and the more you know about how to observe carefully, objectively, and thoroughly, the more you will understand the children, yourself, and your interactions with them.

Summary

Any behavior or event can be studied through observation, but not all behaviors can be studied observationally. This chapter provides a table designed to summarize the following information about each strategy: observation interval required, material covered, recording techniques, major advantages and disadvantages, analysis procedure, and classroom uses. It is important for the teacher or researcher to be familiar with the properties of each observational strategy in order to select the strategy best suited to particular needs and purposes.

The last decade has witnessed a renewed interest in naturalistic research. Direct observation is the cornerstone of naturalistic research. The history of the continuing battle between experimentalists and naturalists is briefly reviewed ending in a discussion of the reasons why naturalistic research is once again "in

vogue." These reasons include the rise in popularity of human ethology and ecological psychology, the move away from quantitative methods of research to qualitative methods, interest in classroom interaction, interest in infant development, the development of technical tools to assist the observer, and increased safeguards in research with human subjects.

Suggestions for Further Reading

Some of the books identified in earlier chapters provide good overviews of direct methods of observation and are worth rereading now that you have more information about observation. The ones that we feel are particularly good reviews are:

Brandt, R.M. *Studying Behavior in Natural Settings.* New York: Holt, Rinehart and Winston, 1972.
Hutt, S.J., and C. Hutt. *Direct Observation and Measurement of Behavior.* Springfield, Ill.: Charles C. Thomas, 1970.
Kerlinger, F. N. *Foundations of Behavioral Research.* 2d ed. New York: Holt, Rinehart and Winston, 1973; Chapter 31.
Wright, H.F. Observational Child Study. In P.H. Mussen, ed., *Handbook of Research Methods in Child Development.* New York: Wiley, 1960, pp. 71-139.

Several recently published articles cogently state the case for more naturalistic methods of research. Two of particular interest are:

Bronfenbrenner, U. Developmental research, public policy, and the ecology of childhood. *Child Development,* 1974, 45, 1-5.

McCall, R.B. Challenges to a science of developmental psychology. *Child Development,* 1977, 48, 333-344.

Classroom Observations

The classroom teacher can use observation in a variety of ways. It is a useful means of getting to know children at the beginning of the year, of describing their learning styles, patterns of interactions, and use of time. It is a means of assessment and evaluation and an important tool for case studies and referrals. We have identified some classroom questions or problems. Your task is to select the observation procedure most appropriate for answering or solving each.

Procedure: Identify the observation strategy you would use to study each of the following questions or problems. State your reasons for selecting this strategy over other possible strategies and identify how the teacher would carry out the observation.

1. You have just had lunch with the school psychologist and are stimulated by her perceptions about why children fail. Some of your discussion focused on the issue of too much pressure from parents and inconsistent expectations in school. These are factors that are largely outside of the child's control. Other factors are more directly controlled by the child. For example, some children fail because they are unwilling to try; others fail because they tackle problems that are too difficult for them. Still other factors seem to be controlled by the teacher. For example, some children fail when asked to perform in front of the rest of the class. You have decided to investigate failure in your own classroom. How would you go about observing it?

2. You will have a group of three-year-olds next term and you know that this will be the first group experience for most of the children. Given that, you are interested in how dominance is established within the group; who are the children that will emerge as leaders and who will be the followers? What observational strategy would you use to study this?

3. You are feeling frustrated by the fact that so much of your day seems to be taken up either with paper work or with interruptions. You feel that there is too little time for teaching. What observational strategy would you use to determine how your time is spent?

4. You have decided that you want to do a classroom profile of the work or study habits of your second graders. You know that you can always count on Jim and Shirley to work well on their own and you can always count on Bonnie to need help right away. You realize, however, that most of the group falls in the middle and you are feeling that you need to know more about the children's individual work habits in order to help them develop the best study habits they can and to be sure you are reinforcing the right behaviors. What kind of observations would you do to gather this information?

5. You have just been informed that you will have a student teacher next semester. You have never supervised a student teacher before and are interested in your own reactions to this new task. You also know that you will be asked to evaluate the student at the end of the term and want to be sure you do this objectively. What kind of observations would you do to record both kinds of information?

6. It is February 1st and Timothy Davis has just been assigned to your classroom. He and his family have just moved to town from Des Moines and Timothy is not at all happy about leaving his friends and coming to a new school. He has good reason to be worried; Timothy is handicapped and is nervous about how his new classmates will respond to him. You want to do your best to help Timothy both academically and socially, but you are also concerned about being overprotective. You decide that you need to start by seeing where Timothy "is at" and how the children react to him. What strategy would you use to observe Timothy's introduction to the group?

7. The local college has offered to have their physical education students work with the less physically coordinated children to help them develop better skills. Your principal has asked you to select five children from your class for the special program. You want to be sure that you select the right children. What observational strategy would you use to help you make your decision?

8. The Gray Panthers have organized a foster grandparent program and each of the senior citizens involved has agreed to adopt a classroom. You are interested in how your children respond to a class grandparent. Many of them do not see their own grandparents often and, in fact, have little contact with senior citizens. What strategy would you select to observe the children's responses?

Research Observations

Observation is an important component of most research studies. It is critical to naturalistic research and is an important component of most experimental studies. Your task in this assignment is to select the observational strategy that is more appropriate for the research questions identified.

Procedure: Identify the observation strategy that you would use to answer each of the following research questions.

1. There has been a great deal of interest in sex-role learning in recent years. You are interested in exploring the ways in which preschool teachers reinforce sex-role learning. What observational strategy would you use to study this question?

2. Researchers, clinicians and child-rearing experts have long studied and written on the topic of sibling rivalry. At a recent dinner party, one of the guests asked you (as the resident expert), "When does it all start?" You had to admit you didn't know and the question has gnawed at you ever since. You have decided to do an exploratory study of children's first responses to newborn siblings to see if this will give you any leads. How would you observe this phenomena?

3. Piaget says that children's learning is enhanced by optimal cognitive conflict arising from discrepancies between the child's knowledge and a new experience. You are interested in studying how children deal with cognitive conflict. What strategy would you use to observe this?

4. Increasing attention is being paid to the role of the father in child development. Your own interest is in comparing the differential behavior of fathers and mothers. You have decided to look at speech patterns and plan to observe how fathers and mothers talk to young children. What strategy would you use to observe this?

5. You know that teachers respond differently to different children. There are those children who are instantly liked and others who are instantly disliked. Some children become teacher's pets and others scapegoats. You want to observe teachers' responses to children the first two weeks of school and then compare this with their own perceptions of how they feel about the different children. How would you study this observationally?

6. As the divorce rate rises, so does the number of children affected by divorce. One of the problems for families experiencing a breakup between husband and wife is that both parents are so involved with coping with their own feelings that they have little energy for helping children cope with the situation. How would you study this problem observationally?

7. Some hospitals have been experimenting with programs designed to explain what is happening to juvenile patients. A special doctor or nurse is assigned to make the rounds in the children's ward just to tell them about what is happening and what is going to happen to them. You want to observe what effect this has on the children's behavior while they are in the hospital. How would you study this observationally?

8. Television, it is said, has dramatically changed family interaction patterns, children's use of leisure time, and even our values. You are interested in what percentage of children's play is influenced by TV. How would you study this observationally?

Bibliography

Ainsworth, M. The effects of maternal deprivation: a review of findings and controversy in the context of research strategy. *Maternal Care* and *Mental Health and Deprivation of Maternal Care*. New York: Schocken Books, 1966.

Allport, G. W., and H. S. Odbert. Trait-names: a psycho-lexical study. *Psychological Monographs*, 1936, 47 (Whole No. 211).

Almy, M. *Ways of Studying Children*. New York: Teachers College, 1959.

American Psychological Association. Ethical standards for developmental psychologists. *Newsletter*, Division of Developmental Psychologists, 1968, 1-3.

Anderson, J. R., and R. M. Bingham. Recording teacher and pupil verbal inquiry: behaviors in the classroom. In A. Simon and E. G. Boyer, eds., *Mirrors for Behavior. Supplement Vol. A*. Philadelphia: Research for Better Schools, 1970, 80.1.

Arrington, R. E. Time sampling in studies of social behavior: a critical review of techniques and results with research suggestions. *Psychological Bulletin* (February 1943), 40(2), 81–124.

Arrington, R. E. Time sampling studies of child behavior. *Psychological Monographs*, 1939, 51, 2, entire issue.

Axline, V. *Dibs—In Search of Self*. Boston: Houghton Mifflin, 1964.

Baldwin, A. L. *Theories of Child Development*. New York: Wiley, 1967.

Bandura, A. *A Social Learning Theory*. Englewood Cliffs, N.J.: Prentice-Hall, 1977.

Bandura, A., and R. H. Walters. *Social Learning and Personality Development*. New York: Holt, Rinehart and Winston, 1963.

Barker, R. C. *Ecological Psychology*. Stanford, Ca.: Stanford University Press, 1968.

Barker, R. G., and H. F. Wright. *Midwest and Its Children: The Psychological Ecology of an American Town*. New York: Harper & Row, 1955.

Barker, R. G., and H. F. Wright, *One Boy's Day*. New York: Harper & Row, 1951.

Barrett, D. E., and M. R. Yarrow. Prosocial behavior, social inferential ability, and assertiveness in children. *Child Development*, 1977, 48(2), 475–481.

Baruch, D. W. *One Little Boy*. New York: Julian Press, 1952.

Berne, E. V. C. *An Experimental Investigation of Social Behavior Patterns in Young Children*. Ph.D. Dissertation, State University of Iowa, July 1928.

Biehler, R. F. *Child Development: An Introduction*. Boston: Houghton Mifflin, 1976.

Birdwhistell, R. L. *Kinesics and Context*. Pittsburgh: University of Pennsylvania Press, 1972.

Blanton, S. The use of behavior charts in the preschool and kindergarten clinics. *American Journal of Psychiatry*, 1925-26, 5, 615-623.

Blurton-Jones, N. G. An ethological study of some aspects of social behaviour of children in nursery school. In D. Morris, ed., *Primate Ethology*. London: Weidenfeld and Nicolson, 1967.

Blurton-Jones, N., ed. *Ethological Studies of Child Behaviour*. Cambridge: The University Press, 1972.

Boas, F. "Anthropological investigations in schools," *Pedagogical Seminary*, 1891, 1, 225-228.

Boas, F. *Ethnology of the Kwakiutl*, 2 Vols. Washington: Thirty-fifth Annual Report of the Bureau of American Ethnology, 1921.

Boehm, A. E., and R. A. Weinberg. *The Classroom Observer: A Guide for Developing Observation Skills*. New York: Teachers College, 1977.

Boyer, E. G., A. Boyer, and G. Karafin, eds. *Measures of Maturation: An Anthology of Early Childhood*

Observation Instruments. Philadelphia: Research for Better Schools, 1973.

Brandt, R. M. An historical overview of systematic approaches to observation in school settings. In R. A. Weinbert and F. H. Wood, eds. *Observation of Pupils and Teachers in Mainstream and Special Education Settings: Alternative Strategies.* Reston, Va: Council for Exceptional Children, 1975.

Brandt, R. M. *Studying Behavior in Natural Settings.* New York: Holt, Rinehart and Winston, 1972.

Bremner, R. H., ed. *Children and Youth: A Documentary History,* Vol. I: 1600-1865. Cambridge: Harvard University Press, 1970.

Brenner, C. *An Elementary Textbook of Psychoanalysis.* Garden City, N.Y.: Doubleday, Anchor Books edition, 1957.

Breuer, J., and S. Freud. On the psychical mechanism of hysterical phenomena (1893). In J. Rickman, trans. *Collected Papers,* vol. 1. New York: International Psychoanalytic Press, 1924.

Breuer, J., and S. Freud. *Studies in Hysteria* (1895), A. A. Brill, trans. New York: *Nervous and Mental Disease Monographs, 61,* 1936.

Bridges, K. M. B. A preschool character rating chart. *Psychological Clinic,* 1928, *17,* 61-72.

Bronfenbrenner, U. Developmental research, public policy, and the ecology of childhood. *Child Development,* 1978, *49*(4), 1163-1173.

Brown, H. W. Some records of the thoughts and reasonings of children. *The Pedagogical Seminary,* 1892, *2,* 358-396.

Brown, J. A. C. *Freud and the Post-Freudians.* Baltimore: Penguin, 1961.

Bühler, C. *The First Year of Life,* P. Greenbert and R. Ripin, trans. New York: Day, 1930.

Burgess, R. L., and R. D. Conger. Family interaction in abusive, neglectful and normal families. *Child Development,* 1978, *49,* 4, 1163-1173.

Burnham, W. H. A scheme of classification for child study. *The Pedagogical Seminary,* 1892, *2,* 191-198.

Byers, P., and H. Byers. Nonverbal communication and the education of children. In Courtney Cazden, Vera P. John, and Dell Hymes, eds., *Functions of Language in the Classroom.* New York: Teachers College, 1972, pp. 3-31.

Caldwell, B. M. Child development and social policy. In Myrtle Scott and Sadie Grimmett, eds., *Current Issues in Child Development,* Washington, D.C.: National Association for the Education of Young Children, 1977, pp. 61-87.

Caldwell, B. M. A new APPROACH to behavioral ecology. In J. P. Hill, ed., *Minnesota Symposia on Child Psychology,* vol. 2. Minneapolis: University of Minnesota Press, 1969, pp. 74-109.

Caldwell, B. M., and A. S. Honig. *APPROACH: A procedure for patterning responses of adults and children.* Little Rock: University of Arkansas Center for Early Development and Education (no date).

Carthy, J. D. *The Study of Behavior.* London: Edward Arnold, 1966.

Champney, H. The measurement of parent behavior. *Child Development,* 1941, *12,* 131-166.

Cohen, D. H., and Stern V. *Observing and Recording the Behavior of Young Children.* New York: Teachers College, 1958.

Compayré, G. *The Intellectual and Moral Development of the Child,* Mary Wilson, trans. New York: Appleton, 1896.

Cronbach, L. J. *Essentials of Psychological Testing,* 3d ed. New York: Harper & Row, 1970.

Darwin, C. A biographical sketch of an infant. *Mind,* 1877, *2,* 285-294.

Darwin, C. *The Origin of Species by Means of Natural Selection.* London: Murray, 1859.

Darwin, C. *Expression of Emotion in Man and Animals.* London: Murray, 1872.

Davis, C. M. Results of the self-selection of diets by young children. *Canadian Medical Association Journal,* 1939, *41,* 257-261.

Dawe, H. C. An analysis of two hundred quarrels of preschool children. *Child Development,* 1934, *5,* 139-157.

Dearborn, G. V. N. *Moto-sensory Development: Observations on the First Three Years of a Child.* Baltimore: Warwick & York, 1910.

Dennis, W. A bibliography of baby biographies. *Child Development,* 1936, *7,* 71-73.

Dennis, W., and M. G. Dennis. Behavioral development in the first year as shown by forty biographies. *Psychological Record,* 1937, *1*(21), 349-361.

de Santillana, G. *The Crime of Galileo.* Chicago: University of Chicago Press, 1955.

Dickens, C. *David Copperfield.* New York: St. Martin, 1892.

Dickens, C. *Oliver Twist.* New York: Holt, Rinehart and Winston, 1969.

Dresslar, F. B. A morning's observation of a baby. *Pedagogical Seminary,* 1901, *8,* 469-481.

Eibl-Eibesfeldt, I. *Ethology: The Biology of Behavior*, 2d ed. New York: Holt, Rinehart and Winston, 1975.

Erikson, E. H. *Childhood and Society*, 2d ed. New York: Norton, 1963.

Erikson, E. H. *Identity: Youth and Crisis*. New York: Norton, 1968.

Fagot, B. I. Reinforcing contingencies for sex-role behaviors: effect of experience with children. *Child Development*, 1978, *49*(1), 30-36.

Flanders, N. A. *Analyzing Teacher Behavior*. Reading, Mass.: Addison-Wesley, 1970.

Flanders, N. The use of interaction analysis to study pupil attitudes toward learning. In R. A. Weinberg and F. H. Wood, eds., *Observation of Pupils and Teachers in Mainstream and Special Education Settings: Alternative Strategies*. Reston, Va.: Council for Exceptional Children, 1975, pp. 41-74.

Flavell, J. H. *The Developmental Psychology of Jean Piaget*. Princeton: Van Nostrand, 1963.

Frank, Anne. *The Diary of Anne Frank*. Garden City, N.Y.: Doubleday, 1952.

Frank, L. K. The beginnings of child development and family life education in the twentieth century. *Merrill-Palmer Quarterly*, 1962, *8*(4), 207-228.

Freud, S. *Gesammelte Werke*. 18 vols. London: Imago Publications, 1950. Einstein letter in Vol. 16:20, quoted in Eibl-Eibesfeldt, I. *Ethology*, 2d Ed. New York: Holt, Rinehart and Winston, 1975.

Freud, S. *New Introductory Lectures on Psychoanalysis*, W. J. H. Sprott, trans. New York: Norton, 1933.

Frodi, A. M., and M. E. Lamb. Sex differences in responsiveness to infants: A developmental study of psychophysiological and behavioral responses. *Child Development*, 1978, *49*(4), 1182-1188.

Froebel, F. *The Education of Man*, W. N. Hailman, trans. New York: Appleton, 1896.

Gesell, A. *The Mental Growth of the Pre-school Child: A Psychological Outline of Normal Development from Birth to the Sixth Year, Including a System of Developmental Diagnosis*. New York: Macmillan, 1925.

Ginsberg, H., and S. Opper. *Piaget's Theory of Intellectual Development*. Englewood Cliffs, N.J.: Prentice-Hall, 1969.

Good, T. L., and J. E. Brophy. Analyzing classroom interaction: a more powerful alternative. *Educational Technology*, 1971, *11*, 36-40.

Goodall, J. Life and death at Gombe. *National Geographic*, 1979, *155*(5), 592-621.

Goodenough, F. L. *Developmental Psychology*. New York: Appleton, 1934.

Goodenough, F. L. Inter-relationships in the behavior of young children. *Child Development*, 1930, *1*, 29-47.

Goodenough, F. Measuring behavior traits by means of repeated short samples. *The Journal of Juvenile Research*, 1928, *12*, 230-235.

Guilford, J. P. *Psychometric Methods*, 2d ed. New York: McGraw-Hill, 1954.

Haggerty, M. E., W. C. Olson, and E. K. Wickman, Haggerty-Olson-Wickman behavior rating schedules. Yonkers, N.Y.: World Book, 1930.

Hall, G. S. *Aspects of Child Life and Education*. New York: Appleton, 1907.

Hall, G. S. The contents of children's minds. *Princeton Review*, 1883, *59*, 249-272.

Hartshorne, H., and M. A. May. *Studies in the Nature of Character*, 3 vols. New York: Macmillan, 1928-30.

Haskell, E. M., ed. *Child Observations; First Series: Imitation and Allied Activities*. Boston: Heath, 1896.

Heathers, G. Emotional dependence and independence in nursery school play. *Journal of Genetic Psychology*, 1955, *87*, 37-57.

Herbert, J., and C. Attridge. A guide for developers and users of observation systems and manuals. *American Educational Research Journal*, 1975, *12*(1), 1-20.

Hilgard, E. R., and G. H. Bower. *Theories of Learning*, 4th ed. New York: Appleton, 1975.

Hill, W. F. *Learning: A Survey of Psychological Interpretations*, 3rd ed. New York: Crowell, 1975.

Hollander, P. A. *Legal Handbook for Educators*, Boulder, Colo.: Westview Press, 1978.

Holm, R. A. Techniques of recording observational data. In G. P. Sacket, ed. *Observing Behavior*, vol. II. Baltimore: University Park Press, 1978, pp. 99-108.

Horn, E. *Distribution of Opportunity for Participation among the Various Pupils in Class-room Recitation*. New York: Teachers College, 1914.

Hough, J. B. An observational system for the analysis of classroom instruction. In A. Simon and E. G. Boyer, eds. *Mirrors for Behavior*, vol. 3. Philadelphia: Research for Better Schools, 1967, 9.1.

Huston-Stein. A., L. Friedrich-Cofer, and E. J. Susman. The relation of classroom structure to social behavior, imaginative play, and self-regulation of economically disadvantaged children. *Child Development*, 1977, *48*(3), 908-916.

Hutt, S. J., and C. Hutt. *Direct Observation and Measurement of Behavior.* Springfield, Ill.: Charles C. Thomas, 1970.

Hutt, C., and C. Ounsted. The biological significance of gaze aversion with particular reference to the syndrome of infantile auttion to Piaget. New York: Agathon Press, 1972.

Isaacs, N. *A Brief Introduction to Piaget.* New York: Agathon Press, 1972.

Isaacs, S. *Intellectual Growth of Young Children.* New York: Harcourt, 1930.

Isaacs, S. *Social Development in Young Children.* New York: Harcourt, 1933.

Itard, J. M. *The Wild Boy of Aveyron.* New York: Appleton, 1962.

Jersild, A. T., and M. F. Meigs. Direct observation as a research method. *Review of Educational Research* (December 1939), 1-14.

Johnson, H. M. *School Begins at Two.* New York: Agathon, 1970.

Jones, M. C. A study of the emotions of preschool children. *School and Society,* 1925, *31,* 755-758.

Kerlinger, F. N. *Foundations of Behavioral Research,* 2d ed. N.Y.: Holt, Rinehart and Winston, 1973.

Kessen, W. *The Child.* New York: Wiley, 1965.

Kohl, H. *36 Children.* New York: New American Library, 1967.

Kozol, J. *Death at an Early Age.* New York: Bantam, 1967.

Levin, G. *A Self-Directing Guide to the Study of Child Psychology.* Monterey, Calif.: Brooks/Cole, 1973.

Locke, J. *Some Thoughts Concerning Education,* 4th ed., enlarged. London: A. & J. Churchill, 1699. The first edition was published in 1693.

Lorenz, K. The fashionable fallacy of dispensing with description. In *Konrad Lorenz: The Man and His Ideas,* R. I. Evans, ed. New York: Harcourt, 1975, pp. 152-180.

Lorenz, K. Der Kumpan in der Umwelt des Vogels. *Journal für Ornithologie,* 1935, *83*(2), 137-215, 289-413.

Lorenz, K. *On Aggression,* M. K. Wilson, trans. New York: Harcourt, 1966.

Maier, W. *Three Theories of Child Development,* 3d ed. New York: Harper & Row, 1978.

McCall, R. B. Challenges to a science of developmental psychology. *Child Development,* 1977, *48,* 333-344.

McCullers, C. *Member of the Wedding.* Boston: Houghton Mifflin, 1946.

McGrew, W. C. *An Ethological Study of Children's Behavior.* New York: Academic Press, 1972.

Marston, L. R. *The Emotions of Young Children.* Iowa City: State University of Iowa Studies in Child Welfare, 1925.

Mead, M. *New Lives for Old.* New York: Mentor, New American Library, 1956.

Mead, M. *Sex and Temperament in Three Primitive Societies.* New York: Morrow, 1935.

Medley, D. M., and H. E. Mitzel. Measuring classroom behavior by systematic observation. In N. J. Gage, ed. *Handbook of Research in Teaching.* Skokie, Ill.: Rand-McNally, 1963, pp. 247-328.

Mowat, F. *Never Cry Wolf.* New York: Dell, 1963.

Murphy, L. B. *Social Behavior and Child Personality.* N.Y.: Columbia University Press, 1937.

O'Gorman, N. *The Wilderness and the Laurel Tree.* New York: Harper & Row, 1972.

Olson, W. C. The measurement of nervous habits in normal children. Minneapolis: University of Minnesota Institute of Child Welfare Monographs, 1929.

Olson, W. C., and E. M. Cunningham. Time-sampling techniques. *Child Development,* 1934, *5,* 41-58.

Parten, M. B. Social participation among preschool children. *Journal of Abnormal and Social Psychology,* 1932-33, *27,* 243-269.

Pavlov, I. P. Lectures on conditioned reflexes, 3d ed. Excerpted in R. J. Herrnstein and E. G. Boring, eds. *A Source Book in the History of Psychology,* Cambridge, Mass.: Harvard University Press, 1965.

Pestalozzi, J. H. *A Father's Diary.* Cited by R. De Guimps, *Pestalozzi, His Life and Work.* New York: Appleton, 1906.

Pestalozzi, J. H. *How Gertrude Teaches Her Children,* Lucy E. Holland and F. C. Turner, trans. Syracuse, N.Y.: Bardeen, 1894.

Peterson, C. C. *A Child Grows Up.* New York: Alfred, 1974.

Piaget, J. *The Language and Thought of the Child,* M. Gabain, trans. New York: World, 1955.

Piaget, J., and B. Inhelder. *The Psychology of the Child,* Helen Weaver, trans. New York: Basic Books, 1969.

Pren, 1893.

Preyer, W. *The Mind of the Child: Part 1: The Senses and the Will,* 3d ed., H. W. Brown, trans. New York: Appleton, 1888.

Puckett, R. C. Making supervision objective. *School Review*, 1928, *36*, 209-212.

Rasmussen, V. *Diary of a Child's Life: Birth to the Fifteenth Year*, M. Blanchard, trans. London: Gyldendal (n.d.)

Read, K. H. *The Nursery School: Human Relationships and Learning*, 6th ed. Philadelphia: Saunders, 1976.

Remmers, H. H. Rating methods in research on teaching. In N. L. Gage, ed., *Handbook of Research on Teaching*. Skokie, Ill.: Rand-McNally, 1963, 329-378.

Rosenthal, R. and L. Jacobson. *Pygmalion in the Classroom: Teacher Expectation and Pupils' Intellectual Development*. New York: Holt, Rinehart and Winston, 1968.

Rousseau, J. J. *Emile*, or *On education*, Barbara Foxley, trans. London: Dent, 1911.

Russell, E. H. The study of children at the State Normal School, Worcester, Mass. *The Pedagogical Seminary*, 1892, *2*, 343-357.

Salinger, J. D. *Catcher in the Rye*. Boston: Little, Brown, 1945.

Schoggen, P. H. A study in psychological ecology: structural properties of children's behavior based on sixteen day-long specimen records. Unpublished doctoral dissertation, University of Kansas, 1954.

Schulman, Anne Shaaker. *Absorbed in Living: Children Learn*. Washington, D.C.: National Association for the Education of Young Children, 1967.

Sears, R. R. Your ancients revisited: a history of child development. In E. M. Hetherington, ed., *Review of Child Development*, vol. 5. Chicago: University of Chicago Press, 1975, pp. 1-73.

Senn, M. J. E. Insights on the child development movement in the United States. *Monograph of the Society for Research in Child Development*, vol. 40:3-4. Chicago: University of Chicago Press, 1975.

Serbin, L. A., I. J. Tonick, and S. H. Sternglanz. Shaping cooperative cross-sex play. *Child Development*, 1977, *48*, 924-929.

Sherif, M. *Social Interaction: Process and Products*. Chicago: Aldine, 1967.

Sherif, M., O. J. Harvey, B. J. White, W. R. Hood, and C. W. Sherif. *Intergroup Conflict and Cooperation: The Robbers Cave Experiment*. *Overland Monthly*, 1894, *23*(133), 2-19.

Shinn, M. W. *The Biography of a Baby: The First Year of Life*. Boston: Houghton-Mifflin, 1900.

Shinn, M. W. *The Development of the Senses in the First Three Years of Childhood*. Notes on the Development of a Child, University of California Publications in Education, vol. 4, (July 1908), 1-14.

Simon, A., and E. G. Boyer. *Mirrors for Behavior*, Philadelphia: Research for Better Schools, vol. 1-6, 1967; vol. 7-15, 1970; Supplements vol. A. & B, 1970.

Skinner, B. F. *Science and Human Behavior*. New York: Macmillan, 1953.

Skinner, B. F. *The Behavior of Organisms: An Experimental Analysis*. New York: Appleton, 1938.

Skinner, B. F. *Walden Two*. New York: Macmillan, 1948.

Sluckin, A. M., and P. K. Smith. Two approaches to the concept of dominance in preschool children. *Child Development*, 1977, *48*(3), 917-923.

Smith, B. *A Tree Grows in Brooklyn*. New York: Harper & Row, 1947.

Smith, P. K., and L. Daglish. Sex differences in parent and infant behavior in the home. *Child Development*, 1977, *48*(4), 1250-1254.

Smothergill, N., F. Olson, and S. G. Moore. The effects of manipulation of teacher communication style in the preschool. *Child Development*, 1971, *42*, 1229-1239.

Stallings, J. Follow Through program classroom observation evaluation, Final report for Bureau of Elementary and Secondary Education, U.S. Office of Education, 1971-72. Menlo Park, Ca.: Stanford Research Institute, 1973.

Stallings, J. A. *Learning To Look; A Handbook on Classroom Observation and Teaching Models*. Belmont, Ca.: Wadsworth, 1977.

Stern, W. *Psychology of Early Childhood: Up to the Sixth Year of Age*, 2d ed., A. Barwell, trans. New York: Holt, 1930.

Stevenson, H., ed.: *Sixty-second Yearbook of the National Society for the Study of Education, Part I, Child Psychology 1963*.

Thomas, D. S., and associates. Some new techniques for studying social behavior. *Child Development Monograph*, 1929, 1.

Thorndike, E. L. A constant error in psychological ratings. *Journal of Applied Psychology*, 1920, *4*, 25-29.

Thorndike, E. L. Animal intelligence: An experimental study of the associative processes in animals.

In R. J. Herrnstein and E. G. Boring, eds., *A Source Book in the History of Psychology.* Cambridge, Mass.: Harvard University Press, 1965.

Tiedemann, D. *Beobachtungen ueber die Entwickelung des Seelenfahrigkeiten bei Kindern.* Altenburg: Bonde, 1787.

Tinbergen, N. On aims and methods of ethology. *Zeitschrift für Tierpsychologie,* 1963, 20, 410-433. Cited in Eibl-Eibesfeldt, *Ethology: The Biology of Behavior,* 2d ed. New York: Holt, Rinehart and Winston, 1975.

Twain, M. *Huckleberry Finn.* New York: Dodd, 1953.

van Lawick-Goodall, J. *In the Shadow of Man.* New York: Dell, 1971.

Wann, K. D., M. S. Dorn, and E. A. Liddle. *Fostering Intellectual Development in Young Children.* New York: Teachers College, 1962.

Watson, J. B. *Behaviorism,* 2d ed. New York: Norton, 1930.

Watson, J. B., and R. Raynor. Conditioned emotional reactions. *Journal of Experimental Psychology,* 1920, 3, 1-4.

Watson, R. I., and H. C. Lindgren. *Psychology of the Child,* 3d ed. New York: Wiley, 1973.

Weinberg, R. A., and F. H. Wood, eds. *Observation of Pupils and Teachers in Mainstream and Special Education Settings: Alternative Strategies.* Reston, Va.: Council for Exceptional Children, 1975.

Whipple, G. M., ed. *Twenty-eighth Yearbook of the National Society for the Study of Education: Preschool and Parental Education.* Bloomington, Ill.: Public School Publishing Company, 1929.

Whiting, J. W. M., and I. L. Child. *Child Training and Personality.* New Haven: Yale University Press, 1953.

Woodcock, L. P. *Life and Ways of the Two-Year-Old.* New York: Dutton, 1941.

Wright, H. F. Observational child study. In P. H. Mussen, ed. *Handbook of Research Methods in Child Development.* New York: Wiley, 1960, 71-139.

Wright, H. F. *Recording and Analyzing Child Behavior.* New York: Harper & Row, 1967.

Yussen, S. R. and J. W. Santrock, *Child Development.* Dubuque, Iowa: William C. Brown, 1978.

Index